Russell Jester

The Modern Message
of the
Minor Prophets

As he spake by the mouth of his holy prophets.

LUKE 1:70

For the prophecy came not in old time by the will of man: but holy men of God spake as they were moved by the Holy Ghost.

II PETER 1:21

The Modern Message
of the
Minor Prophets

By

RAYMOND CALKINS

HARPER & BROTHERS

New York ———————————— *London*

THE MODERN MESSAGE OF THE MINOR PROPHETS

~~~ Contents ~~~

Contents

~~~ *Preface* ~~~

THE TWELVE Books of the Minor Prophets are for the most part little understood and little used by the average Bible reader. Though he read his Bible faithfully, he rarely turns for inspiration to Zephaniah, Nahum, Habakkuk or Obadiah. Indeed, these are often names of books to him but little more. There are real reasons for this. The language of these books is often obscure and sometimes even repellent. The ideas seem archaic and remote from present-day interest and problems. The situations with which the books deal belong to a history in the past which it is not easy to understand. One finds oneself enmeshed in the social and political problems of a day long behind us. True, there are verses in most of these books that are dear to the Christian heart. Certain passages and chapters are familiar because of being read in church. But the books as a whole are not understood and they remain like antiquities in a museum, interesting survivals of a past age, but having no particular meaning for life today.

As a matter of fact, these Minor Prophets share the characteristic of the Bible as a whole: the timelessness and universality of its message. The Bible is ancient, but it is also modern. Its books have a message for its time, but that message is also for all time. The lessons contained in the narratives of its heroes are as valid for our day as in the day in which they were written. The Psalms are the confessional of the world. Just so with these Minor Prophets. When we get within them and behind their historical settings, it is astonishing to discover how applicable they are to modern human and social problems. They are seen to have almost startling relevancy to the world in which today we live.

The different books of the Minor Prophets are presented in the chronological order accepted by the most recent scholarship. In the discussion of the many perplexing problems presented by the authorship, date and unity of composition of these books, care has been taken both to avoid unnecessary attention to detail and to indicate divergent opinions. Acknowledgment is made of frequent quotations

vii

from R. H. Pfeiffer's *Introduction to the Old Testament,* and Rolland E. Wolfe's *The Editing of the Book of the Twelve* and *Meet Amos and Hosea.* Indebtedness to other writers on these prophets is acknowledged in footnotes.

The authorized King James version has been used throughout.

, For the better understanding of obscure and unintelligible passages the reader is referred to the exegesis of the text in the appendix. In the preparation of this material much use has been made of the Cambridge Bible for Schools and Colleges and other sources. The reader may also consult the forthcoming Revised Standard Version of the Old Testament, the modern translation by James Moffatt and the American Translation of the Bible, University of Chicago Press, 1931.

I am very grateful to Dr. Robert H. Pfeiffer of Harvard University, who has generously read the introductions to these chapters and made many valuable suggestions; and to Mrs. Carrie Fogg Hudson for expert stenographical service.

To recover for the Bible reader and student the understanding, appreciation and use of the Twelve Books of the Minor Prophets is the purpose of the present publication.

Cambridge, Massachusetts   R. C.
August 10, 1946

B.C.	785–744	Reign of Jeroboam II
	735–720	Reign of Ahaz
	732	Fall of Damascus
	722	Fall of Samaria
	720–692	Reign of Hezekiah
	692–641	Reign of Manasseh
	638–608	Reign of Josiah
	630–624	Invasion of the Scythians
	621	Reform of Josiah
	612	Fall of Nineveh
	608	Battle of Megiddo
	605	Battle of Carchemish
	586	Fall of Jerusalem
	538–537	Fall of Babylon
	537–536	First Return from the Exile
	516	Completion of the Temple
	458	Ezra
	444	Nehemiah

The Modern Message
of the
Minor Prophets

1. AMOS   (750–   B.C.)

2. HOSEA   (745–734 B.C.)

3. MICAH   (*c.*   701 B.C.)

4. ZEPHANIAH   (628–626 B.C.)

5. NAHUM   (614–612 B.C.)

6. HABAKKUK   (605–600 B.C.)

7. HAGGAI   (520   B.C.)

8. ZECHARIAH I–VIII (520–519 B.C.)

9. MALACHI   (460   B.C.)

10. OBADIAH   (400–350 B.C.)

11. JOEL   (*c.*   350 B.C.)

12. JONAH   (*c.*   300 B.C.)

THE TITLE, "The Minor Prophets," we owe to St. Augustine who so designated the last twelve books of the Old Testament "on account of their brevity as compared with those which are called the Major because of their ampler volumes." And this name has passed into general use today. In Hebrew literature, however, they are uniformly called "The Book of the Twelve," and we have every reason to believe that they were gathered together in four volumes before their reception into the final and authoritative Canon of the Prophets about 200 B.C. The twelve books may have been differently arranged from time to time; their contents may have been altered, but the Twelve have always stood together. Their unity has never been lost. In our English Bibles they come at the very end of the Old Testament, preceded by the Three Major Prophets. Why they were placed there we do not know. Possibly it was felt that prophecy was a fitting prelude to the New Testament. In the Hebrew Bible they come after the Pentateuch and the historical books (sometimes called the Earlier Prophets) and they are followed by the other "Writings": Psalms, Proverbs, Ecclesiastes, etc.

The collection and arrangement of these twelve books are "wrapped in obscurity." As nearly as it is possible to trace this process, it ran somewhat as follows:

1. Between the fall of Samaria in 722 B.C. and that of the Southern Kingdom in 586 B.C., the books of Amos and Hosea were well known. The Book of Hosea probably appeared in two parts (chaps. 1–3 and 4–14) of which the first was the more widely read and circulated. When these two parts were put together we do not know. It may have been shortly before the Exile. At the same time the books of Amos and Hosea were probably combined. Here we have the Book of the Two.

2. The period of the Exile was one of intense literary activity. It was then that the ancient traditions and manuscripts relating to the early history of the Hebrew people were assembled and combined.

3

During this same period it is quite likely that considerable attention was given to the early prophetic writings, gathering them into a larger collection, to include not only Amos and Hosea, but also the other pre-exilic prophets—Micah, Zephaniah, Nahum and Habakkuk. Here we have the Book of the Six.

3. Three centuries later, about 300 B.C., three more prophecies were added—Joel, Jonah and Obadiah. These, however, were not appended to the Six, but were inserted among the others. Thus the historical sequence was broken.

4. For the next seventy-five years this Book of the Nine was studied and re-edited. But then other prophetic books and anonymous prophecies remained to be accounted for. Until 250–225 B.C. the books of Haggai, Zechariah and Malachi were not in popular use. Why, we do not know. Thus the next step was to add these three prophecies to the Nine, and to append the anonymous prophecies—Micah 4–5, 6–7 and Zechariah 9–14, to existing prophetical books, to which subsequently it was assumed that they belonged. Thus the Book of the Twelve was completed.

5. For fifty more years the Book of the Twelve was subject to further revision by the scribes. But by the year 200 B.C., or a little later, the number of the books and their contents became fixed and unalterable.

It is difficult to determine why these twelve books were arranged in their present order in the Hebrew Bible.[1] Some have felt that they were arranged in what the editor thought was their chronological order. Others find no evidence for this, and suggest [2] that the first six books were arranged according to size (Micah being out of place) alternating between the prophets of Israel and those of Judah. Still others point to certain affinities between books placed side by side, as between Joel and Amos. In the Septuagint, the Greek Version of the Old Testament, the arrangement of the first six books is in a slightly different order: Hosea, Amos, Micah, Joel, Obadiah, Jonah. Here the arrangement according to size is clear, except that Jonah comes last.

[1] See H. E. Ryle, *The Canon of the Old Testament*, p. 229.
[2] So R. H. Pfeiffer.

May there have been other prophets whose work has not been preserved? This we do not and cannot know. Between Amos and Jonah was a long stretch of five hundred years. Are we to assume that during all this time the Word of the Lord came to but fifteen men, the Three Major Prophets and the Twelve? The possibility that it may have burst from the lips of others during the period when it existed must always be borne in mind. If so, their names and their message have been forever lost.

How were these twelve books originally composed? The prophets had three ways of communicating the Word and Will of God to their contemporaries: through speech, through the written word, and through symbolical action. The third of these, often found in Jeremiah and Ezekiel, was not used by any of the Twelve. Therefore their prophecies must have been spoken, and later transcribed by their hearers and thus preserved; or they were written by the prophets themselves. In the case of only one of the Twelve can we be sure which method has been followed. The Book of Jonah is unquestionably a literary composition written by its anonymous author from beginning to end. Nahum's poem, too, was surely composed by its author. Also the authentic prophecies of Zephaniah and of Habakkuk bear the marks of literary composition. The "Dies Irae" of Zephaniah—and there is no solid reason for not ascribing it to him—is a poem of such matchless pathos and power that it must have been written by its author. And the literary structure of the Book of Habakkuk leads us to the same conclusion.

As for the other prophets, there are various possibilities. It seems unlikely that these prophecies were all written out before they were uttered. But the prophets may have made notes for their oral discourses and these they may have later expanded in writing. So were Amos and Hosea probably composed. By some it is claimed, without being able to prove it, that the prophets did no writing at all, and what we possess is what was remembered by their hearers. Here we have the analogy of the words of Jesus which were not written down at the time they were spoken, either by him or by anyone else, but were preserved by oral tradition and only later assembled in our four Gospels. If in this way these prophecies have come down to us, we should be careful not to regard them as stenographic reports, the texts presenting the substance rather than the actual words of the prophetic message except as these may have been exactly recalled.

In any case it is well to remember that the books of the prophets, except Jonah, do not contain the whole of their teaching. They must have said much that either they themselves did not later reproduce or that was not recalled by their hearers. Yet just as we may be sure that the fundamental religious ideas of Jesus are preserved for us in the fragmentary reports of his teaching, so we may be sure that in these books we have preserved for us the core and essence of the prophetic messages of the Twelve. We may have only a collection of excerpts from the prophetic discourses, but this collection represents adequately the minds of the prophets.

But if these books do not contain all that the prophets did say, it is even more important to remember that they do contain much that does not belong to them. At this point we confront a literary practice which is completely foreign to all our modern ideas of literary ethics. To us an author's book as it has come from his pen is inviolable. If it has not been copyrighted by law, it is still copyrighted by custom. No one would think of altering in any way a book written by another, and still circulated under his name, in order to add certain ideas to it, to improve it, or to make it agree more fully with one's own ideas. In the age, however, in which these prophetical books were written, these literary standards did not exist. Subsequent editors felt perfectly free to add to them from time to time, supplementing the ideas of their original authors, bringing the books "down to date," making them reflect more adequately the moods of a later age. These twelve books were read and reread, studied again and again by devout men who, throughout the centuries that followed, interpolated their own religious ideas into the original discourses of the prophets. To such vicissitudes were these exposed. And there were others. The manuscripts of these prophecies had to be copied by the hands of scribes. Sometimes these scribes made comments on the margin. Subsequent scribes would insert these comments into the body of the text. These insertions when detected are called "glosses." It is clear also that the order of the original text has sometimes been altered, with the result that the logical connection of ideas has been disturbed. The result of all this is that we have in these twelve books a "confused literature." The original prophecy has been obscured by these insertions, alterations, and the accumulation of later additions.

A vast amount of the most painstaking scholarship in recent years has been devoted to the work of restoring these prophecies to their original form by removing these successive layers of later deposits of material, and deleting the inapt scribal insertions which have crept into the text. To this scholarship the Bible student is deeply indebted. Instead of viewing it as laying a rough hand on sacred and inviolable books, one should rather regard it as a reverent effort to give to us of this day the authentic messages of these inspired men just as they fell from their lips.

Needless to say, this work of revision and of restoration has been one of much difficulty and delicacy. Certain criteria of judgment have been quite clear. Beyond these, however, there is an area in which opinions may easily differ. We cannot expect unanimity of judgment. This work of restoration cannot be carried out with the exactitude of scientific analysis. Hence the experts often disagree. There is always room for doubt. No hard and fast decisions can in every case be made. An approximation to the original text is all that we can expect.

Still, it is possible to follow the work of subsequent editors with some degree of probability.[3] This work may have begun even before the Exile in certain revisions of Amos and Hosea. Then came the postexilic editors, who in the light of the glowing hopes of the future of Israel sought to supplement the gloomy outlook of the pre-exilic prophets with glowing expectations of a restored and redeemed nation. Then followed the Messianic ideas of the coming of a supernatural Messianic king to set up a new kingdom of which he would be the ruler. Later came elaborations of the idea of a "Day of the Lord," specializing in pictures of the final Day of Judgment. "Old expectations become tinted with a new [lurid] hue. All historical setting has been lost sight of and free license is given to the imagination." Still later editors

---

[3] An elaborate and scholarly attempt to do this has been made by Rolland E. Wolfe in his essay "The Editing of the Book of the Twelve," published in *Die Zeitschrift für die alttestamentliche Wissenschaft*, N. F., vol. 12, 1935. What follows is an abbreviated summary of his conclusions.

reflect intensely nationalistic and antiforeign ideas especially with regard to Edom. Then come the Psalmists and the "Doxologists." And finally the later scribes, in putting the Book of the Twelve together, prefixed an introductory verse (note the similarity between the first five words in Hosea, Micah, Zephaniah, Joel) and introduced some historical notations in harmony with their concept of the religious development of the Hebrew people. Dr. Wolfe estimates that no less than thirteen different and successive editors amended and added to the original prophecies, each interpolating his own ideas. And if this number seems large, we are reminded that this work of revision went on for nearly five hundred years, a new editor on the average every forty years.

Such, in roughest outline, is the progress of the gradual editorial revision of the original work of the Twelve Minor Prophets. Where historical inaccuracies in the text are plain, as in Hosea 6:5, for example, where reference is made to the great prophets who followed Hosea, or where historical allusions are found to events which we know occurred subsequent to the age in which the prophet wrote, then we can be sure of our ground. When ideas which we know gained currency only at a later time are found in any of the prophets, we can be less sure. For may not a prophet have anticipated those ideas by immediate and personal inspiration? When it is a question of difference in style we may be even less confident. For an author does not always limit himself to one style of writing. All these questions are discussed briefly in the introductions to the books themselves.

At first, with the possible exception of Amos and Hosea, the interest in these prophetical books was faint. They were not nearly so popular as the historical books and they were overshadowed by the "Law." After the Exile, in the fifth century, however, they came into their own. The fall of Jerusalem had vindicated the truth of the stern messages of the pre-exilic prophets and they were studied afresh and venerated in the faith that God would intervene to rescue His people from the punishment they had so richly deserved. With this growing popularity of the prophets went a new zeal for re-editing and revising them in the light of these glowing expectations. Indeed, it may be said that the more popular a prophetic book became, the more new material was likely to be inserted in it. This may account for the large amount of these later additions to be found in Amos, Hosea and Micah.

A word may be said about the value of this "secondary prophecy" added to the authentic work of these prophets. Some of it is on the same high level as the original prophecies, as in Micah 6 and 7. Much of it is of an inferior quality as in Zechariah 9-14. Yet all of it has an importance which warrants its inclusion in Scripture. For one thing, it has great historical significance. Often it is our only source of knowledge of conditions in the life of the Jewish people in periods not covered by the original writings. Again, it was, because of its appeal to the expectation of the coming of a Messiah, the overthrow of pagan powers, and the restoration of the Jewish kingdom, a source of great inspiration to later Jewish and to New Testament writers. Indeed, it has been computed that there are far more references to this "secondary prophecy" in the New Testament than to the authentic messages of the prophets themselves.

In view of these repeated editorial revisions and interpolations, it is not surprising that considerable portions of some of the books of the Twelve are discovered to be the work not of the prophet whose name they bear, but of later writers. This discovery should not lessen our veneration for these prophetical books. For whenever written or by whom, they are a "word of prophecy; whereunto ye do well that ye take heed, as unto a light that shineth in a dark place, until the day dawn, and the day star arise in your hearts." And again it is not surprising in view of the composite character of these books, if, in the form in which they are preserved for us in our Bibles, they should often seem obscure and even unintelligible. But if this material is properly sifted, put in its original form and setting so far as this is possible, these twelve books become some of the most gripping, most intensely interesting, most immediately applicable to present needs and problems, to be found in the whole range of Bible literature.

The Book of the Twelve covers the whole prophetic era. From Amos (c. 750 B.C.) to Jonah (c. 300 B.C.) we have a period of approximately five hundred years. The first Isaiah is a contemporary of Micah. Jeremiah is a contemporary of Zephaniah, of Nahum and of Habakkuk. Ezekiel and Second Isaiah precede Haggai and Zechariah. Daniel was not reckoned among the prophets. For, believing that prophetical inspiration had at last ceased, the scribes had closed the Canon of the Prophets before the book of Daniel had been completed.

"Old Testament prophecy is a phenomenon to which the history of religion affords no real parallel." [4] It cannot be classified with any other literature of the soul. The prophets belong in a class by themselves, a series of inspired men who present to us a unique spiritual phenomenon. Prophecy is the most remarkable fact not only in Hebrew history but in the moral development of the human race down to the coming of Jesus Christ. Into the nature of this prophetic inspiration we are unable to penetrate beyond saying that these were holy men, sensitive to the fact of sin, in intimate relation to God and convinced that God spoke through their lips. This close and permanent association between religion and prophetic inspiration is its distinctive feature. Prediction was a minor note in its message to men, and always it also had a religious basis and motive. These men were not primarily foretellers, but forthtellers. They uttered God's truth as it was given them to know it, in sheer disregard either of the popular mood or of their own fortunes. Their message, too, was brought to bear with precision upon concrete political and social problems. It was not an abstract principle that was declared, but a pronouncement upon definite moral emergencies in personal and social life. It is this combination of truth in its eternal aspects as related to the Being and Will of God with concrete human necessity that gives the quality of timelessness to the message of the prophets. Because the sins, social and personal, which the prophets condemn are in root and essence the same as those which still degrade the soul of man and of society; because the truths which have their source in the holiness and justice of God are immutable and eternal; because the way of repentance and of a return to God's Word and Will remains the only hope of redemption and of salvation— therefore, the inspired messages of these prophets are not for their time only but for our time and for all time.

The casual reader of these twelve books, if indeed the casual Bible

---

[4] Skinner, *Prophecy and Religion,* p. 1. See also the author's *Jeremiah the Prophet,* pp. 40-54.

reader ever reads them at all, may be tempted to say, how ancient is all this; how uninteresting and unimportant in the urgent problems of our modern world are these situations in the little Jewish community of so long ago, which bears no resemblance to the world in which we live today. Thus it happens that many a modern reader knows of these twelve books only a few isolated verses which stand out in mind and memory. This is a vast loss in what the Bible has to offer. Anyone who earnestly desires a knowledge of Bible truth should apply himself to the recovery of the sublime truths which lie within these books, truths as applicable to the days in which we live as to the days in which they were written.

The title "Minor Prophets" must not suggest to us that they are of minor importance. Of course it is true that no one of the Twelve can rank with Isaiah, with Jeremiah or with Ezekiel in the broad scope and reach of his teaching, or in his influence on the political and religious history of the Jewish people. Yet it remains true that the messages of the Twelve, within the narrower sphere of their activities, are no less sublime, no less trenchant, no less meaningful. Indeed, it is only as we traverse them all that we come into a full knowledge of what prophecy has to teach us concerning our duty both to God and to man.

How different were these prophets the one from the other! Amos was a herdsman and Micah a countryman. Zephaniah was an aristocrat of royal blood, and Zechariah a leader of his people in Palestine; Zephaniah was a young man and Haggai an old man. Habakkuk was sensitive and introspective. Nahum was a thunderbolt, the whole force of whose invective was let loose against Nineveh. The author of the Book of Jonah is one of broad charity and humanitarianism. Joel seethes with an intense nationalism. Hosea, we say, tells us of the love of God. Obadiah is the incarnation of hatred. No set of men could have been more dissimilar in outward circumstances. But God finds His workmen, then as now, when He wants them, whether they are plowmen or princes. No set of men could have been more dissimilar in inward mood or temperament. But God can use men of different type and character. Each teaches his lesson in his own way. But all alike reason "of righteousness, self-mastery and judgment to come." The same Word of God spoke through them all. Each uttered it in terms of his own experience, and of his own personality. Together they cause us to hear both the deep diapason notes of the divine judgment and the sweet overtones of the divine mercy and love.

All the Twelve wrote in days of darkness and of tragedy. The whole stretch of five hundred years was one of almost unbroken calamity, relieved by only a few fleeting years of brightness and of transient prosperity. Not one of these prophets spoke in other than evil days. Not one of them but confronted a social order that was full of corruption and a political situation that invited despair. Hardly a ray of light shone on the landscape on which rested the eyes of these prophets. Hence their message came *de profundis*. It plumbed to the depths. It got beneath the nethermost of man's need. This characteristic it shares with the rest of the Bible, but of it the Twelve are the supreme exemplars. This constitutes their title to immortality. The world can never know darker days than those in which these men spoke. And if in such an age these prophets could point the way to salvation, if they could show how society could be cured of the disease that threatened its very existence, then they have shown men that, however low they may fall through sinful neglect of God's Word and Will, the power of self-recovery is not lost, the hope of redemption still remains.

For this is the grandeur of their message. Never, even in the darkest hour, did these men wholly despair. Never did they believe that all was irretrievably lost. God was still in the midst of His people, however faithless they had been. "The just Lord is in the midst thereof . . . he faileth not." Always, too, there remained "the remnant." The soul of goodness never became extinct. There was always a flicker of light left shining which needed only a breeze of God to fan it into flame. Dean Church, of England, once said that the Bible is an unbroken call to hope. Even when we have discounted all later additions to the original prophecies of these men, we find in their authentic work words which redeem even the saddest, the sternest of them from the darkness of despair. What gives their message its permanent significance for us of this day is its realization of the devastating effect of sin on personal and social life, combined with its firm hold on the possibilities of the final redemption of mankind.

~~~ *Amos* ~~~

I. INTRODUCTION

AMOS IS the first of the great classical, literary and reformatory prophets of Israel. There had, of course, been prophets before Amos: Samuel, Elijah, Micaiah son of Imlah (I Kings 22:8). But none of these left any written record of their teachings and none of them inaugurated any prophetic movement. Amos, on the other hand, has left a book containing what is doubtless an authentic account of his message, which announces truths that were nothing short of revolutionary, truths which influenced the whole course of Hebrew thought and determined the development of Hebrew religion. And Amos awoke a prophetic inspiration which lasted for five hundred years, an era without parallel in the history of religion.

There was nothing to presage what was about to happen. No prophetic development led up naturally to Amos. There is no record of written prophecy down to the day of Amos and there is no reason to believe that there was any. Neither was Amos the product of any prophetic school. He himself is very precise on this point: "I was no prophet, neither was I a prophet's son" (7:14). In a word, we find in the career of Amos a break with the past, the beginning of a new epoch in the religious history of the Hebrew people and so of the world. Precisely as in the development of the organic world we come upon certain points where one cannot explain the transition from one form of life to another by the orderly processes of evolution, so here we reach such a moment in the development of the religious idea. Thus Amos becomes a phenomenon, an original spiritual genius. He has been called "one of the most marvellous and incomprehensible figures in the history of the human mind." [1]

The background and previous career of the man only add to the mystery. The name "Amos" occurs only here in Scripture. It is not to be confounded with the quite different name of "Amoz," the father

[1] Cornill, *The Prophets of Israel*, p. 46.

13

of Isaiah (Is. 1:1). An "Amos" is mentioned in Luke 3:25, but
it is an open question if "Amoz" is not the correct form of the name
of one of whom, in any event, we know nothing. The meaning of the
name "Amos" has been variously explained.[2] Its most probable sig-
nification is "burden-bearer" or "burdened." If so, Amos certainly
lived up to his name. The fact that his father's name is not mentioned
leads us to believe that his was a humble parentage. He was a shepherd
or perhaps a sheep breeder ("herdman," 1:1, 7:14), and owned a
flock of "ugly and short-footed sheep valuable for their excellent
wool." To this occupation he added that of a tender of "sycomore
fruit" (7:14). These were not like our trees which bear the same
name. They were a fig-bearing tree, the fruit of which was not highly
esteemed. Because these trees are not to be found in the region where
he lived, it has been thought that he may have owned a plantation in
the hill country leading down to Philistia (I Kings 10:27).

Amos was a native of the Southern Kingdom of Judah and lived
at Tekoa, a settlement of shepherds. Tekoa lies—the place with the
same name still exists—about six to eight miles south of Bethlehem
and twelve miles from Jerusalem, in the midst of a barren and rugged
country. He lived, in the atmosphere of a desolate region, of a moor-
land desert, the solitary life of the shepherd. Yet this is probably not
the whole story. His book reveals an intimate knowledge of social
conditions in the Northern Kingdom and of impending political
events. It is possible, of course, that this knowledge of the outside
world came to him through others, travelers who had arrived from
the north or members of his own community who traded there.[3] It
is far more probable, however, that Amos himself in his capacity as
wool trader had made journeys among the markets in the Northern
Kingdom. Bethel and Samaria were only a day's journey from Tekoa.
And Amos had such a minute acquaintance with the social and political
situation there that it is hard to believe that all this came to him by
hearsay. He met with men of many lands, and thus by close observation
and retentive memory gained precise and detailed information about
localities and events. And this knowledge he brought home when he

[2] See Hastings' Bible Dictionary, "Amos," note.
[3] See R. E. Wolfe, *Meet Amos and Hosea,* p. 6.

returned to his "mountain-top village in the wilderness of Judah."

Such, as well as we are able to reconstruct it, was the background and early career of a man destined to become one of the great religious teachers of mankind: a humble shepherd, without distinction in parentage or pedigree, without other education than came to him from the natural world in which he lived under the open sky, in the desert solitude. Yet within his soul there seethed the sense of the sins of the people as he had witnessed them, the sense too of the impending and inevitable judgment that awaited the recreant nation of the North. "And the Lord took me as I followed the flock, and the Lord said unto me, Go, prophesy unto my people Israel" (7:15). God had found the man whom He needed. And the men whom God finds are often men whose origin is obscure, who, according to human standards, are men of no repute. Impossible of psychological analysis is this sudden and overpowering irruption of the life of God in a human soul. Efforts to trace its origin either to the impact of external events —in this case the threat from the growing Assyrian power coincident with the thin veneer of prosperity that veiled the inner corruption of Israel—or to purely human conviction and emotion are futile. Here is sudden Fact, Reality, a fresh, authentic manifestation of the Divine Life—a Reality which can be neither questioned nor denied. We have to deal here with an elemental and wholly supernatural spiritual phenomenon.

It is interesting to compare the varied ways in which this Inspiration came to the prophets. With Hosea, it was born out of poignant personal experience; with Isaiah, it came as a kind of theophany during a temple service; with Habakkuk, it came in an hour of brooding over the problem that evil presents to faith. But with Amos, out in the wilderness, it came like the roar of a lion (3:8). It may have been an actual lion's roar that caused the voice of God to reverberate in Amos's soul. One thing is sure: from the moment that he heard it, it took complete possession of the man's whole nature. From that moment he became one of this world's deathless heroes. He became a selfless, fearless instrument of the Word and Will of God. He attacked the most hoary, revered and until then unquestioned religious beliefs of his day. He faced people, priests and princes with a courage born of his sure knowledge that the Divine Fiat was behind his every utterance. "Deus vult" was his battle cry.

He may have been a young man, in his twenties or early thirties, when the word of the Lord came to him. His career as a prophet was a short one. It may have lasted only a few months, whereas the career of Jeremiah covers well-nigh forty years. Yet within those few months that was done which altered the moral life of the world.

It is not difficult to date the period of the prophetic activity of Amos. The mention of an earthquake (1:1, see Zech. 14:5) does not help us much, for no one knows when this tremor is supposed to have taken place. However 1:1 fixes the date as during the reign of Uzziah, king of Judah, whose contemporary in the Northern Kingdom was Jeroboam II (785-744 B.C.). And social and political conditions in the Northern Kingdom as described in the Book of Amos point definitely to the latter part of Jeroboam's reign, after 760 B.C., when the kingdom was still prosperous outwardly, before the disorders that followed the death of Jeroboam in 744 B.C. had begun. Thus 750 B.C. is a probable date for the prophetic ministry of Amos.

Under Jeroboam II, Israel (as the Northern Kingdom was known as distinguished from Judah, the Southern Kingdom) had risen to a height of prosperity which recalled the palmy days of Solomon. He restored the territory that Syria had taken from Israel, and the borders of the nation were extended from "the entering of Hamath unto the sea of the Plain" (II Kings 14:25, Amos 6:14), i.e., from the Lebanon mountains to the Dead Sea. The power of Syria had been definitely broken by Assyria, which did not yet threaten the independence of Israel. Thus under Jeroboam the people of the Northern Kingdom enjoyed a period of prosperity and peace. "The nation witnessed an unprecedented expansion in trade and a large merchant class came into prominence." Wealth increased and luxuries abounded. Israel enjoyed an economic boom. Materialism was the order of the day with all the social abuses that follow such a rapid development in wealth. Politically the kingdom was apparently secure. Samaria, its capital, was considered impregnable. It was the last glorious period in the history of the kingdom of Israel. The hopes and expectations of the people were lifted to the highest pitch. The Lord was with them and the great "Day of the Lord" when final victory over their enemies would be achieved was eagerly anticipated (5:18). Such was the situation into which, without warning, was catapulted the dynamic personality of Amos.

Apparently he did not hesitate after the Word of the Lord came to him like the roar of a lion, but departed immediately on his sensational mission, traveled into the Northern Kingdom, went from place to place uttering his message of judgment and of impending doom until the land was unable to endure all his words (7:10). It is impossible to follow with any precision the itinerary of Amos in his prophetic mission. We know that he visited Samaria, perhaps more than once, and he may have visited Gilgal (5:5) and other shrines. The climax came when he arrived at Bethel and foretold not only the destruction of the kingdom but the death of Jeroboam himself (7:9). That was too much for Amaziah, chief priest of the royal sanctuary there. He sent a message to Jeroboam reporting these traitorous utterances of Amos, told Amos himself to go home and do his prophesying there, and ordered him to cease preaching at Bethel. In reply, Amos declared that he had done only what the Lord had told him to do, and once more predicted the utter destruction of the Northern Kingdom. That prediction was fulfilled in 722 B.C.

This positive assurance of Amos in the coming doom of Israel can be traced in part to his keen insight into the rottenness of its social order beneath the surface of its apparent prosperity, and to his discernment of the impending threat to the kingdom from what was going on in the far north. It is true that Amos does not mention Assyria, nor name the nation destined to devastate Israel. Yet it is evident that he realized that the same pagan pressure which already had crushed Syria would continue its course southward and ultimately reach the Hebrew kingdom. With this said, however, room must be made within the prophetic consciousness for divine inspiration which reached farther than deduction from outward circumstance and lent finality and terrific impact to his message.

We know nothing about the rest of the life of Amos. That he died a martyr [4] is pure supposition. Far more likely is the idea that he went

[4] R. E. Wolfe, *op. cit.,* p. 60.

back home as Amaziah bade him, his mission completed, and then wrote out for the people of his time, and so for all time, the words he had uttered. There is no reason to suppose [5] that Amos was unable to write; that he formulated his addresses in advance, memorized them and delivered them orally; that the report of them which his book contains is only what was recalled by some who heard them and set them down as they remembered them. Amos was a master of literary style and his book betrays the authentic marks of his own authorship. In the quietness of his retreat at Tekoa, while what he had uttered still seethed in his soul, he set down in glowing language what the Lord had commissioned him to utter. And if the question be raised how could a humble shepherd, without formal schooling, be a writer of consummate skill and eloquence, the answer must be that academic training is not essential to command of language. One has only to cite Abraham Lincoln as a well-known illustration of this possibility. And there are many others, such as John Bunyan, in the history of literature.

We come then to the Book of Amos itself. That this contains an authentic record of his preaching is doubted by no one. We may have here a digest of his teaching only. Yet what we do possess beyond question gives us the gist of it. Again it is not to be doubted that there is in these chapters material which does not belong to Amos: additions, later interpolations, glosses, and scribal annotations. The only question is, how much of this additional material does the book contain? Here is a wide divergence of opinion among scholars. Conservative opinion has ascribed nearly the whole of the Book to Amos, deleting only a few passages. George Adam Smith [6] questions only 26 or 27 verses out of 146, and in this judgment Driver,[7] and J. Taylor in Hastings' Dictionary of the Bible, substantially agree. At the other extreme is the modern scholar, R. E. Wolfe, who holds that only half or less of the book as it now stands can belong to Amos. The truth of the matter probably lies between these two opinions. If we scan the book carefully we discover many interpolations and additions to the text

[5] So R. E. Wolfe, *op. cit.*, p. xxiv.
[6] "Amos" in his *The Book of the Twelve Prophets*.
[7] *Introduction to the Old Testament* and to *Amos* in Cambridge Bible series.

made doubtless by Jews of the Southern Kingdom who did their work some two centuries later and certainly after the Exile. Their purpose was to make its message applicable to the Southern Kingdom as well as to the Northern; and especially to relieve its somber message of final doom with some word of hope and promise of future restoration and salvation. There are difficulties in the text too, corruptions due to the carelessness of copyists or to accident. It would be futile here to endeavor to explore the work of the scholars as they seek by critical analysis to restore the original form of these prophecies of Amos. It is a delicate operation, and one wonders if it is necessary to deal so radically with the text as some have done. To reject a verse, for example, because we do not see the connection, is surely arbitrary and "critical operations may easily do violence to literary forms."

Certain tests, however, may legitimately be applied to these chapters. First, there are the scribal annotations and editorial additions, which must be detected and deleted (1:1; 4:7,12,13; 5:25-27). Then there are historical allusions which cannot be synchronized with the age in which Amos lived, which indicate a later date (1:9-12; 5:1,2; 6:2,14; 8:11-13, etc.). Again, there are the repeated references to Judah. Now, that Amos who belonged to the Southern Kingdom should have thought of and mentioned his own land in the course of his prophecies is so natural that the elimination of every reference to it is surely an arbitrary judgment. Still, it appears likely that these references later received considerable amplification (2:4, 5; 6:1). Once more, we find various ascriptions to the might of Jehovah which reflect the theological ideas of a later age and remind us of Job (4:13; 5:8-9; 9:5-6). And finally there are the promises of hope and deliverance that are found here and there and come to their climax in the very end of the book. The question of how much of the idea of Hope can be assigned to the prophets of justice and doom is a nice one. The possibility that even they cherished the idea of ultimate redemption for the people of God must be admitted. At least it cannot be denied. Yet the suspicion that many of these glowing promises were later insertions is always there. On the whole, it seems unlikely that the reference to the remnant of Joseph (5:15^b) belongs to Amos, whatever may be said of the rest of verses 14, 15. And the final words in

9:8 certainly appear to be a later addition. As for the closing verses of chapter 9 (11-15), these are in such glaring contrast to all the rest of his book that we have no difficulty in deciding that they were appended by a later writer, who found the words of Amos so somber that he felt they must be lightened by a promise of final redemption. There are also doubtless expansions of the original text, although just where the line is to be drawn is not clear. With all this said, however, and with every allowance made, we may be sure that we have preserved in the Book of Amos his essential message.

The book as we have it consists of three sections. The first of these (chaps. 1 and 2) contains a series of prophecies against the nations. The order in which these are arranged is not geographical, beginning at the north and coming southward, and we cannot know why this order was followed. In each instance, however, the nation named is excoriated for sins against humanity, atrocities of cruelty and barbarism for which they are to be punished by God. The second section (chaps. 3-6) deals with the sins of Israel that he had beheld with his own eyes, which had aroused in him the deepest sense of indignation, the sure conviction of impending punishment and doom. Here is a clap of thunder that must have startled Amos's hearers. That he should have denounced the pagan nations for their barbarities was natural enough. But that he should condemn Israel in equal fashion for its immoralities and social sins and have predicted for her the same fate that awaited the Syrians and the Philistines, this was not only treason but blasphemy. Yet in a series of terrific denunciations prefaced by the words "Hear ye," Amos indicted the whole nation, princes, priests, merchants, women, and the people themselves. The sight of sacred prostitution openly practiced in the sanctuaries in imitation of Canaanitish rites; the moral deterioration of Israel, due to the luxurious living of the wealthy, and callous disregard of the sufferings of the poor inflicted by remorseless creditors and dishonest traders; the venality of judges, who were bribed to flagrant acts of injustice; the corruption of the priesthood; the indifference of rulers to social conditions: these he denounced with a passion which must have stupefied his hearers. The idea, however, that evoked his sharpest sarcasm (4:4-6; 8:4-6) and bitterest invective (5:21-24) was the belief that sacrifice and ceremonial was the essence of religion rather than righteousness and justice. The conventional notion among his contemporaries was that sacrifices were both a thanksgiving to God for mercies received and a means for securing His future favors. Personal and social ethics did not enter into the relationship between God and His people at all. As against all this Amos proclaimed that ritual without righteousness was abhorrent to God and a degradation of the very idea of religion itself. In the third section of the book (chaps. 7-9) we find a series of visions,[8] interrupted by an account of what took place at Bethel (7:10-17). These visions reinforce the message of sin and retribution. But for the intercession of the prophet, locusts and a scorching drought will devour the land; a plumb line sent down to the center of the nation's life reveals that it is tottering to its fall; a basket of fruit, the name of which is a pun equivalent of "end" presages the fate of Israel; famine shall overtake the land, and the temple itself shall be destroyed. They that trust that Samaria is impregnable, "even they shall fall and never rise again" (8-14). The "Day of the Lord" is not a day of triumph, but a day of ruin. Israel's doom is sealed. "The prophet intones the funeral dirge over the Virgin of Israel as if she were already dead" (5:1).

Such was the message of Amos. If now we seek to understand the revolutionary contribution that Amos made to theology, we must start with his basic idea, his overpowering conviction that God is absolute righteousness. "In the strength of that principle he does what was absolutely new in Israel." [9] The inevitable conclusions resulting from this conception of God as righteousness may be roughly summarized as follows:

(1) Righteousness is a universal principle. Thus, if God be righteousness there can be but one God. This idea runs counter not only to the polytheism of the pagans of his day, but to the prevailing idea among the Hebrews that while Jehovah the god of Israel was God of gods, these other gods existed. Each was god in his own sphere, of his own land. In a word, we have in Amos the germinal idea that was to produce in time the full monotheism of the later prophets.

---

[8] "The authenticity of the last three visions, notably the third, is by no means certain." —R. H. Pfeiffer, *Introduction to the Old Testament*, p. 580.
[9] George Adam Smith, *op. cit.,* "Amos."

(2) If God be righteousness, then the idea that as their national God Jehovah would defend their political interests must be swept away. Unrighteousness will be punished in Israel as surely as in the heathen nations. God plays no favorites. It is not true that because they are God's people they will not be punished; rather, it is true that because they have been God's people is added reason why they will be punished (3:2).

(3) If God demands righteousness, then only righteousness can satisfy Him. The idea that by offering sacrifices, observing the outward rites and ceremonies of religion, the people can please God and secure His favor is rank superstition. Ritual and sacrifices of themselves were not the service God demands. This is a new interpretation of the essence and function of religion according to an ethical principle.

(4) If God is universal righteousness, then there is introduced the idea of a new relationship of God to the heathen nations. His providence is over all and is to be seen as truly in His direction of their destinies as in His leading of His own people (9:7). Here is the emergence of a new spiritual universalism. There is no place for a favored people. God makes the same moral requirements of all nations and displays equal solicitude for all.

Now, every one of these ideas was absolutely new in the day of Amos. Every one of them contradicted what were the accepted, settled and cherished convictions of those to whom he spoke. Yet he uttered them with a clarity, a passion, a fearlessness which make him one of the greatest spiritual prophets of all time. He taught with singular clearness and eloquence truths which could never again become obsolete. He was a pioneer in religious thought, and he laid deep moral foundations on which the whole structure of later Hebrew theology was built. He was one of the greatest preachers the world has ever known. In his command of language, forms of expression, effective illustration, and well-chosen images, in the directness of his addresses, and in the variety of presentation, he ranks among the masters of human speech.

In some of these respects, Amos was greater than all who came after him. But there is this lack in Amos which later prophecy supplied. "Ihm fehlt die Liebe." There is no note of love in Amos. Whether this was

due to the fact that he was not a native of the Northern Kingdom and
so could not love it as if it were his own land; or whether it was due
to his own nature, rugged, robust, trained to hardship but uninfluenced
by the softer elements of human experience, this we cannot know. We
know only that we do not find in him, as we do in Hosea and Jeremiah,
the heart that breaks over the sin and failure that must be condemned,
the love that would ransom the people whose punishment must be
decreed. The first of the great prophets of Israel stands a stern, tower-
ing figure, whose words reverberate in tones of thunder unrelieved by
light or love. The real complement of Amos is found, marvelously
developed, in Hosea, who came after him.

II. THE PROPHECY

The Book of Amos, in spite of certain obscurities and interpolations,
is clear and absorbing reading. It is [10] "one of the best arranged of the
prophetic books." The literary style is superb. Its picturesque illustrations drawn from the life of a shepherd, its vivid sketches of life as
he saw it in the cities and sanctuaries of Israel, its flashes of irony and
satire, all lend color and interest to the book. It takes high rank in the
prophetic literature of the Old Testament.

In Amos, too, we find incorporated the ideals of a truly prophetic
ministry. His speech is simple, homely, direct, and easily understood.
It is directed to definite moral ends, to the urgent moral problems of
the time. His soul is freighted with the sense of sin. The evils of the
world in which he lives press heavily upon him. He cannot walk
through Samaria and behold what is going on at Gilgal and Bethel
without an overpowering conviction of the tragic meaning of it all, of
the destruction to which it surely leads. And behind all his preaching
there lay the sense of a divine and irresistible compulsion. Preachers
today would do well to study the personality and career of Amos. He
became a preacher only because he could say: "The Lord God hath
spoken, who can but prophesy?" God took him. The Lord said unto
him, "Go, prophesy" (7:15). In an arresting figure he compares
himself with a bird trapped in a net (3:5). He is held by the divine

[10] R. H. Pfeiffer, *op. cit.*, p. 583.

impulse. He may struggle to escape from it, but always he is pulled back again. Hence his moral passion, his fearlessness as he attacked the most cherished convictions of his hearers. No one in the world's history ever spoke more daringly than Amos. His courage was derived from his conviction of the reality, the dignity of his message when the Lord had spoken. That is the starting point of Hebrew prophecy. The same sense of inescapable necessity must lie at the heart of any truly prophetic ministry. No other motive, no lesser consideration can equip a true prophet for his task. No man has a right to speak for God unless he believes that God has chosen him to be His spokesman.

In one respect, Amos is not the model preacher, any more than was John Knox. His passion was not tempered by love, sympathy, pity. He warns, he condemns, he threatens, but this he does "without a sob." He does not take upon himself the sins that he condemns, nor seek to identify himself with the people who have forfeited their claim on the divine compassion. He attacks evil with passionate directness. But he does not sow the soil which he has scorched with the seeds of a new and regenerating life. The modern prophet may well remember that a purely minatory preaching can never accomplish the full ends of a truly evangelical message. Only as warning and rebuke are accompanied by sympathy, by personal humility, by selfless love which breaks the heart of the preacher as truly as it seeks to penetrate the hearts of his hearers, can the way of salvation be made plain, can man be won to walk in it.

No one can ponder the prophecies of Amos without discovering how directly they bear upon the problems of our modern world. Amos preaches today as truly as when he lived. The writings of all these prophets exhibit a unique timelessness. For they deal not only with the issues of their day but with the fundamental problems of life. The message of Amos, if heeded and obeyed, would solve for us of today problems that vex and disturb us.

The fundamental idea underlying all the preaching of Amos was, as we have seen, the conception of God as righteousness and justice. From this were derived the convictions that bore so directly upon the life of the world in which he lived, which have so much meaning for us of today. If God be righteousness, then the whole of history is but the unfolding of the righteous purpose of God in the affairs of men. In all the terrible events that he foretold, in the downfall of nations, the ruin of Israel's hopes, Amos saw that the ultimate purpose of God was being fulfilled. It was not mere muddle and chaos. Rather, it was a movement and a march, controlled by a divine purpose. God's truth was marching on. This is the real note of optimism to be found in Amos. He may have no word of hope for Israel herself. For God is not concerned about the fate of nations. Samaria might be destroyed, Israel as a nation might disappear. Yet these are but negligible episodes in the great drama of the vindication of God's truth and righteousness which nothing can defeat. Hence Amos and the prophets who came after him reached their magnificent heights of faith in the face of the most terrible political convulsions. It was their innermost and most passionate conviction that the final purpose of God was being wrought out through all contemporary disaster—a purpose which the sin of man might delay but could never defeat. Hence, while Amos never compromised in his denunciation of evil or flinched in his pronouncement of punishment and justice, still he preserved the unshakable persuasion that the final victory belonged to God. That victory did not depend upon the deliverance of even His chosen people. Indeed, it may have demanded the destruction of a people who had forfeited the right to His favor and defense. High above the wreck of an earthly kingdom stood the kingdom of His truth and righteousness.

It would be well if we of today could recapture this mood of Amos. Too often we are prone to link the idea of moral victory with the triumph of earthly kingdoms, to identify it with the welfare of our own nation. Not at all. God, teaches Amos, is not concerned with the prosperity of any nation on earth. The only way in which any nation can hope to survive is by identifying itself with the truth and righteousness of God. Only the men and women who share this conviction are the true prophets in our modern world. They face the possibility that modern nations, even our own, may turn to ways and purposes which are not of God's choosing and hence may come into judgment. Yet always beyond "the wrecks of time" they behold the final fulfillment in the sphere of history of God's purpose, which is grounded in truth and justice.

Amos disposes also in his grand way of the idea that the providence of God is limited to any one people or peoples on earth. How deeply rooted that idea was in the minds and hearts of the Hebrew people any reader of the Old Testament is well aware. In a sense it was true that they were God's chosen people. In them had been implanted a knowledge of God not vouchsafed to other nations, an idea that was to grow in process of time until it burst out into full bloom in the knowledge of God in Christ. Yet, so teaches Amos, the providence of God was directing the destinies of other nations as truly as that of Israel. His providence was over all. The same Hand which had led the people of Israel across the Red Sea and through the desert into Canaan had brought the Philistines from Caphtor and the Syrians from Kir (9:7). The universal movement was under God's direction and control. Amid "all the events of earth and all the tangled processes of history" [11] we find God's providence at work shaping everything to His divine ends.

Here we find the ultimate denial of the idea of favored races, of the superiority in God's sight of one race, one people over another. The notion still lingers in the minds of many that the Anglo-Saxon has been divinely appointed to be the master race; that there is a fundamental difference in the eyes of Providence between the races of the earth. This is the hidden root idea within the whole program of imperialism which still curses the earth. We shall be rid of it only as we understand that the purpose and providence of God is as surely manifest in the aspirations of other races as in our own; that these have the same dignity in His sight and that their destinies are as surely wrought into the fabric of His total purpose for the world as our own. Here is the final foundation of that human equality and spiritual democracy which alone can create the world community for which we hope and pray.

The principle of judgment which Amos applied to Israel is an eternal principle to be applied to every nation. "Thus he shewed me: and, behold, the Lord stood upon a wall . . . with a plumbline in his hand . . . Then said the Lord, Behold, I will set a plumbline in the midst of my people Israel . . ." (7:7,8). It was the plumbline of justice and truth. That means that "there is a principle of moral gravitation operat-

[11] George Adam Smith, *op. cit.,* "Amos."

ing in the universe." [12] Only that nation can stand on a firm foundation whose whole life from top to bottom is true and straight according to the plumbline test of justice and righteousness. That plumbline Amos let right down through the whole life of Israel: through its religious life, its political life, its economic and industrial life, its social life. And that plumbline revealed that the whole of it was untrue and was tottering to its fall. Its religion was shot through with superstition, hypocrisy and degrading immoralities; its political life was guided by motives of expediency and self-interest; its economic life was a travesty upon the simplest principles of justice and fair dealing; its social life reeked with frivolity and self-indulgence. The life of the whole people rested on rotten foundations.

The same plumbline is let down into the life of the nations today. Is their political relation to other nations governed by selfish motives with cynical disregard of the ideas of brotherhood and the rights of minorities? Is their religious life a matter of form and outward observance rather than a spirit which penetrates every phase of the existing order and seeks to shape it according to the principles of righteousness and justice? Is their economic life filled with inequalities causing the rich to become richer while the underprivileged suffer from want and poverty? Is their social life one of frivolity and self-indulgence, of extravagance and immorality? If so, then judgment swift and sure awaits them as surely as it did Israel. Such is the modern message of the Book of Amos.

Amos has been called "conscience incarnate." He insists always and everywhere that true religion begins in recognition of the holiness of God: a holiness which must find its expression, its embodiment in the personal and national life. He saw with astonishing clearness the evils by which society was corrupted: the love of pleasure, the love of gain, the oppression of the poor, the callousness of the rich, the lust of power, reliance on force. He perceived that the physical and intellectual strength of a nation can be sapped by the twin vices of intemperance and impurity. Away with all this, he cries; "Seek good, and not evil ... Hate the evil, and love the good, and establish judgment in the gate" (5:14, 15). Only a thorough moral reformation can avert national dis-

[12] *Ibid.*, "Amos."

aster. Amos asks us of today, Is the religion which we have in the land "rooted in conscience and expressible in conscience"? [13] The message of Amos goes to the heart of things. It tears pretense from law courts, where lingers favoritism rather than justice; from industry and commerce, where the love of gain has ousted the love of man; from altars of religion, where officials are busy with their services and are indifferent to reality. It must have astonished those who listened to Amos to have him call sins such as these as heinous as the barbarities of the heathen nations. Yet the same formula, "Thus saith the Lord," precedes the catalogue of the sins of Israel as had preceded his excoriation of the inhuman cruelties of the Syrians and the Philistines. And today Amos would declare that the inhumanities of our present social order are as truly to be condemned as the atrocities of the Japanese or of the Germans in the late war. If any reader of these pages resents this statement, then he simply shares what must have been the indignation of the hearers of Amos.

There remains to be mentioned what Amos has to say about ceremonial and religion. This subject will be discussed again when we come to the prophets of the Restoration, who present the other side of the picture. Only when we grasp what both they and Amos have to say will we have the whole matter in its true perspective. There are those who feel that Amos taught that ritual has no place in a true religion.[14] They point to a verse (5:25) of doubtful authenticity in which the prophet declared that in its very beginnings the Hebrew religion had provided no place for sacrifices. Ceremonial is not only unnecessary in religion, it is foreign to its essential meaning as the practice of the righteousness demanded by the Word and Will of God. Hence Amos banished it from religion. "Emphasis upon morality as the sum of religion to the exclusion of sacrifice is the most original element in Amos." [15] This statement of the case, however, is probably too broad. It was not sacrifice and ritual themselves that Amos was denouncing, but rather the abuse of them. Amos did not explicitly deny that ritual has any place in religion although religion may do without it. But to substitute ceremonial for righteousness was to degrade the very idea of religion itself.

[13] *Ibid.*, "Amos."   [14] *Ibid.*, "Amos."   [15] *Ibid.*, "Amos."

And that is precisely what the Israelites had done. For them, religion consisted solely of a cloak with which to cover transgression. They had become penetrated by the idea of their heathen neighbors that rites and sacrifices were the indispensable element in religion. Thus they were assiduous in their ritual, punctilious in their sacrifices, yet because of sensuality, worldliness, pride and hardness of heart they never felt that clear summons to duty and to righteousness which a true religion always makes men hear. Hence sacrifice and lavish ritual was an abomination in the sight of the Lord.

If, then, real religion embodying an ethical course of conduct was to become a reality, a robust repudiation of a hollow and insincere ceremonial was necessary. And this we find in Amos. And in his indignant protest against a false use of religion he has given us "one of the few immortal statements of the essence of religion itself" [16]: "Let judgment run down as waters, and righteousness as a mighty stream" (5:24). "His was the first voice raised in antiquity to utter a forceful call to an ethical religion." [17]

The same voice was raised again by Jesus in his day. The religion of the Pharisees had degenerated into a formal observance of the externals of religion without any regard for its ethical and moral meanings. Hence the terrific excoriation of it which we find in the twenty-third chapter of Matthew's Gospel. And the same voice needs to be raised in every age and in our age. For the temptation is always present to imagine that orthodoxy and ecclesiastical conformity are the credentials of the religious man.[18] Our churches today are doubtless filled with people, as Stanley Jones once said, who would be equally shocked to have the truths of Christianity doubted or to have them practiced. There are many who will take their Bibles to church, but are not likely to put them in their pockets when going to business. Phillips Brooks once told a parishioner of his that there did not seem to be much connection between his churchgoing and his business practices. He received this good-humored reply: "I do not see what you have to complain of. I divide things up. I cannot go to church all of

---

[16] *Ibid.*, "Amos."
[17] *Ibid.*, "Amos."
[18] See R. B. Y. Scott, *The Relevance of the Prophets,* p. 207: "The prophets make it plain that religion and ethical behavior must form a vital unity."

the time. So on Sunday I go to church and sing hymns and say my prayers. Then on Monday I go to my business." There in simplest terms is the situation precisely as Amos found it. In Ruskin's *Crown of Wild Olives* occurs this passage: "Nothing can be accomplished unless, first of all, both servant and master are resolved that, come what will of it, they will do each other justice . . . That is the one thing constantly reiterated by our Master, the order of all orders that is given oftenest: 'Do justice and judgment.' That's your Bible order; the 'Service of God,' is not praying nor psalm-singing . . . He loves honest servants, not beggars . . . And yet we are impudent enough to call our beggings and chantings 'Divine Service'; we say 'Divine Service will be performed' (that's our word—the form of it gone, though) 'at eleven o'clock.' Alas! Unless we perform Divine service in every willing end of our lives, we never perform it at all. The one Divine work—the one ordered sacrifice—is to do justice; and it is the last we are inclined to do." Thus the voice of Amos summoning men to an ethical religion needs to be heard today as truly as in the day in which he lived. Amos does not substitute morality for religion. On the contrary, he taught that all morality finds its roots, its spiritual source and its compelling power over the consciences of men in the character of God Himself, that is, in religion. Neither the reconstruction of society nor the re-formation of human character can be achieved without the sanctions of a true religion. Both social and personal morality if it is to be stable and adventurous must be derived from a conscious relationship between God and man. But this religion must be rooted also in conscience. It must hate evil both in oneself and in the world wherever found. It must love justice and seek the good. For neither morality without religion, nor religion without morality, can ever avail to bring salvation either to man or to society. Such is the message of Amos to our modern world.

~~~ *Hosea* ~~~

I. Introduction

ALONE of these Hebrew prophets, Hosea was a native of the Northern Kingdom, and only he and Amos prophesied there. The name "Hosea," with its variants "Hoshea" and "Oshea" (Num. 13:8; II Kings 15:30), and "Osee" (Rom. 9:25) appears to mean "salvation." Of his family background we are told only that his father's name was Beeri. That he belonged to the priestly class, or, like Zechariah, may himself have been a priest, seems possible from his frequent references to the intrigues and evil doings of the priesthood. He was certainly a man of culture and education, competent to follow with keen intelligence the policies of his country and to pass judgment on them. If inferences may be drawn from the illustrations and figures of speech in which his book abounds, it appears likely that he belonged to the country rather than to the city. For Hosea was clearly a lover of nature and was sensitive to its moods. "The poetry of Hosea clings about his native soil." [1] He speaks of wool and flax and oil, of sowing and reaping, of the dews and the early and latter rain, of fig trees and olives, the wild vine and the scent of Lebanon, of birds and beasts, of home life and occupations. "Where do we find anything like this, save in the parables of Jesus?" [2]

His was evidently a difficult and stormy career. He placed himself in open opposition to all religious leaders (5:1) as well as to kings and princes (7:3,7; 8:4,10). A rather obscure passage (9:8) seems to indicate persecution. No real prophet in those days or in ours has had an easy time of it, and Hosea is no exception. This is the price a prophet has to pay for living ahead of his time.

The date of his ministry can be fixed with some precision. We are told (1:1) that he prophesied "in the days of Jeroboam . . . king of Israel." (The names of the kings of Judah from Uzziah to Hezekiah

[1] George Adam Smith, *op. cit.*, "Hosea."
[2] *Ibid.*, "Hosea."

31

are a later interpolation.) Since Jeroboam II died about 744 B.C., Hosea's work must have begun before that date. And it must have ended before 735-734 B.C., for Hosea makes no mention of the invasion of Judah by Resin, king of Syria, and by Pekah, king of Israel (Is. 7:1; II Kings 16:5), or to the raid of the Assyrian Tiglath-pileser III upon Gilead and Galilee (II Kings 15:29) in 734 B.C. There is no sign in Hosea that Israel has as yet broken with Assyria. Thus we have the nine years between 744 and 735 B.C. within which falls the work of the second of the great Hebrew prophets. Five years before Hosea had begun to prophesy, Amos had completed his sensational tour of the Northern Kingdom. It is certain, however great the dissimilarities between the two, that Amos had made a profound impression on the mind of Hosea. It is possible that the two may have met, or that Hosea had been among those who listened to the preaching of Amos. On the whole, it appears more likely that Hosea had learned of the message of Amos by hearsay, and that this had awakened deep echoes in his own soul.

Indeed, this may have been the origin of Hosea's call to prophesy, precisely as the preaching of John the Baptist summoned Jesus from Nazareth to the Jordan. On this point students of Hosea differ. How shall we interpret the words (1:2): "The beginning of the word of the Lord by Hosea. And the Lord said to Hosea, Go, take unto thee a wife," etc.? To some this affirms that Hosea's call came before his marriage,[3] while others are equally sure that the words assert that the call came out of his domestic experience.[4] It is a question not easily resolved and may well be left in the twilight of the mysteries of prophetic inspiration.

Since the days of Amos, things had gone from bad to worse in the Northern Kingdom. Amos prophesied in the earlier years of Jeroboam II when a transient prosperity was at its height. Within, beneath, and beyond it, Amos with sure insight had descried the inevitable ruin that confronted the nation. That ruin Hosea was destined to witness with his own eyes. The earlier portion of his prophecies fall within the last

[3] So R. H. Pfeiffer, *Introduction to the O. T.*, p. 568.
[4] So George Adam Smith, *op. cit.*, "Hosea"; and R. E. Wolfe, *Meet Amos and Hosea*, pp. 74, 117.

years of Jeroboam's reign and reflect the waning glory of Israel as the sun of its splendor goes slowly down. The later chapters give us vivid glimpses of the debacle that followed the death of Jeroboam, the chaos and anarchy into which the whole nation was plunged. Details are supplied by II Kings 15. In rapid succession Zechariah, Shallum, Menahem and Pekakiah mounted the throne. Shallum murdered Zechariah, and he in turn was murdered by Menahem, who bribed the Assyrians to keep him in power (II Kings 15:19). His son Pekakiah was assassinated by Pekah (735 B.C.). At this point Hosea disappears, just before the final plunge of the nation into oblivion. Pekah was disposed of by Hoshea, the last of the kings of the Northern Kingdom. Assyria was now on the march. Hoshea bought off Tiglath-pileser for a time (II Kings 17:3,4). Then, relying unwisely upon the support of Egypt, withdrew tribute. Swift vengeance followed. Samaria fell in 722 B.C., and the doom so confidently predicted by both Amos and Hosea overtook the recreant nation.

Historically the book of Hosea is important because it gives us this vivid picture of social conditions in the Northern Kingdom during the period between 744 and 735 B.C. We read of crime waves, of corruption and immorality, of the degradation of the priesthood, of the impotence of rulers, of chaos and disorder. Hosea is the prophet of the decline and fall of the Northern Kingdom.

The Book of Hosea falls into two unequal parts: 1-3 and 4-14. It is probable that the two parts appeared separately and were only later —just when, we cannot know—combined in the book as we now have it. Which of these two sections first came from Hosea cannot be known with certainty. Some feel that the autobiographical section (1-3) must have been written at the end of Hosea's life, and that place must be found for it somewhere in the course of his prophecies in 4-14. This, however, is a question which need not detain us. It is best to take up the book as it is presented to us in our Bibles.

1. *Chapters 1-3.*

Here we have described the personal domestic story of Hosea's marriage and of the bearing of it, in the prophet's mind, upon the relation of God to His people Israel. The story reads in simple, straight-forward fashion. The prophet was bidden of the Lord to marry a profligate woman, Gomer by name. This he did. Three children were born, of whom presumably only the first was the child of Hosea. All three were given symbolical names, descriptive of God's future dealings with His people. Discovering that his wife was unfaithful to him, Hosea put her away; or she may herself have deserted her home. In any event, she became a common dissolute woman and was finally sold as a slave. In this plight Hosea saw her, had compassion on her, bought her and brought her back to his home, where she lived under discipline and without full status as wife and mother. So seems to run the story. The question is, what shall we make of it? The various answers may be briefly summarized as follows:

(1) The story must be taken exactly as it appears to read. God commanded Hosea to marry a woman whom he knew to be a prostitute, whom he endeavored to reclaim. This was done in order that Hosea might learn from such a bitter experience what was the love of God toward a sinful nation. The objections to this interpretation seem conclusive. It is unimaginable that God would command a course of action so abhorrent to every normal human impulse. Had Hosea done such a thing, the sensation that it would have created would have prevented the people from listening to his prophetical interpretation of it. Moreover, to imagine that Gomer was an impure woman before her marriage spoils the analogy, since the whole idea is that Israel was pure at the beginning of the covenant between her and God, and only later became unfaithful to Him. For these and other reasons this interpretation now has few adherents.

(2) The whole thing is allegory.[5] Prophets often represent themselves as performing actions which they could not have performed (Ezek. 4:1ff.). So here, Hosea puts in pictorial form an action he was never called upon to perform and did not perform. He cast in the form of a dramatic parable the truth of Israel's faithlessness and of God's redeeming love. And yet the story certainly reads as if it were a real story. Is it likely also that a man would deliberately invent such a story about himself and his wife? And the whole passionate message

[5] See Hastings' Bible Dictionary, "Hosea."

of Hosea to his people seems to stem from some personal and poignant experience, whether or not this constituted his call to prophesy. It therefore seems probable that some substratum of fact underlies the narrative.

(3) Gomer was not a profligate woman when Hosea married her, but became one after her marriage to him. His wife must have been pure or she could not have served as a type of Israel whose early relations to God he describes as innocent. How now are we to reconcile this with the explicit statement in 1:2 that at the command of God he married a woman whom he knew to be dissolute? Some seek to solve this apparent contradiction by pointing out that what may be meant is that the woman was not actually but only potentially an impure woman. She had it in her to be such. Others reason that Hosea when he discovered that his wife was unfaithful to him, and what was God's purpose in such a bitter experience, pushed back his own knowledge of that purpose to the very time of his betrothal to Gomer. God had commanded him to marry a woman who subsequently became what she did become. The rest of the story is taken as it is set down for us. In spite of its difficulties, this interpretation of the story seems to the writer to be on the whole the most probable. It will be followed in the exposition of these chapters.

(4) A variant of this interpretation is concerned with the fate of Gomer. R. E. Wolfe holds that once Gomer left her home she never returned to it. Her fate was sealed. She was stoned. The story of her final reclamation by Hosea when she was exposed for sale as a slave (chap. 3) was the work of later editors who inserted this invention in order to hold out hope thereby for the final redemption of Israel. Hosea's repudiation of Gomer was final, just as his judgment of doom for Israel was without promise of redemption. But if this revolutionary idea is adopted, what then has become of Hosea's basic idea of the long-suffering and redemptive love of God? It provides no adequate explanation of what after all is the supreme thing in Hosea's understanding of God. Is this, indeed, Hosea?

(5) Dissatisfied with any of these interpretations, R. H. Pfeiffer in his *Introduction to the Old Testament* advances the idea that Gomer was a pure woman when Hosea married her and remained so to the

literary style – 1. not clear
2. pathos – long-suffering
3. language – crude

36   THE MODERN MESSAGE OF THE MINOR PROPHETS

end. She is called "a wife of whoredoms" figuratively because she belonged to a people who were faithless to God and therefore was herself faithless to Him because of her organic and inseparable connection with and participation in their sin. The woman mentioned in chapter 3 is a different woman altogether, not Gomer at all. The word of the Lord came again to Hosea and bade him purchase this common slave and take her to his own home, where she was kept in seclusion, as a symbol of Israel's impending slavery and of God's continuing love. The difficulty here is that in thus removing the element of tragedy in the domestic life of Hosea we are left without due explanation of the sense of poignant and personal emotion that pervades these chapters and gives depth and passion to his interpretation of the relation of Jehovah to His people. Also we lose the pathos and beauty of the love of Hosea for his wife in spite of her degradation, a symbol of the all-suffering and redeeming Love of God.

Among these different interpretations, the reader of the first three chapters of Hosea will make his choice. Whichever he chooses will determine in a measure his interpretation of the message of God to Hosea, and of Hosea to his people.

The authenticity of the bulk of these chapters is doubted by none except those few who reject the whole of chapter 3. However, in addition to the editing of v. 1 in chapter 1, we see clearly that verses 7, 10, 11 of this chapter are by a later hand. They seem to reflect the deliverance of Jerusalem from Sennacherib in 701 B.C. The promises of restoration in 2:14-23 and 3:5 are also of doubtful authenticity. Still, this first part of Hosea's book is well preserved for us. It probably appeared in a manuscript by itself, was much read, and new copies of it were made before the text became worn and illegible.

2. Chapters 4-14

Coming now to the second part of Hosea, we find ourselves in much difficulty. The composition of these chapters falls during the chaotic period following the final collapse of the house of Jehu after the death of Jeroboam II. They consist of a series of discourses illogically arranged which can be only a reproduction by the prophet himself of the

Hosea – tenderhearted
reflects grief over the apostasies of his people

main parts of his addresses on different occasions and in relation to different events. We have a multitude of variations on one theme: Israel's apostasy and punishment. But the poor textual transmission, the large amount of interpolated material and the fact that Hosea's thoughts are set down in such confusion make these chapters obscure reading. Various efforts have been made to bring some order out of all this. Perhaps the best that can be done is to arrange the different items in the general arraignment which Hosea brings against Israel. In chapters 4-6 he is chiefly engaged in condemning her religious institutions, cultus and worship. The genuine spiritual conception of God has degenerated into the nature worship of the Baalim and immoral rites are practiced in place of the pure worship of Jehovah. The present cultus is a sin, and for this the priests are responsible. The following chapters, 7-10, contain vivid descriptions of a disorganized society in which different factions contend for the mastery. Hosea alludes to incidents which are obscure; but they all reveal that internal convulsions were breaking the nation into pieces. The prophet assails kings and princes who have not been able to maintain order. He is weary of the impotency of secular politics and seems to foreshadow as his ideal a theocracy of which the Lord alone will be King (8:4). In these and in following chapters the external policies of Israel are condemned. This reliance on foreign alliances, Assyria and Egypt, is unfaithfulness to God (8:9), a distrust of Him, alienation of the mind from Him. And the issue of all this is certain. Jehovah will drive Israel out of the land. This will be done both by the sword of the enemy (8:3; 5:8,9) and by internal decay (7:8,9; 9:16). Assyria (9:3) or Egypt (8:13) will swallow them up. The wages of sin is death. Moral law operates (8:7; 10:13). The closing chapters, 11-14, reflect the grief of Hosea over the apostasy of his people, his deep conviction of the unwearying love of God that bears with Israel in spite of her sin, his despair lest Israel's incapacity to repent will seal her final doom.

Chapters 4-14 were not so popular as the first part of the Book of Hosea. Good care was not taken of this section when it appeared, and the restoration that was made was not true to the original. Thus these chapters are probably one of the most disordered sections of the whole Bible. It is hard to bring order out of this chaos. The text is dilapidated

Religion is life —

almost beyond repair, and the question of authenticity is raised to a pitch of great difficulty.

In seeking to decide how much of these chapters is the authentic work of Hosea and how much of it must be assigned to later additions to the original text, the same criteria are used that were applied to the Book of Amos. Thus, to a Judean editor will be credited the frequent references to Judah, although it is by no means certain that Hosea never once mentioned the Southern Kingdom. The whole of chapter 12 seems to be the work of a Jew with strong antipathy for the Samaritans, who justifies the intensity of his feeling by a historical retrospect which is not at all in the manner of Hosea. Historically, certain references to the Assyrians and Egyptians, as in 11:11, seem to belong to a later time. Then there is always the question of whether interpolations were not inserted tempering the final judgment of God upon the people, as in 1:10-2:1; 2:14-23; 4:16[b]; 11:8[b], etc. Yet to deny to Hosea any of these promises of future restoration, any of these glimmerings of hope, might be to err in that direction and to be untrue to the wavering moods of the prophet as love struggles with justice. Some of them, perhaps later expanded, may well belong to him.

Into the intricacies of this attempt at restoration of the original text it is unnecessary for us to go. But a major question is whether the beautiful epilogue in chapter 14 describing the final redemption of the people belongs to Hosea or not. The authenticity of this chapter is passionately defended by George Adam Smith [6] who had decided against the authenticity of a similar ending of the book of Amos. He feels that the two cases are not parallel. The closing verses of Amos are opposed to the whole temper of his book and announce no ethical conditions for salvation. Hosea, on the other hand, has not only continually preached repentance but has an inward conviction, born of his own experience, of the unwavering love of God, a conviction to which Amos was a total stranger. For these reasons this profound Old Testament scholar declares that he cannot "conceive of the possibility of a stronger case for the genuineness of any passage of Scripture." Yet the same scholar, in commenting on the words "repentance shall

[6] *Op. cit.*

be hid from mine eyes" (13:14), writes: "The statement that His people will not be saved, for God cannot save them, is in thorough harmony with all of Hosea's teaching." Here we touch the antinomy in the thought of Hosea that constitutes the inmost tragedy of his experience: on the one hand, a people who not only do not repent but seem incapable of repentance; on the other hand, a Love that will not let them go. To the present writer it seems truer to the experience of Hosea to leave this tragical antinomy unresolved than, by denying to Hosea any expressions of possible redemption, to assume that he, like Amos, was at the end a prophet without hope of the salvation of his people; or, by admitting the authenticity of chapter 14, to resolve it in the glowing expectations of the epilogue. Precisely as we are not told when Gomer came back home again what was the final story of her life with Hosea, so we are not told what was the final issue of the struggle of Sin against Love. Therein lies the final mystery of the Book of Hosea. At the beginning of his ministry he had hoped that discipline would turn the hearts of the people. Yet even when he came to believe that their sin was incurable, still he retained his unswerving faith in the love of God. Although convinced that God must execute the death sentence against the people, yet Love remains unconquered and unconquerable. That is Hosea.

The fate of the man is enshrouded in obscurity. Whether he survived the fall of Samaria is not known. Probably he had passed away before Assyria invaded the land. His grave is still regarded as a shrine on the top of Mount Hosea, east of the Jordan.

The importance of the message of Hosea in the development of Hebrew thought may be roughly summarized as follows:

(1) Religion with Hosea becomes inward and spiritual. Before his time the element of fear had predominated. God was King and worshipers were His subjects. He was master and they were servants. Obedience was the keynote in religion. Thus in Amos the ethical element is uppermost. But in Hosea we have a concept entirely new of a spiritual relationship between God and His people. The phrase "the Lord thy God" was coined by Hosea, and the essence of religion is found to consist in this spiritual bond between God and man, pre-

sented in the figure of the marriage relation, "the most original and the most important contribution of the prophet." [7] This idea was never again lost in Hebrew theology. If Amos was John the Baptist among the prophets, Hosea was St. John the Evangelist.

(2) Thus Hosea presents us with an idea of God new to Hebrew thought. The God of righteousness becomes the God of a long-suffering Love. This conception of the essential nature of God was carried to new heights by Jeremiah, between whom and Hosea there is strong affinity. For, whereas in Hosea the love of God applies to the nation only, Jeremiah carries it into the life of the individual as well. The initial discovery, however, of the Fatherhood of God, the sonship of man, a Divine Love operating in all the permutations of human experience belongs to Hosea. And this places him in the front rank of the world's religious geniuses. This is the fundamental idea that runs through and determines the whole message of Hosea to his world and to ours. The problem left by Amos was how to match Law with Love. Hosea has a conscience as keen as that of Amos. Yet love is even stronger than sin. "No truth uttered about the Divine Grace by later prophets that is not found in Hosea." [8] He is Israel's earliest evangelist. This is the tragedy of Hosea's life: The struggle between justice and mercy.

(3) Hosea was the first prophet to attack idols. Elijah and Amos were concerned only that Israel should worship Jehovah and not idols, against which they had no word to say. But in Hosea we hear for the first time the note of mockery of idols (8:4,5,6; 10:5,6; 13:2) which sounds through later Hebrew prophecy. And in one of these passages (8:6) the prophet speaks as if these gods had no real existence at all. Thus the foundation was laid for the complete monotheism of Hebrew religion.

(4) In Hosea we find the first foreshadowing of the idea of theocracy, of a nation governed by God alone (7:16; 8:4ª; 10:2,3; 11:5,7.). One has to pick his way carefully through these chapters in the discovery of this idea, for many passages—as, for example, 1:11 and 3:5 —are certainly spurious. Still, the complete failure of a secular govern-

---

[7] George Adam Smith, *op. cit.,* "Hosea."
[8] *Ibid.,* "Hosea."

ment seems to bring Hosea to the contemplation of a State ruled only from above. This idea comes to its full fruition in later Hebrew thought, but has its beginnings here.

When we remember that all four of these cardinal ideas were absolutely new, we understand the importance of Hosea in the development of Hebrew thought. It is not too much to say that "the entire faith and theology of later Israel grew out of Hosea, that all of its characteristic views and ideas are first found in his book." [9]

The style of Hosea is in sharp contrast to that of Amos, who was direct, simple, logical; whose addresses move in a straight line, as it were. But with Hosea, the emotional element brought confusion into his style. "Le style, c'est l'homme." And because Hosea was the man that he was, his style is what it is. His writing is surcharged with feeling. Hence he passes without any transition from tenderness to ferocity, from a sob to a curse. Essentially he was a poet, a poet of the heart, and we find outbursts of exhaustless sorrow, endless grief, wild cries of anguish, bold poetic flights, with only rarely a distinct connection between them. He was a man controlled by his moods, and these find full and lyrical expression in his writing. He does not so much address the people as commune with himself "in shuddering disjointed monologue."

For these and for other reasons, which have been stated, the Book of Hosea is immensely obscure and difficult. It is not easy and intelligible reading. Neither is it altogether pleasant reading. For Hosea does not hesitate to use a harsh, a coarse, and even a vulgar vocabulary as with extreme frankness and candor he exposes the sins, the shames of the people, their infidelities toward an ever-loving God.

II. THE PROPHECY

1. *Chapters 1-3*

No figure in the prophets' frieze by Sargent in the Boston Public Library is so arresting as that of the prophet Hosea, whose fine, sensitive and ascetic face is half shrouded by the long white garment in which

[9] Cornill, *The Prophets of Israel*, p. 53.

he is clothed. His indeed is a tragic figure and his theology was born out of bitter personal experience. One will never understand Hosea unless one remembers that "tears fall upon every page that he wrote, not the tears of sentiment, but the terribly different tears of a strong man." For Hosea was indeed a man of sorrows and acquainted with grief. His is a sad book from first to last, yet with a wonderful undertone of love. Hosea tells the story of the compassionate love of God.

Married, then, to a woman of his love, he began a life of domestic happiness. A child was born to them, to whom was given the name of Jezreel. It was in the valley of Jezreel that Jezebel had met her fate. And Hosea, called of God to be His prophet, already seething with indignation at the sins of Israel, symbolized in the name he gave by divine commandment to his son the fate that awaited the dynasty of Jehu, and of the people of Israel. Two other children were born. But were they Hosea's? The first, a daughter, received the name Lo-ruhamah, signifying "no mercy"; the second, a son, was called Lo-ammi, "not my people." In these names is suggested the tragedy that had befallen Hosea, the faithlessness of his wife, who no longer was permitted to live, who no longer may have wished to live, in what had been their home.

Out of the bitterness of this experience, Hosea was made to see, not perhaps for the first time but now in all the starkness of reality, the changed relation between God and His people. No longer did the covenant relation exist as in the days of Israel's innocency, but a union which had been ruined by faithlessness, a situation which demanded that Israel be driven from her home, her happiness and glory gone, given to shame and desolation. All of this in poignant phrase is spread before us in chapter 2:1-13.

Follows the story (chapter 3) of Gomer's degradation, her exposure as a common slave for sale, Hosea's compassion on her, her reclamation and home-coming once more. And there the story ends. Did Gomer become a regenerate woman? We are not told. Neither are we told whether Israel was to become a regenerate people (v. 5 is spurious). But we are told the story of Love, deep, compassionate and sacrificial.

In all of this Hosea saw mirrored the relation of God to His people.

Whether or not his prophecy originated in his personal experience, it was given depth and passion by it, human, moral and personal color. God had joined His people to Himself in their innocency, in holy covenant. They had been faithless to Him, and therefore the bond that had united them had been broken. As Gomer no longer could remain at home, neither could Israel remain in what had been a promised land. As Gomer went in her degradation into slavery, so must a degraded people go into captivity. Yet as Hosea had had mercy on Gomer and had sought to redeem her from her fate, so the long-suffering love of God would follow and seek to ransom Israel. Hosea had learned what no prophet had learned before, what no prophet perhaps could have learned except through his own personal experience, that the essence of God's nature is not justice alone, but justice and love.

Thus there was double tragedy in the life of Hosea. For he loved his land and his people with a depth only equaled but not surpassed by Jeremiah himself. Amos had come into the land a stranger, and he could utter his invectives without pain to himself. But the love of Hosea for his land and people is spread open upon every page. Hence his very heart is wrung with grief and pity. His condemnation of their faithlessness and sin is accentuated by his love. For the more one loves another, the sharper and more piercing will be one's detestation of the sin that defiles and degrades him. It is precisely this correspondence between his personal relationship with Gomer and that of his people with God that made the cup of his suffering to overflow.

In all of this, also, we see mirrored the whole drama of the Bible story, the whole drama of human experience. Sin, judgment and love, these are the three great themes of the Bible from Genesis to Revelation; these are the three elemental experiences of the human soul. Sin appears in the second chapter of the Bible record and it does not disappear until the last chapter of it was written. In between, the fact and the nature of it remains unaltered and unabridged. Sin is willful disobedience of man to the Word and Will of God, which results in a severing of the filial relationship of man to God, in the alienation of man from God. The whole message, theology and evangel of the Bible rest solidly on its conception of the nature and meaning of sin. All

Bible writers, historian, psalmist, prophet, agree in their definition of sin. Each has his own way of describing it; of describing, too, its effects. But not one who does not plant it solidly at the basis, place it as the ultimate cause, of the tragedy of human experience. Yet no one of them has done this so convincingly, so appealingly, with such poignancy and pathos as the prophet Hosea.

The inevitable result of sin is judgment and punishment. And this consists in banishment from the presence of God. Paradise is lost. Gomer leaves a home where she might have found her happiness. Israel goes into exile. The Prodigal Son finds himself in a "far country." The wages of sin is death. "For they have sown the wind, and they shall reap the whirlwind" (Hos. 8:7). Retribution follows moral disobedience, swift and sure. A flaming sword bars re-entrance into Paradise. "The soul that sinneth, it shall die."

If this were all, the Bible would but repeat in its own fashion the doctrine of Fate as we find it expounded in Greek thought and given dramatic illustration in the Greek tragedies. But the Bible presents us not with three Fates but with two Fates and an Angel. To its concepts of sin and retribution is added its doctrine of the Love of God. That idea was not altogether original with Hosea. From the first, Hebrew thought had within it a deep conviction of a Providence that guided the destinies and shaped the course of a chosen people who were under His special care and protection. But by Hosea that idea was given warmth and color and was clothed with emotion such as the human heart feels for the object of its affection. This makes up the poetry and the beauty of Hosea's description of the love of God for His people. It was not a flaccid or superficial love. Love at its holiest and best does not exclude severity. Hence these two conflicting moods of tenderness and sternness which we find on every page of Hosea's writing. Justice to the fact of sin lies at the heart of this love of God. There is something profound and terrible and adequate about it. It reaches to the depths. Doing so, it suffers. Hosea portrays the suffering love of God. "Aimer, c'est souffrir." "Plus on aime, plus on souffre." Love never exonerates the sinner, nor seeks to set aside deserved and righteous punishment for sin. To do so would not be to love. But out of his sorrow Hosea learned the sorrow of God. And out of his forgiveness he learned the sacrificial and forgiving love of God. "The Love of God is a terrible thing: that is the last lesson of the book of Hosea . . . Quivering with his own pain, Hosea has exhausted all human care and affection for figures to express the Divine tenderness" [10] toward the people whom He loves, forgives and yearns to win back to Himself. That agony of Love is never ended until it has won its victory over sin and reclaimed the sinner.

The final note of tragedy in the experience of Hosea lies here: that he cannot glimpse that sure and final victory. Sin can withstand and defeat the love of God. And Hosea sees no sure sign that Israel will return and be saved. He cannot compel, he can only "allure and woo" the people back to God. Yet his eye, which pierces to the center of his people's infamy, cannot pierce beneath it and discover infallible proofs of a repentance that leadeth unto life. Sin and love struggle together. We see the struggle but we do not see the victory, either in the life of Gomer or in that of Israel.

Thus Hosea anticipates but he does not reach the heights of the New Testament evangel. The victory of love was proclaimed only by the Cross of Christ, the symbol of a Love that taketh away the sin of the world. Because of this transcendent fact Paul could say: "Love never faileth." That assertion Hosea could never make. Thus his sad book ends not in exaltation but in grief and lamentation.

2. *Chapters 4-14*

These chapters contain the record of the full indictment that Hosea brings against Israel. It is a dark and dreadful picture, relieved only by rays of light which come from a heart of pitying love, a heart in which hope struggles with despair. The chapters are obscure and difficult reading. Also one is abashed by the frankness of the language in describing the immoralities of the people. This characteristic of Old Testament preaching will be fully discussed when we come to the prophet Nahum. Here it need only be said that the Bible does not shun realism in its description of sin. Its vocabulary seeks to lay bare the heinousness of the offenses of which the people were guilty.

[10] George Adam Smith, *op. cit.,* "Hosea."

When we traverse these chapters we find ourselves in an outburst of tumultuous and emotional feeling, from a heart surcharged with both wrath and pity. There is little logical connection. Thus is revealed Hosea's personality, so distinctive among the prophets. "What Hosea gives us are really monologues, the ebullitions of a deeply moved heart, torn by grief, in all its varying moods and sentiments . . . But it is exactly this subjectivity and this individuality which gives to the book of Hosea its special charm and irresistible efficacy." [11]

The first accusation which Hosea brings against his people is that they have honored the Baalim and false gods instead of the spiritual worship of Jehovah. These Baalim were nature gods. The people worshiped them because they received from them the fruits of the earth, the harvests, material blessings which enriched their lives. Hosea's first appearance as a prophet may have been in Samaria, noted for the worship of golden calves. This degeneration of worship aroused the prophet's indignation. He excoriated the priesthood (4:4-10) as Amos had done before him, and exposed the insincerity of a worship which looked to false gods for material favors. He was sickened also by the immoral rites that accompanied pagan forms of worship (4:13,14) and by superstitious veneration of idols. The true worship of the one God of righteousness and love was not to be found in the land. Hence the punishment that was sure to overtake them.

All this exposes the fundamental failure of our contemporary civilization. If we look beneath the surface for the ultimate cause of the chaos and confusion in the world of today, it must be found in our modern paganism. We, too, have worshiped false gods: the gods of wealth, of success, of outward prosperity, of materialism, of national aggrandizement. No single element of our life today, industrial, economic or political, has been God-controlled. The religion for which the churches have stood has failed to penetrate or to influence the policies that have guided our destinies. And this is due, at least in part, to the inefficiency of the clergy. An English bishop recently declared that it is impossible to exaggerate the gulf existing between the Church and the ordinary life and thinking of the English people. "The clergy's spiritual anemia has left half of our countrymen worse than heathens

[11] Cornill, *op. cit.*, p. 51.

in that they believe in nothing—not even in themselves." Irreligion is at the root of all our troubles today as truly as it was in the days of Hosea. And in order to reinstate religion it is necessary to have an intelligent, a competent, a courageous and devoted ministry. This perhaps is the greatest need of the Church today.

The second item in Hosea's indictment has to do with the nation's moral life. It is noticeable that, unlike Amos and Micah, Hosea was not so much concerned with social questions, the sins of men against their fellow men, as with their sin against the love of God. They have not shown their constancy, their loyalty to Him by lives of purity, of right living, of sobriety and self-control. On the contrary, they have given themselves over to self-indulgence, to perjury, lying, adultery. Thus their sacrifices are meaningless. They are a faithless and adulterous generation, guilty of every crime abominated by a just and loving God. The result of all this is that they are corrupt in mind and heart (5:11). Immorality has destroyed both intelligence and conscience (4:12). With insight and passion Hosea presses home this close connection between sins of immorality and the integrity of the personal life, and so of the social order.

And we of today need to heed this preaching of the ancient prophet. We have come to understand that we shall never have a new kind of world until we have a new and a better type of man. Outward reorganization of the world is futile and meaningless except behind it be the moral purpose of the moral man. The golden age waits for men of golden character and motive. And what we see all about us is the weakening of high intelligence and of moral fiber by self-indulgence, frivolity, disregard of high and austere standards of conduct, the elevation of self-gratification above the sanctions of the moral law. The seriousness of these aspects of contemporary life lies in their inevitable effect upon that kind of character which alone can work our salvation. Terrible as are the resulting tragedies in personal experience, even more terrible is the realization that this kind of living destroys the foundation upon which the whole future organization of society must rest. This solemn and eternal truth of the relation of right living toward God to the salvation of the world is brought sharply home to mind and conscience by the preaching of Hosea.

The inevitable result of moral decay, he saw, was political decay. Hosea has been called the first great political prophet of the Old Testament. He is at once the most spiritual and the most political of these Minor Prophets. He perceived the close connection between social morality and political stability. Sins such as he condemned he saw were "the gangrene of the nation," which had lost its moorings and was adrift on a threatening sea. Its policies consisted largely of diplomatic intrigues. Hosea was not opposed to monarchy as such. What he discerned and decried was the failure of the monarchs of his day. They failed to promote domestic stability, allowed crime to run riot, failed to suppress insubordination and social anarchy and to create order out of chaos. In international relations, "like a silly dove," they relied on alliances often made in secret with their threatening neighbors (7:11-13), played fast and loose with principles of honor, and put no reliance whatever upon God, whom they had forgotten and whose covenant with them they had betrayed. Thus with grand gesture, Hosea sweeps away kings, princes, governors who had proved themselves to be incompetent and faithless alike to God and people, and envisages a State ruled by God alone and founded upon His truth and righteousness.

Applied to conditions in our modern world, this message of Hosea is sharply pertinent. Kings and princes, statesmen and rulers have created a world in chaos and confusion. Each has worked, schemed, plotted, for the interest of his own land. Secret diplomacy, intrigues, cynical disregard not only of the rights of other nations but of the principles of truth and honor, have lain at the very center of international relations all through modern history. Failure to do justice to the underprivileged, to provide for their security, has created social unrest and industrial instability. In a word, secular statesmanship stands condemned by its record of misgovernment. It has become increasingly apparent that a continuation of such a regime can result only in world disaster. Hence the demand in our day for an end to this order of things; for government based not on the selfish sovereignty of separate and independent nations, but founded on the idea of a community of nations bound together by common needs, interests, aspirations, not ruled by a selfish statecraft but governed by spiritual principles which have their source in the Word and Will of God. Only death and destruction await mankind except we can break with the old order and create a new world of which the Lord alone is King.

Interspersed through these chapters of condemnation of sin and prediction of punishment are words of pity and of sorrow, of trembling hope that Israel may yet turn and be saved. Only a rigid and ruthless theory which holds that all these are to be ascribed to postexilic interpolation will deny that at least some of them belong to Hosea, who loved his people so passionately and had such unswerving faith in the love of God. The most touching of all these passages is to be found in chapter 11, one of the most tender and beautiful to be found in Scripture. At least the core of this chapter must belong to Hosea. Another verse (13:14), however, dear to the Christian heart, of which Paul made use in his Ode to Immortality has doubtless been mistranslated and misunderstood. As its final words show, this verse was not a promise but a threat. Here the prophet's real meaning is: "Shall I rescue them from the power of the grave? Shall I redeem them from death? Bring forth your plagues, O death, and your destruction, O grave. Compassion is hid from my eyes." So pity and wrath, hope and despair, struggle in the soul of the travailing prophet.

Two other cardinal ideas of Hosea remain to be mentioned. The first of these is Hosea's concept of the knowledge of God. By it Hosea means more than an apprehension of the being of God. He means an inward and spiritual understanding of God's nature and the responsive loyalty of the soul to God. Hosea himself suffered the pain of not being understood. A man of deep tenderness, tact, delicacy, Gomer had not understood him and neither had the people of his love of whom she was the symbol. Just so, Hosea lays emphasis upon the people's essential ignorance of God, His love, His patience, His tenderness. And this lack of understanding of God led to disloyalty to Him in their way of life. Thus when Hosea says (4:1) that "there is no knowledge of God in the land"; or (4:6) "My people are destroyed for lack of knowledge"; or (6:6) "I desired . . . the knowledge of God more than burnt offerings," this is his meaning. The basic error of the people lay in their lack of understanding of the nature of God and their consequent faithlessness to Him. Thus a true knowledge of God begins in feeling, which in turn prompts conscience, and this finally issues in character, in love, in service. Hosea's only hope for his people, his deepest prayer for them, is that the seeds of such knowledge of God might be sown in their hearts.

It is our deepest prayer today. It is probably true that there are few theoretical atheists among us. In one way or another, most people aver that they believe in God. But such knowledge of God as many people possess seems to be consistent with a practical atheism. Their theoretical ideas of the existence of God have no relation to their actual living. They neither understand the nature of God nor do they order their lives by the simple dedication of their wills to God.

Such knowledge of God can come only through repentance. And "so thoroughly has Hosea dealt with this that no preacher since has surpassed his insight." [12] To know God, in the sense in which Hosea uses the term, evidently involves a complete re-formation of the inward man so that he is capable of seeing God for what He is, capable too of turning to the God whom he thus sees, and giving himself to God in loyal and loving obedience. Hosea's reiterated definition of repentance is "returning unto God" (3:5, 6:1, 7:10, 14:1). Repentance, that is, must be thoroughgoing and of the heart. Thus Hosea anticipates the idea of repentance as found in the gospel: a *metanoia,* a change, that is, in the very temper and disposition of the soul whereby it enters into a new relationship with God and hence into a new and higher type of life. Nothing can save Israel, teaches Hosea, and nothing can save man today except such a returning unto God.

Hosea's tragic doubt concerning his people lies in his deep questioning not only of their desire, but of their capacity for such repentance. Nothing is more significant in Hosea than the insight into the difficulty of such repentance upon the part of those long immersed in evil. For this involves not only regret for past mistakes, not only a realization that these mistakes have led to disaster, but a resolute turning away from past habits and practices, an equally resolute turning to God, His Will and His Way. Is Israel capable of such repentance, or has she sinned against God to the extent that the capacity for it has been destroyed within her? Because Hosea does not know the answer to that question, he cannot proclaim in confident hope the salvation of

[12] George Adam Smith, *op. cit.,* "Hosea."

Israel. The love of God remains unaltered. But can the hearts of those whom He loves be so altered as to embrace God's mercy and find salvation in His redeeming grace and power? And the question that haunted the soul of Hosea in his day haunts our souls in the tragic days in which we live.

In all of this it is easy to see how Hosea advances beyond Amos. With Amos, all is Law. With Hosea, it is Love beneath the Law. With Amos, the people had sinned against moral law. With Hosea, their nethermost sin was against divine love. Amos warns and threatens. So does Hosea, but he also pleads. With Amos, doom is destruction. With Hosea, it is discipline. Amos closes the door upon Israel without a pang.[13] Hosea's soul is wrung with pity and with grief. He must have felt sick at heart when he spoke his final message (13:10-16). For his book ends in a deep minor key. If it began with hope of repentance and so of restitution, that hope has faded in the terrible days of Israel's complete collapse before her final fall. The morally corrupt nation simply did not have sufficient strength to give birth to a new spirit. So God must be deaf to her imploring cries in her death hour. Hosea does not, because he cannot, close in benediction. Instead, his final word speaks of the inevitable fate that awaits a recreant people. Yet, though Love may be defeated, Love is still there. And for us the true Christian element in the book consists in that far-reaching intuition of God's forgiving love which was revealed in its fullness in Jesus Christ, the Saviour of mankind.

Hosea is more frequently quoted by New Testament writers than any other of the Minor Prophets. More than thirty direct or indirect quotations from the Book of Hosea may be found in the Gospels and the Epistles. And no wonder. For none of these inspired men, unless it be Jonah, bring us so close to the heart of the evangel as Hosea the son of Beeri.

[13] Or, shall we say, except for the "touching elegy" in Amos 5:1,2?

Know similarities of amos + Hosea

Micah

I. INTRODUCTION

MICAH IS a common Hebrew name. It appears frequently on the pages of the Old Testament. Readers of the Book of Judges will recall the name in the quaint narrative recorded there in chapters 17 and 18. We are told that Micah the prophet was a Morasthite, that is, a native of Moresheth. The site of this village, nowhere else mentioned, has not been identified. Its conjunction with the name of Gath (1:14), however, shows us that it lay in the maritime plain between the Judean hills and Philistia by the sea. This was a fertile territory, with rich soil, cornfields, and olive groves. Micah, then, was a countryman and everything in his book shows us how dear the countryside was to him. It was a region of small villages, remote from the life of large towns and from the political activities that centered in Jerusalem. Micah was a younger contemporary of Isaiah. We are told (1:1) that he prophesied "in the days of Jotham, Ahaz and Hezekiah." Of his activity during the reign of Jotham we have no record; that he prophesied when Ahaz was king (735-720 B.C.) is apparently indicated in verses 6 and 7 of chapter 1, which contains a prediction of the fall of Samaria, which occurred before the accession of Hezekiah in 720 B.C. Hence some critics assign this portion of chapter 1 to a date shortly before 722 B.C. However, this prediction may refer to the final razing of the city of Samaria which followed by many years its capture and the deportation of its inhabitants. And the passage is in close conjunction with the following verses describing the impending fate of Jerusalem. The whole chapter trembles with the imminent destruction of both the Northern Kingdom and Judah. In verses 9-16, the disaster has reached not only to Jerusalem but to the territory in which Micah himself lived. The question remains, did Micah utter these words while Samaria was tottering or had already fallen, and anticipate what was to follow for Jerusalem or Judah, or did he speak while Jerusalem itself was being besieged by Sennacherib in 701 B.C.? We learn from Jeremiah 26:17 ff. that Mi-

:ah prophesied "in the days of Hezekiah, King of Judah." While this
does not exclude the possibility that he may have prophesied earlier or
even later, it seems most likely that the authentic prophecies of Micah
were uttered around 701 B.C. The length of Micah's career is uncertain.
Some would limit it to a few months. Others have wondered if he may
not have prophesied not only as early as Ahaz, but as late as the reign
of Manasseh (692 B.C.), thus accounting for Micah's authorship of
certain portions of the book bearing his name, which, it is said, could
have been written only in that period.

The days in which Micah lived were ominous ones. Samaria fell in
722 B.C. The buffer state which thus far had protected the Southern
Kingdom from the invader no longer existed, and the Assyrians were
sweeping all before them as they advanced toward Egypt, Jerusalem
lying mid-between right in the path of the conquerors. The political
situation was tense. We can compare the state of mind of the people of
Jerusalem with what would have been that of the people of Washing-
ton in the days of the Civil War if Lee had won at Gettysburg and if
Baltimore had fallen into his hands. Even more exposed than Jerusalem,
however, was the broad and open maritime plain where dwelt Micah
of Moresheth. It lay in the very center of the region that would bear
the brunt of the attack of the invader who undertook the conquest of
the Southern Kingdom. Such were the days in which Isaiah and Micah
prophesied. But with this difference: that whereas Isaiah remained immovable in his conviction that Zion was inviolable, Micah was equally
persuaded that nothing could halt the advance of the Assyrian through
the land he loved, which was to feel the full force of heathen invasion
because of her infidelity. Both were right, Isaiah for the moment, but
Micah in the end. We find, then, in Micah a tragical union of love of
country and of indignation for her iniquities which are sure to result in
her punishment. Nothing is more remarkable in the work of the prophets than this power of detachment from personal or national prejudice. Their moral sense is neither dimmed nor diverted by instincts
natural to the human heart. No man ever loved his native soil more than
Micah. Yet no one ever uttered a sterner or more uncompromising message of merited retribution for flagrant sins than he.

The sins he excoriated were those which bore upon the plain people whom he knew, the farmers, the agriculturists, the small landowners. These were made the victims of the rapacity of the wealthy. The sins of sensuality and immorality characteristic of urban life find little mention in Micah. But the social sins of cruelty and inhumanity bulk large in his writing. No one of the prophets has left a message more applicable to our modern world than Micah the Morasthite.

As might be expected from his quiet country life, political events and problems did not concern him as they did the great religious statesman Isaiah, or later Jeremiah. He was aware of the meaning of all that was happening in the great outside world. But his attention was fastened primarily on what was going on right around him in his own little world. And he looked upon what was imminent in the incursion of the Assyrians as punishment for sins against his own people rather than on their ultimate effect on the destinies of the Jewish state. Micah is provincial to the core. When we study him we do not survey the political prospect in its broad dimensions. We see a soul wrung with pity for the misery of his near neighbors and filled with burning indignation against those who have caused it, are responsible for it, and are to be punished by God according to their deserts.

The Book of Micah as it stands has presented a difficult problem to the scholars. All are now agreed that the whole of it cannot have come from Micah himself. The question is how much of it does belong to him. And here opinions vary. Only a brief summary of these different points of view need be given here.

(1) No one doubts the authenticity of the bulk of the first three chapters. Verses 1-5a of chapter 1 may have been a later addition. Verses 12 and 13 of chapter 2 seem to presuppose the Exile. They are certainly out of place where they stand.[1] With these exceptions we can safely accept these chapters as the message of Micah to his age and to ours.

(2) When we come to chapters 4 and 5, we find ourselves involved at once in much perplexity. For one thing, it is hard to make consecutive sense out of these chapters as they stand. The transitions are so abrupt, the connection is so poor, that it is difficult to believe they can

---

[1] Driver in his *Old Testament Introduction,* p. 328, suggests that they may belong after v. 8 of chap. 4.

have been written by the same hand just as we find them. There must have been insertions, interpolations, glosses, even if we hold that the body of the chapters come from Micah. Let the reader compare, for example, 4:6-8 with verses 9ff, and 4:11-12 with 5:1-3. Again, there is the strange correspondence between 4:1-5 and Is. 2:2-5. Either Micah must have taken this from Isaiah, which may be true, or vice versa, which is far less likely; or both of them incorporated an earlier existing prophecy; or in each of them must have been inserted a later prophecy, and this seems the most probable of these possibilities. Aside from all this, however, the ideas contained in these chapters do not belong to the time in which we know that Micah prophesied. The idea of a Messianic era, for example, as described in 4:6-8 and 5:1ff. did not become current until after the Exile. And there is the further question whether Micah, the prophet of the doom and punishment of his people, would also be the author of these glowing predictions of the future restoration of Israel. This of course is not impossible. Yet the contrast is so complete between the content of chapters 1-3 and 4-5 as to raise grave question whether all of them could have come from the same author. The alternate conclusion is that chapters 4 and 5 were a postexilic insertion to relieve the somber threats of chapters 1-3. Some critics like George Adam Smith,[2] conclude that, with the exception of certain interpolations (as, e.g., 4:11-13), there is nothing in chapters 4 and 5 that might not have been written during the seventh or the eighth century. More recent scholarship, however, tends to the opinion that, with the possible exception of 4:9-10 and 5:9-13, these chapters consist of a collection of short prophecies which belong to a later age.

(3) It is generally agreed that chapter 6 and verses 1-6 of chapter 7 report social conditions which did not exist until the reign of the evil king Manasseh.[3] The reference to the sacrifice of children (6:7) is especially noteworthy, since this was not common until the time of Manasseh, who is said to have made his own son pass through the fire (II Kings 21:6). So far as the general contents of this section are con-

[2] *Op. cit.,* "Micah."
[3] George Adam Smith and others hold that we are not "shut up" to the age of Manasseh and that the body of this section may well be Micah's.

cerned, it might conceivably have been written by Micah. This presupposes, however, that the prophet lived into Manasseh's time. Furthermore, the complete change of style from chapters 1-3 presents real difficulty. Here, instead of the rugged and forthright denunciation of Israel's sins with their bitter invective, we have dramatically presented a court scene in which the Lord is judge, and also prosecutor. He presents His case. He has saved Israel from bondage. How can the nation explain its faithlessness to Him? It all reads like a written composition complete in itself, differing radically from the known prophecies of Micah. On the whole, it seems most likely that it was composed by an unknown author about the middle of the seventh century or even much later.

(4) Precisely as the first three chapters of the book are universally admitted to belong to Micah, with general unanimity it is now agreed that the concluding section 7:7-20 is not his. Some scholars have assigned it to the times of Manasseh. More probably it was composed in the postexilic era. For what in 6:1-7:6 is yet in prospect has now actually come to pass. Zion has now suffered for its sins. Shame has covered her. She must bear the indignation of the Lord until He shall again bring her forth to the light. The book closes with a bright picture of the day of her redemption.

In general, then, we find that chapters 1-3 (except for two brief passages) belong to Micah; that portions of chapters 4-5 may be his; that, while the authenticity of 6:1-7:6 is still defended with some degree of plausibility, the likelihood is that it is the work of a later unknown author; that 7:7-20 is quite certainly not by Micah.

Micah's style has none of the simplicity of Amos or the originality of Hosea. It is rhetorical and emotional as well as forceful and direct. Like Amos, he exhibits deep moral earnestness. Unlike Isaiah, he shows little interest in political movements. Micah is exclusively an ethical and religious teacher. It is not clear whether he anticipated the destruction of the whole Southern Kingdom as might appear from 3:12. His anger did not extend to the whole nation, but fell primarily upon its aristocracy because of its injustice toward the landfolk whom Micah loved. Whether he looked forward to a day when Israel would be redeemed and know the blessedness which can come only by righteousness must remain uncertain. In verses which may have been his, 4:9, 10 and 5:9-13, we have at least a hint of deliverance by the Lord who will Himself remove the iniquities of His people.

This reminds us of a feature in Micah's theology which he shares with other prophets both before and after the Exile. The restoration of Israel, its triumph over the nations, is to be achieved by direct intervention of the Lord, without the intervention either of a Messiah or of any other intermediary being. By the fiat of His own will, the "remnant" will become again a strong nation of which He will be the ruler.

II. The Prophecy

1. *Chapters 1-3.*

The Book of Micah begins with an emotional outburst, a passionate cry from the heart. How he loved his countryside we have seen. And he is sure that punishment and destruction are about to overtake it. The Lord has come out of His place and will tread upon the heights of the earth. Samaria is to fall and her idols will be broken in pieces. Judah's turn will come next, for the enemy is at the very gates of Jerusalem. Then the prophet turns his eye upon his own countryside. He names its villages over one by one, all dear to him. The most to be expected is that their bitterest foes will not exult over their destruction. One must put on the deepest mourning, for only captivity is in store for them. Thus, as with Hosea, love, on the one hand, and the pronouncement of doom, on the other, struggle together in the heart of the prophet. Only as we comprehend this bitter inward experience can we enter into the tragical meaning of the opening chapter of the Book of Micah.

Those early prophets were real preachers. Their fearlessness amazes us. Their moral courage was immense. They did not seem to care what might happen to themselves. They uttered their message in sublime disregard of consequences. They are models in this respect for the modern preacher. They sober him. They make him ask himself whether or not he is as true to his calling as they were to theirs, or whether he simply echoes, more or less unconsciously, the opinions of the day. Who is it who said: "Today we do not kill the prophets, instead we ask them to dinner"? Never perhaps has the preacher had greater need of a sense of dignity, of the solemnity of his calling, than today. He must speak with a certain detachment, from a perception of truth which is above debates and policies. His words will proceed not from a self-assumed egotism but from a renunciation of self, from a profound and self-evident humility in which he identifies himself in any judgment he passes upon what he feels to be the moral failure which he condemns. Yet always there will be something to compare with the uncompromising way in which these prophets of old uttered the Word and Will of God, however unwelcome or unpopular their words may have been.

In chapters 2 and 3 Micah specifies the sins because of which calamity is in store for the people of God. A terrible moral indignation reverberates throughout these chapters. And because Micah is a countryman, it is the oppression of the poor, of the peasant, of the farmer, that preoccupies him. Whereas Isaiah "satirizes the fashions of the town and intrigues of the court, Micah scourges the avarice of the wealthy and the injustices which reduce the peasant to penury and slavery." [4] Unlike Amos and Hosea, too, he has nothing to say about idolatry or hideous immoralities. But he condemns the rich, the nobles, for their inhuman practices which deprive the small landowner of liberty, security and economic well-being. He flays judges who permit themselves to be bribed by the wealthy, and false prophets who are governed by expediency and self-interest rather than by ethical insight and moral principle. Micah is the prophet of the people, and he denounces the social wrongs from which they suffer.

Here lies the relevancy of Micah to the problems of the day in which we live. The sins against which Micah inveighed were the social sins that degraded society. He reminds us that a man today may be living a "good" life in the narrow, personal meaning of that term and still be the blackest of sinners because he is violating in his business life the elementary ideas of human brotherhood: the manufacturer who gets goods out of sweatshops; the industrialist who employs child labor; real estate owners who make large profits out of unsanitary dwellings; employers of labor who have more regard for personal gain than for

[4] George Adam Smith, *op. cit.*, "Micah."

an adequate wage. From this point of view, what Micah has to say about the sinners of his day has a very modern message to the real sinners of our day.[5] He talks about the "scant measure that is abominable"; we use the word "profiteering." He talks about "wicked balances and deceitful weights" (6:11); we use the words "extortionate prices" and "oppressive cost." He says that "the rich men thereof are full of violence and lies" and that "their tongue is deceitful in their mouth" (6:12); and we remember that only recently certain wealthy men were convicted of conspiracy against trade, and of defrauding the government by making a false return of their incomes. He says "The prince asketh, and the judge asketh for a reward" (7:3); and we recall that in our day a learned jurist declared that, while our courts are not venal, it is true that a poor man does not stand the same chance as a man with a princely income, to have justice done to him. He says, "They covet fields, and take them by violence; and houses, and take them away: so they oppress a man and his house, even a man and his heritage" (2:2); and we think of economic conditions that bear heavily upon the wage earner and prevent him from having a good roof over his head and gathering his family about him in his own home. These are the sins that make up the burden of the Book of Micah. And he dared to stand up and tell his countrymen that for these sins, the hand of the Lord will be as heavy against Judah as it was against Samaria, that foreigners will get what the rich landowners vainly imagine belongs to them; that sins of social wrong and injustice are as heinous as the sins of irreligion and personal immorality; that the mouths of the respectable who say "none evil can come upon us" shall be stopped, and "Zion shall be plowed as a field, Jerusalem shall become heaps and the mountain of the house as the high places of the forest." (3:11, 12.)

Thus Micah is the prophet of social righteousness. He is modern in his every accent. He does not hesitate to declare that the organized religion of his day was on the side of the oppressor (3:11): an accusation which needs definite refutation in our day. Such is the social message of the book of Micah.

[5] Closely connected in idea with chaps. 2 and 3 are chap. 6:10-16 and chap. 7:1-6. These sections were quite certainly written at a later time and most probably by another author. They are out of place where they stand and should be read as a supplement to the earlier chapters.

2. *Chapters 4 and 5.*

Whether the main body of these chapters belongs to Micah or not is a problem for the scholars to decide. Their decision, however, in no wise affects the beauty of this prophecy nor its meaning for us of today. The authorship of the Bible books is not a matter of major concern. What we need to ask, and all that we need to ask is, What does the Bible have to say, what does it teach?

Here, then, we have the glowing prophecy of a new day, "the last days," the Messianic era. Here is held before our eyes the promise of the ultimate salvation of God's people, the sure coming of God's kingdom. This is the wonderful thing about the Bible: its utter condemnation of sin, upon the one hand, and its inextinguishable hope, upon the other. And these must go hand in hand with us: no compromise with evil, no despair of redemption. If the picture of external conditions which the Book of Micah draws is black as night, so is the picture it draws of final salvation bright as sunrise. The Messianic age is presented in the terms of universal peace. The Old Testament is a warlike book. But the reiteration in the prophets of the ultimate extinction of war must not be overlooked. In this passage (v. 3) is added the idea of arbitration, "The Lord shall judge between the nations." In the post-exilic prophets war becomes the spiritual symbol of the overthrow of evil by the hosts of the Lord, an idea which is preserved in our militant Christian hymns. Today we have advanced beyond the idea that peace will be attained only in a distant Messianic age, and we are grappling with the problem of achieving peace in the actual life of the world. Thus we perceive how in spite of all setbacks and disappointments definite advance has been achieved in the moral life of the world. No one in Micah's day expected peace in his time. It was to come only "in the last days." How unthinkable a United Nations Association consisting of the Assyrians, the Egyptians, the Ninevites, the Babylonians, the Scythians! The idea of Universal Peace existed only as a utopia in an era to which prophetic inspiration looked forward as the final day of redemption. In all the difficult and tangled problems confronting the intelligence and conscience of men in the days in which we live, the very fact that the obliteration of war for us of today is a present and practical problem offers us ground for encouragement and optimism. War has been revealed as the instrument of the world's final destruction. Hence it must not be in a distant day but in the very days in which we live that the nations must learn to "beat their swords into plowshares and their spears into pruninghooks."

The concluding portion of chapter 4 [6] describing the coming capture of Jerusalem under Sennacherib interrupts this description of the redemption of God's people, but this is continued in even more eloquent fashion in chapter 5. For the first time in the Old Testament we find in this passage of the Book of Micah a classic expression of the Messianic hope: not only that God's people were to be saved, but that their salvation was centered in a Person. This idea took early root and grew gradually in the Hebrew consciousness. It began in an idealization of David, the first king in all their checkered history to rule over a fully united kingdom. Thus the mystical idea developed that out of the "root of Jesse" would come the saviour of God's people. Bethlehem was the birthplace of David. It is an interesting conjecture of George Adam Smith,[7] who defends the authorship by Micah of this passage, that in naming Bethlehem Micah "means . . . to emphasize the rustic and popular origin of the Messiah: 'too small to be among the thousands of Judah.' " To the Christian the Messianic Idea was realized in the Person of Christ, and no less, nay even more, than to the Jew, remains the ground of his social hope. This passage from Micah is appointed to be read on Christmas Eve. It speaks of the coming of the world's Saviour; born in humility but destined to put all things under his feet. And as we watch Him coming down through the centuries, traveling in the glory of his strength, wielding upon the moral customs of society his irresistible Power, slowly forcing the civilized world out of its injustices and inhumanity, we find in Him the complete fulfillment of the ancient prophecy: "He shall stand and shepherd his flock . . . and shall be our peace."

[6] It is an open question whether v. 1 of chap. 5 is to be connected with what precedes in v. 13 of chap. 4 or with what follows in chap. 5.
[7] *Op. cit.*

3. *Chapters 6 and 7*

The sixth chapter consists of two sharply contrasted sections. The second of these, verses 9-16, rehearses the sins of Judah in much the same fashion as in chapters 1-3. The state of society therein described, however, seems to be that of the later reign of Manasseh. And this holds even more decisively with respect to verses 1-6 of chapter 7 with which it is closely connected, and in which the sins of Jerusalem are exposed and condemned, "one of the most poignant criticisms of a commercial community which has ever appeared in literature." Whether or not these passages belong to Micah, they are to be considered as an addition to his castigation of social conditions as contained in chapters 1-3.

There remain, therefore, only the first section of chapter 6, verses 1-8, and the concluding section of chapter 7:7-20.

The first of these passages is one of the most familiar and famous to be found in the whole range of the Old Testament scriptures. Whether or not it belongs to Micah himself is a matter of unimportance. Its splendor and beauty is in no wise affected by questions of authorship. Here is an argument between the Lord and His people. He pleads His own cause: "My people what have I done unto thee?" In other words, "What have I not done for thee?" And the people, in reply, admitting their moral obligation toward God, inquire how it shall be discharged. Here lies the immense significance of the Lord's reply in verse 8, which has rightly been called one of the greatest words to be found in the Old Testament. It gives us a definition of a true religion. There is but one higher than this to be found in the Bible: Jesus' immortal summary of the Law.

Simple as the verse is, it contains two profound truths which we of today need to lay to heart as surely as they to whom they were first uttered. The first of these is the truth Amos drove home in his day, that real religion consists in something higher than religious observance. The Lord requires something more of us than going through the forms of religion. Jesus carried this idea to its highest levels when he said: "God is a spirit: and they that worship him must worship him in spirit and in truth"; "Not every one that saith unto me, Lord, Lord, shall enter into the kingdom of heaven; but he that doeth the will of my Father which is in heaven." Not outward sacrifice but the dedication of the will to God is the test of a true religion.

The other truth is equally significant: what the Lord requires of us is that which every man can render if he will. Nothing is said in this immortal sentence about the requirement that a man shall assent to any intellectual statement of faith. Here is where many stumble and fall. But this Old Testament preacher never mentions any such requirement at all. Neither is anything said about the requirement that a man should have certain religious feelings or emotions or raptures or anything of that sort. He is not required to feel in a certain fashion. We make the life of religion too complicated, too involved, too mysterious. But this verse sets us straight. The Lord requires of us nothing that we are not able immediately to render. No man, whatever his intellectual difficulties or his emotional inabilities may be, but can enter at once, wholly and with entire conviction into the blessedness of the life of real religion. For this definition of religion contains but three simple phrases. And two out of the three have to do with our relation to our fellow men. First, we are to do justly. The Lord requires of us that in our business, in our friendships, in our work and in our leisure we are to do just right. We are to live up to our capacity, live out the best that is in us. Now, that is a splendid and an exacting ideal. But God does not lower His standards to our weakness. He appeals to the noblest that is in us. And if a man is to rise level to this ideal and live the "just right life," he must live it in close association with Him who in the Book of the Acts is described as "that Just One who was crucified." In the next place, it is required of us that we love mercy: that means being tenderhearted, really sensitive to need and suffering that causes us to be the helpers of the weak, the handicapped, the underprivileged. This must be a central instinct, a controlling impulse in our life. It is one of the noblest qualities of a godlike human life, and only close association with Him who was the lover of men will clothe men with such a garment of mercy. And then we are to walk humbly with our God. That is the motive out of which the others spring. To keep our lives close to God's life; to keep step with God; to keep near to Him in "closer, dearer company"; to link our lives with His, this is the true centre of all true living. And anyone can do that who really wants to do it. Such is the reasonableness of a true religion. God has shown us what is good. There is much that He has not shown us. But what He has not shown us is not necessary to a good and faithful life. To live uprightly, to act nobly, to do our duty toward God and man, such is our task. And He has shown us how we may perform it. Perhaps that is all that we have any right to expect of God: that He shall show us what is good. As Whittier has written:

> What asks our Father of His children, save
> Justice and mercy and humility,
> A reasonable service of good deeds,
> Pure living, tenderness to human needs,
> Reverence, and trust, and prayer for light to see
> The Master's footprints in our daily ways.

Such is the message of the Book of Micah, to its day and to ours.

~~~ *Zephaniah* ~~~

I. INTRODUCTION

ZEPHANIAH WAS a contemporary of Jeremiah and prophesied (1:1) during the earlier part of the reign of Josiah (638-608 B.C.). Politically, socially, religiously, the fortunes of Judah were at a low ebb. The long reign of King Manasseh (692-641 B.C.) had come at last to an end. It was marked by a violent popular reaction against Hezekiah's abortive attempt to suppress the rural sanctuaries and to make the temple at Jerusalem the one center of the nation's worship. It was a time also of religious disillusionment. The glowing promises of Isaiah seemed to have been falsified by events. Accordingly, the old idolatries reappeared: the adoration of the sun and of the stars, and other degrading rites were sanctioned and practiced. It was an era of general degradation. The short reign of Amon was followed by the reign of the good King Josiah. He was but eight years of age when he came to the throne, and conditions for the next ten years on the whole remained what they had been under Manasseh. Only years later was he able to inaugurate reforms. These might have led to a new era in the life of the people. But in 608 B.C. Josiah died in the fateful battle at Megiddo, and Jehoiakim, after a reign of three months by Jehoahaz, succeeded him and once again turned to evil ways which led directly to the fall of Jerusalem in 586 B.C. Such, in general, was the state of affairs when Jeremiah, Zephaniah, Nahum and Habakkuk uttered their prophecies. The work of Jeremiah covers practically the whole period; that of Zephaniah falls between the accession of Josiah and the Great Reform; Nahum and Habakkuk wrote after that event.

Zephaniah is not a common Hebrew name and is borne by only three others mentioned in the Old Testament (II. Kings 25:18, I Chron. 6:36, Jer. 21:1). It means "he whom God has hidden." He had royal blood in his veins, being a direct descendant in the fourth generation from Hezekiah (1:1), whose name was too well known to require the addition of the words "King of Judah." He was a young man, perhaps twenty-one years old, when he prophesied, about the age of Josiah himself. It is clear that he lived in Jerusalem, for he is perfectly familiar with its localities and customs (1:5, 8-11). It is generally agreed that he prophesied before the Great Reform under Josiah (621 B.C.). The social and religious corruption which he describes could hardly have existed after the reforms instituted by Josiah had been carried out. This date, before 621 B.C., is further confirmed by the plain reference in Zephaniah to terrible invasions. Between the years 630 and 624 B.C., the Scythians invaded Palestine along the Syrian coast and struck terror into the hearts of its inhabitants (Jer. 4, 5ff). There can be little doubt that it is to this event Zephaniah refers (2:4-12). Therefore his book can be dated approximately 628-626 B.C. Possibly Jeremiah and Zephaniah began to prophesy in the same year. The first chapter of the book is universally regarded as an authentic prophecy of Zephaniah. Doubt has been thrown in recent years on the genuineness of portions of chapter 2 and the whole of chapter 3. The first three verses of chapter 2 belong by close connection with chapter 1, of which they are therefore a part. It is true that verse 3 has "a late ring," yet it may well belong to Zephaniah. As for the rest of the chapter, with its denunciations of foreign nations, insertions were evidently made in it. For the prophecy against Moab and Ammon clearly refers to the hostility of these nations at the time of the destruction of Jerusalem, 586 B.C., and verse 15 can hardly have been written before the overthrow of Nineveh in 612 B.C. All that can be said therefore of 2:4-15 is that it probably was an original prophecy of Zephaniah against the nations, uttered at the same time as chapter 1, but suffered certain "dilapidations and intrusions."

As for chapter 3, many scholars have felt that no part of it can be Zephaniah's. Certainly the concluding portion of it, verses 14-20, bears no resemblance to the rest of the book. Evidently the editor felt that its dark and ominous message should not remain unrelieved by a word of hope. This psalm, beautiful in itself, was therefore added as an assurance that God would yet come to the rescue of His people and that Jerusalem would have a place of glory among the nations of the earth. It may have been written after the Exile. There seems, however, to be no decisive reason why verses 1-13 of this chapter should not belong to Zephaniah. It is true that verses 1-8 are but a pale reflection of the fierce indignation of chapter 1. Yet may not this be understood as the ebb of strength of a spirit that has spent itself? And as for verses 9-13, shall we deny even this sob of hope to the heavy heart of Zephaniah?

Historically the book has immense importance. It gives us the best picture found in the Old Testament of the degradation of the Jewish religion in a period in which the effort was made to introduce into it the rites and customs of the Canaanitish religions, which were wholly foreign to its spirit and genius. Zephaniah is unequaled in his denunciation of this "religious syncretism" which was eating the very heart out of the Hebrew faith. He denounces the religious "collaborationists" of his day whether they be princes or priests or the common people. He pronounces the coming of a terrible judgment as the inevitable punishment of the people for forsaking the pure worship of the God of their fathers. "The thunder of his last judgment rolls in his powerful words whose dithyrambic lilt and wondrous music no translation can render." [1] The incursion of the Scythians is to precipitate a world catastrophe which Zephaniah envisages with unflinching eye. Out of it only a remnant of the humble and meek, the true and the faithful, is to be saved.

Again, Zephaniah is important because in his words we see the first "tinging of prophecy with apocalypse." He borrows the idea of a Day of the Lord from Amos (5:18, 20). But whereas with Amos this has a definite point in history, with Zephaniah it has a supernatural character with all kinds of "vague and solemn terrors from another sphere." Only with an effort can the prophet think of a rally of Israel beyond. The "Day of the Lord tends to become The Last Day." [2] "A day of wrath is that day." Thus in Zephaniah we find ourselves at the watershed where the current of prophecy increasingly assumes an apocalyptical character. That is "the moment which Zephaniah supplies in the history of Israel's religion."

Unlike the prophets of the eighth century, there is in Zephaniah no call to repentance, no interest in social reform. In verse 3 of chapter 2,

---

[1] Cornill, *The Prophets of Israel*, p. 76.
[2] George Adam Smith, *The Twelve Prophets*, "Zephaniah."

if this belongs to Zephaniah, the humble and meek are, it is true, exhorted to seek the Lord and to seek righteousness in the hope of being spared when the dreadful day of the Lord shall come. But this is all. For Zephaniah the day of grace was definitely past. The Scythian was at the gate. Catastrophe was impending. The Day of Wrath and of Divine Visitation was at hand. Why, then, talk of practical reforms? These could in no way alter or deflect the blow that was about to fall upon the people as a punishment for sin. Thus, the unique and dramatic interest of the book of Zephaniah as distinguished from the prophecies of Amos, Micah, Hosea, Isaiah, and even of Jeremiah, lies in this abandonment of any expectation that the people by a recovery of moral purpose, by a mending of their ways, could hope for salvation. Doom pitiless and sure awaited them. This prophecy was fulfilled forty years later in the capture and destruction of Jerusalem.

Thus the Book of Zephaniah is somber throughout. There is only a hint of brightness, of beauty, of hope. There is no mention of the Messianic idea of later prophecy. As a townsman Zephaniah has no eye for natural beauty. Belonging to the aristocracy and never having himself felt the pinch of poverty, his utterances lack that note of sympathy for the poor and the downtrodden which we find in Amos and Micah. The austerity of the book and the author's personal detachment from the sufferings and sins of the people are maintained throughout. The style of Zephaniah is clear and forceful. It lacks the imagination of Amos and Isaiah. Yet his picture of life as he saw it and knew it is vivid and abounds in striking phrases. He seems to have borrowed considerably from his predecessors, as we see by comparing Zephaniah 1:2, 3 with Hosea 4:3; Zephaniah 2:14-15 with Isaiah 2:19-21, Amos 5:20; Zephaniah 1:18b with Isaiah 10:23, 28:22; Zephaniah 2:4-15 with Amos 1:3, 2:1-3. If we compare Zephaniah with his contemporary Jeremiah, we find that Zephaniah's "bold, positive, unflinching nature differs radically from the introspective emotional temperament of Jeremiah. The message of the two is subtly different even when both are prophesying under the appalling menace of the Scythian invasion." [3]

[3] R. H. Pfeiffer, *Introduction to the Old Testament,* p. 601.

II. The Prophecy

The Book of Zephaniah is perhaps the saddest book in the whole Bible. Except for a touch of hope here and there, it reads like unrelieved melancholy from beginning to end. For the book ends with verse 13 of chapter 3. The rest of that chapter is a Hymn of Hope, a peaceful epilogue which was later appended to it. Upon the prophecy of Zephaniah the shadows rest so heavily that hardly a ray of light is permitted to break through. From the lips of this young aristocrat, who has brooded over the sins of his people and sees in the onrushing Scythians the impending judgment of God, falls the dismal dirge of these chapters.

That so young a man should have unfolded such a scene of darkness and of judgment should not surprise us. For there is no sadness in life, as biography and experience abundantly prove, to compare with the sadness of youth.[4] That is the time when the tragedy of all earthly things is likely to crowd down on one in almost overwhelming measure. Without the larger outlook, without perspective, the knowledge of those compensations which alleviate suffering and temper the aspect of evil, these appear to the mind in their blackest form. The pessimism of youth is one of the most familiar and one of the most tragic facts in life. So also is the severity of youth's judgments. A youth of twenty is likely to be much more severe in his moral judgments than a man in middle or later life. From this point of view, a distinguished trustee of one of our colleges has questioned the wisdom of student government, of having penalties visited by the students upon themselves, which he often found to be unduly and unwisely harsh. The students would judge each other much more severely than they would be judged by their elders. Age is more tolerant, more lenient than youth. When a man is young, his condemnation of wrongdoing is likely to be untempered by the compassion with which longer experience turns the edge of judgment.

[4] "There is no hopelessness so sad as that of early youth when the soul is made up of wants and has no long memories, no superadded life in the lives of others."—George Eliot, *The Mill on the Floss*, p. 251.

When we open the Book of Zephaniah, therefore, we are confronted with a somber mind, with the harsh and untempered condemnation of a youthful soul, oppressed by an overpowering sense of evil and on fire with the conviction of swift and final judgment. That is the Book of Zephaniah. Its opening words are these: "I will utterly consume all things from off the land." From this opening verse, the roused soul of the prophet gathers strength with every line until it utters one of the most eloquent and soul-piercing passages in all literature: "The great Day of the Lord is near, the Day of Wrath, the Day of Trouble." Then the prophet breaks out in a series of awful judgments over the heads of Judah and the enemies of Judah including Nineveh the Terrible, and finally he ends in almost a sob of hope that God the Righteous may still have pity on a remnant of the people who have remained humble and meek, who "shall feed and lie down, and none shall make them afraid." If we traverse carefully these succeeding moods of the young prophet, it will not be difficult to discover what permanent place they occupy in any true religious experience.

In the first place, then, there is the sadness of this sensitive soul in the face of the evil and suffering of the world. Zephaniah saw plenty of it, and he had not far to look for it. Nowhere in all prophetic literature is a more graphic picture given of the moral corruption of Jerusalem than in the first few verses of Zephaniah. In them we see the people upon their housetops bowing down to and worshiping the stars; the rulers of the people, sworn to uphold the national faith, dressing themselves in all kinds of foreign apparel and mimicking all sorts of pagan customs. In his pen picture of the general corruption, Zephaniah uses striking and trenchant phrases. The Lord will search Jerusalem with candles to ferret out wrongdoers. And these are not only those who perpetrate positive crimes, but also the sodden, the indifferent, "men that are settled on their lees," men, as we might say, who have "gone to seed": the complacent, encased in their own torpid lethargy, exhibiting what has well been called the putrescence of respectability. Such is the picture from which Zephaniah's soul revolts. Superstition, sensuality, selfishness, the three great sins that make up the suffering of the world, produced in the soul of Zephaniah and must produce in every earnest soul today the most profound spiritual sadness.

The heart-heaviness of Zephaniah is a part of the experience of every true son of God. It was a part of the experience of God's only Son. The mood of Zephaniah is reproduced in the soul of Christ, and in the soul of every Christlike man. If we call up before us the faces of the prophets of our time, Charles Kingsley, George Eliot, Phillips Brooks, Jane Addams, we find imprinted upon them the selfless sadness of all prophetic souls. The face of Kingsley was said to reflect his exquisite suffering when he watched children at play: he was thinking of what they had still to endure. Oliver Wendell Holmes once said that he never really laughed: "The world is too sad for that." It is only a facile optimism which is first cousin to frivolity, only the dilettantism secure in its own comfort and blind to all the world besides, only the cynicism which makes a ghastly joke of the unsolved mystery of pain, that can wear day by day the mask of jollity in an encompassing world of woe. The sadness of Zephaniah is inextricably woven into the total spiritual experience of anyone who even remotely shares the sympathies of every true son of God.

The core of Zephaniah's sadness lay, of course, in his poignant sense of sin, the root of it, the meaning of it, the consequences of it. Herein lies the permanent religious value of his message to the world. The time has come to bring home to men this trenchant judgment: the conviction that they are morally responsible for the consequences of the sin that is in them. "The world is ready once more for the declaration of the awful reality of human evil." [5] We need a fresh, keen realization, a piercing sense of the sheer and sinister power of sin in human life: its hard resistance, its inexhaustible versatility, its infinite disguises, the way in which it enters into and corrupts everything. The world has been given in these days an awesome exhibition of the power of sin to produce human misery, to destroy all that men hold dear, to evoke the savage instincts in man himself. Nothing is clearer than that all the dreadful calamities that have befallen our race have their origin in the corrupting power of sin, its destructiveness of all moral sense, its unlimited reach into the very center of man's moral being. Such is the message of Zephaniah to his time, to our time, and to all time.

As a consequence of their apostasy, Zephaniah perceives descending

[5] See R. B. Y. Scott, *The Relevance of the Prophets,* pp. 213-214.

upon the people imminent, terrible and universal judgment. The method of this divine judgment is the impending Scythian invasion. "From the coasts of the Black Sea a storm broke over the world such as man had never before witnessed. Wild tribes of horsemen overran all Asia for twenty years on their fast horses spreading terror and desolation everywhere. The Assyrian world edifice cracked in all its joints." [6] All the coast of Palestine was overrun and Egypt itself was threatened. Here was the judgment of God upon a recreant world and a faithless Israel. "The great day of the Lord is near, and hasteth greatly." With unflinching eye Zephaniah watches the impending doom, and prophesies universal catastrophe. His description of the Day of Wrath and of Mourning has become immortal. It is the source of one of the great enduring hymns of the Christian Church. The "Dies irae, dies illa" is sung by the Roman Church and the whole Christian world, and its solemn measures for a thousand years have been chanted as a requiem over the departed human soul. The author of this great medieval hymn, Thomas of Celano, was a friend and companion of St. Francis. He was not one of his earliest disciples, but the relation between them seems to have been unusually close and intimate. He was the counterpart of Francis in that he was predisposed to look upon the darker side of life and to speak of judgment rather than of mercy. Their sympathies as poets doubtless drew them together. He outlived Francis by thirty years, and it was perhaps in this later period when his own life was drawing to a close and the shadows of the Great Day were gathering around him that he poured out his soul in this great hymn, which is almost a literal reproduction of Zephaniah's words. Its wonderful setting of sense to sound, the roll of organ music that runs through the hymn even unaccompanied, the transitions so clearly marked in sound as in meaning from lofty adoration to pathetic entreaty, impart a dignity to the "Dies Irae" which is indescribable and unparalleled. The translations of this hymn in modern languages run into the hundreds. It is indissolubly associated in the history of music with Mozart's Requiem. All Christendom rejoices in it as a common treasure. Such is the contribution of Zephaniah to the permanent religious literature of the whole human race.

[6] Cornill, *op. cit.,* pp. 76, 77.

So, also, is Zephaniah's contribution to Christian theology. As we have seen, our prophet has no place for social reform in his message. Judgment swift and sure must precede salvation. God was about to visit punishment upon the world, and nothing could halt Him. That was the burden of Zephaniah's message. Salvation is to come not by the slow process of reform but by the quick coming of God in judgment. And Zephaniah, lifting up his eyes above the sin and selfishness and recreancy of the people, saw that judgment coming swiftly. Historically, then, the prophecy of Zephaniah is important as bringing forward the idea of what may be called the "crisis theology" which is a permanent part of a total Christian world view. Here, again, lies the contemporary value of Zephaniah's message. He emphasizes the necessary corrective to the idea of salvation by the slow processes of social reform.

American delegates to the Oxford Conference held in 1938 were surprised and baffled by the attitude of the Continental churches toward the pressing problems of our modern world. They were not at all interested in practical methods of reform, in peace societies, in proposed forms of world reorganization, in efforts to improve the world by human effort. These were all futile, were foredoomed to failure. To a man, these Continental delegates held to a "crisis theology." There is little or nothing to be done but to wait for the Day of the Lord's judgment when with a sweep of His hand He would overturn the injustices of the world and usher in His kingdom. To the British and American delegates, that attitude seemed to be irrational. It was a virtual denial of the necessity and possibility of moral action.

Yet only in a union of both ideas, of ethical reform, on the one hand, and the apocalyptical hope, on the other, do we grasp the total message of the Bible to a world in disorganization and despair. Reform has its place. The slow processes of ethical improvement have their importance: the effort to improve the moral life of the individual on whom the re-creation of the world must depend; the attack on sin in this form or that; the gradual methods of education and instruction: these must always be there also. These all find their vindication in the teaching of Jesus, who often described the coming of the Kingdom as the slow germination of the seed planted in the soil.

But this is not all. This is not enough. Side by side with this doctrine of slow reform by human effort must be placed the "crisis theology" of Zephaniah, this solemn apocalyptical expectation of a great and coming Day of the Lord in judgment when He will stretch forth His arm in the sight of the nations, "even the bitter day of the Lord." We shall hear more of this when we come to Zechariah. Here it needs to be noted that precisely as for Zephaniah the Day of Judgment was not only a great and final event in the moral history of mankind, but also an imminent fact, the impending catastrophe of the Scythian invasion, so for us in our modern world, a Day of Judgment is already upon us. The terrible catastrophes that have overtaken us cannot be otherwise interpreted than as a judgment of God upon the world for its political and social sins. It is a day of visitation in which the descriptions of desolation by Zephaniah have been literally fulfilled: "This is the rejoicing city that dwelt carelessly, that said in her heart, I am, and there is none beside me: how is she become a desolation, a place for beasts to lie down in" (2:15).

There is little of purely nationalistic feeling in Zephaniah's condemnation of the pagan nations. Rather there is discoverable in it a certain philosophy of history: the discernment of a divine purpose, a certain "moral meaning, coherence and movement in relation to an end transcending the experienced present." John Fiske once declared that history is simply His story. Just so in all the permutations of the world Zephaniah, in company with the rest of the prophets of Israel, detects the presence and the activity of the living God. The only way to sanity, to the recovery of stability and orderliness in the midst of chaos is to recognize the reality of God and bring personal and social life into harmony with His principle of righteousness. "Seek ye the Lord . . . seek righteousness . . . it may be ye shall be hid in the day of the Lord's anger" (2:3). The future is entrusted to the faithful and to the honest. Salvation rests upon character and simple trust in God. Such is the contemporary meaning of the message of Zephaniah.

It is a beautiful characteristic of the Bible that even its most somber and austere books are not without at least a ray of light, a note of hope. That is why it is the Bible. The Bible does justice to all the sadness of human life, it does not gloss over its sin and suffering. But the Bible never ends there. That makes the difference between Bible pessimism and secular pessimism; between the Book of Zephaniah, let us say, and James Thomson's *The City of Dreadful Night*. In both cases we have bleak, black descriptions of human life and destiny. But in the latter case we are left there and in the former we are not.

For even in Zephaniah a ray of God's light shines through and illumines the darkness of those dreadful days (2:3; 3:5, 12, 13). The doom is confidently predicted of those nations which stand as the incarnation of evil, against which the conscience of Israel has steadfastly set its face. Even Nineveh is to go down, the destruction of which is the theme of the prophet Nahum, who wrote only a few years later than Zephaniah. Without doubt contemporary events had something to do with this prophetic confidence. Yet we must reckon it among the unexplained marvels of Bible inspiration that its writers even in darkest hours implicitly believe in the ultimate overthrow of evil and the destruction of the enemies of God. How much it would mean for us today if we could catch this inspiration and share in this confidence.

As for Israel, while punishment is to be visited upon her, she will not be utterly destroyed.[7] In the midst of universal corruption and universal ruin, there remains "the remnant" who have not bent the knee to Baal. "I will also leave in the midst of thee an afflicted but pure people, and they shall trust in the name of the Lord. The remnant of Israel shall not do iniquity . . . for they shall feed and lie down, and none shall make them afraid" (3:12–13). This doctrine of the remnant did not originate with Zephaniah, of course. It is found in all the prophets who preceded him: in Amos, Hosea, and Isaiah, as well as in his contemporary, Jeremiah. The significant thing is that even Zephaniah, whose outlook was even darker than theirs, retained it and used it. Even for him there remains a remnant which, however small, is to be the seed out of which a new life is to spring. Here is one of the most precious truths in the Bible. Always, that is, there is soul left. The witness of God in humanity is never wholly destroyed.

---

[7] This interpretation of course will not be allowed by those who deny the authenticity of this passage.

All through the darkest ages since the day of Zephaniah there has remained the remnant, the few, who have retained within them the soul of goodness and of faith. These have been the source, the *fons et origo* of the regenerating influence which has saved the world's life and ushered in better days. Out of the remnant in Zephaniah's day came the new faith that was to rescue Israel in the days of its seeming destruction. Wickedness may do its worst, corruption may seem to have poisoned the very streams of morality, but always there is that left, the indestructible remainder of the love of God which gives hope for the future, which is the pledge and guarantee of ultimate salvation. God and conscience cannot be wholly wiped out of humanity. Ultimately there is that left which shall take refuge in the name of the Lord. Let one believe this wonderful truth of the saving remnant, the divine remainder, and with what faith and courage one can look out upon a disordered world and trust in the re-creating power of the divine life in the heart of our poor humanity.

And underneath all the tragedy of the world as he saw it and knew it, Zephaniah shared the conviction of all the prophets of Israel that "the just Lord is in the midst thereof . . . every morning doth he bring his judgment to light, he faileth not" (3:5). As surely, that is, as the sun rises, so sure is it that God's justice will shine upon the earth. This conception of a living God, of a God living in the midst of the turmoil of events, of the tragic experiences of the race, underlies the final optimism of the Old Testament prophets. God in the midst; God with us; this conviction illumines and transfigures all the dark mysteries of this world's sin and suffering. It is the Bible way out. It is the only way out. And even in the darkness of Zephaniah's night, it was the way out for him.

This idea for the Christian finds its perfect consummation in the fact of the Incarnation. "They shall call His name Emmanuel, which being interpreted is, God with us." "I am struggling," wrote Charles Kingsley, "through infinite darkness and chaos by means of one bright pathway which I find to be the only explanation of a thousand mysteries, I mean the Incarnation of our Lord." That bright pathway even in the darkest days is forever ours. "The Lord is in the midst thereof . . . He faileth not."

prophecy - phenomenon of history of religion
unity of minor prophets has always consisted
but not a completeness

~~~ *Nahum* ~~~

I. INTRODUCTION

IT IS impossible to understand the Book of Nahum without some acquaintance with the historical background. Nineveh was the capital of the great Assyrian Empire which lay on both sides of the river Tigris, north of Babylonia. It had a succession of great rulers and mighty warriors, Tiglath-pileser III, Sargon, Sennacherib, Esarhaddon, Asshurbanipal. The first of these conquered a large part of Syria. Damascus fell in 732 B.C., and Sargon took Samaria in 722 B.C., when the ten tribes of the Northern Kingdom went into captivity. He consolidated the entire Assyrian Empire. Sennacherib, who followed him, reduced Babylonia, and in 701 B.C. penetrated into Judah when its king Hezekiah revolted, captured forty-six fortresses, and carried off 200,000 prisoners. He invested Jerusalem but was prevented from taking it by a pestilence that so crippled his army that he was obliged to return home without delay. The story of all this is told in II Kings 18:13; 19:1–36. His son Esarhaddon captured Sidon, and reduced Edom, Moab, Gaza and Palestine to vassalage and undertook a successful campaign against Egypt. Finally, Asshurbanipal, under whom Nineveh reached the zenith of its power, again attacked Egypt (Nahum 3:8–10) and began a work of plunder and pillage without parallel even in those days. The Assyrians were masters in the art of war. They were a merciless, ferocious, barbarous foe, execrated by all the peoples whom they had ruthlessly conquered and pillaged.

After this, however, the power of Assyria began to wane. After the death of Asshurbanipal in 625 B.C. its decline was rapid. Rebellion within the empire and the growing menace of the Medes and Chaldeans diminished its strength. Subject nations began to throw off the Assyrian yoke, and in 614 B.C. Cyaxares, king of the Medes, made a direct attack upon the Assyrians. He was beaten off, but two years later he formed an alliance with Nabopolassar, king of Babylonia, and an assault upon Nineveh resulted in its final overthrow in 612 B.C.

Didn't know where to
rivers - have civilization
nile
Euphrates

nile - cradle of civ. - not any more
Egyptians - discovered the different cults
advanced civ. art of sculpture
progressed in drama + poetry

Egypt defeated by assyrians + the Euphrates took upper hand

Since Nahum's immortal ode is concerned solely with the impending downfall of Nineveh, its date can be easily determined. There are two fixed dates between which the book must have been written. The first is the capture of Thebes (No-Amon) by the Assyrians in 661 B.C., since this is described in Nahum 3:8. The second is the fall of Nineveh in 612 B.C., since Nineveh had not yet fallen when Nahum wrote his prophecy. Thus the book must have been written at the moment between the actual invasion of Assyria by the Medes and the beginning of an advance upon its capital. The invasion has begun but the foe has not yet begun to invest the city. A probable date is 614–612 B.C.

All that we know about Nahum is that he probably belonged to the Southern Kingdom, was a contemporary of Jeremiah and lived in a place called Elkosh, the location of which we are unable to identify. The name "Nahum" means "full of comfort."

Nineveh was the symbol of cruelty, barbarism, ruthlessness. And against it is directed the invective of Nahum. Judah, his own people, is never once mentioned. Unlike his predecessors, Nahum does not view the suffering of his land by the oppressor as a punishment for sin. He is so preoccupied with the shocking iniquities, with the well-merited and impending doom of Nineveh, that he has no thought for the short-comings of his own people. "Nahum's heart," writes George Adam Smith, "with all of its bigness holds room only for the bitterness, the baffled hopes, the unappeased horrors" which the Assyrians inflicted not only upon Judah but upon the whole of that Oriental world. He voices in his invective "the conscience of mankind," the indignation of an outraged humanity against Nineveh's wanton bloodshed, inhuman cruelty and inherent wickedness. Only when we grasp this fact are we in a mood to understand the depth, the passion of Nahum's terrible invective, his complacency as he reflects that in her hour of doom Nineveh will have none to comfort her, the song of joy that bursts from his heart as he sees the coming final exit of this "city of blood from the stage of history." [1]

Nahum was not an eyewitness of the events he describes. He was

[1] George Adam Smith, *op. cit.*, "Nahum."

redactor - editor

tragically familiar with the kind of warfare which the Assyrians themselves waged, which was now being waged against them. Moreover, communication was easy in those days and the news of the events happening in Assyria were doubtless well known in Judah. Nahum's poetic imagination supplied the rest. Both Isaiah, (30:30–31) and Zephaniah (2:13–14) had prophesied against Assyria, but neither of them attained the sublimity of the fiery and daring spirit of Nahum. Nahum's book is one great 'At last'!"

preface

The genuine prophecy of Nahum is contained in chapter 2:1, 3–13, and chapter 3. This is preceded by a proem, supplied by an editor at a much later date, perhaps as late as 300 B.C. This editor evidently *may have his notes* had before him not only Nahum's ode but also a psalm belonging to his own time which he felt was a fitting introduction to Nahum's prophecy. So he pieced the two together. The psalm itself is incomplete and difficult to reconstruct. There are traces of an alphabetic or acrostic arrangement in the successive distichs, similar to what we find in Psalms 25, 34, 37, 111, 112, 119, 145. The editor in joining together this psalm with Nahum's ode may have inserted some material of his own. Thus the text presents some difficulties to the scholars; but fortunately these do not concern the general reader.

In the first chapter, not by Nahum himself, we find most of the religious ideas contained in the book. It expresses vividly the general principle of God's avenging justice, of which the destruction of Nineveh which Nahum describes is a dramatic illustration. The next two chapters, with the exception of 2:2, which interrupts the connection, belong to Nahum. It is apparent at once that these are not a prophecy in the sense that they contain religious or moral or ethical teaching like those of Amos or Micah or Jeremiah. Rather, they are a magnificent poem depicting in glowing and inspired language the imminent downfall of Nineveh. This poem of Nahum is akin to the Ode of Deborah which we find in Judges 5, and to the Elegy of David over the death of Saul and Jonathan in II Samuel 1:19–27. Nahum may be called the last of the great Hebrew poets. His ode is a paean of triumph expressed in language of great vividness, beauty and power.

The inclusion of this poem in the book of the prophets was probabl
due to the fact that it was felt that with its theological prologue it co
veyed a real religious message to the people of God, as indeed it did.

II. THE PROPHECY

The first chapter of the Book of Nahum, as we have seen, is
theological introduction or background to the Ode of Nahum.
utters a profound faith in the rule of God. The overthrow of tyran
is certain. God's people can be sure of deliverance from brutal empir
by which they had been oppressed. God may be merciful, He may b
patient, but He is also just and will take vengeance on His enemie
"Jehovah must crush the tyrant, else He is untrue." Such is the mot
that runs all through this chapter. It expresses, in terms which ma
seem to be too strong for those whose idea of God has been nurture
by the gospel of Christ, the truth that God is the Avenger who wi
make His enemies to be His footstool. He who has power over th
forces of nature, who has His way in the whirlwind and in the storm
before whom the mountains quake, who rebukes the sea, the sam
God will be furious and take vengeance on His adversaries. He wil
break their yoke: He will break their bands asunder. He will brin
them to an ignominious end.

Thus the prologue to Nahum's Ode announces the indispensabl
truth that behind all the permutations of history, there stands the Go
of Justice, who will vindicate His truth by the overthrow of tyrant:
This truth receives dramatic illustration in the downfall of Nineve
as set forth in Nahum's Ode. And the peculiar value of this prologu
so far as the character of God is concerned is that it does not allov
us to forget His hatred of evil. We think and we talk much of th
love of God: so much that our religion may have grown thin and flac
cid. We need to hear the reverberating words: "Who can stand befor
his indignation? and who can abide in the fierceness of his anger?"
We like to dwell on the thought that the Lord is good and forgivin
and that He is plenteous in mercy. And so He is. Yet, unless balance
by the idea of God that is here set forth, there is likely to be muc
spiritual loss and damage. To think only of the goodness and merc

nd love of God begets loose notions of sin and the eternal yet for-
otten ideas of retribution and justice.

Over against all such loose ideas of the moral character of God
here stands as the eternal corrective the picture of Him preserved in
his just and honest chapter of the Book of Nahum, which tells us
nat He is indeed good and a stronghold in the day of trouble: that
He knoweth them that trust in Him: but that the same God is a God
f righteousness before whose wrath the wicked shall not stand. Thus
Nineveh becomes an object lesson to the empires of our modern world.
Only nations which embody righteousness, civic and personal, can
tand.

> Far-called, our navies melt away;
> On dune and headland sinks the fire:
> Lo, all our pomp of yesterday
> Is one with Nineveh and Tyre!
> Judge of the Nations, spare us yet,
> Lest we forget—lest we forget!

In the midst of this assertion of the indignant wrath of God against
vil there occur two beautiful verses: "The Lord is good, a strong
old in the day of trouble; and he knoweth them that trust in him"
v. 7). Here surely is one of the most beautiful verses in the Bible,
which brings comfort in every time of trouble whether personal or
ocial. The beauty of this verse is all the more wonderful because of
he grim environment in which we find it. "God is good!" Such is
he faith uttered in a dark hour. The goodness of God is not always as
pparent as His power. In nature and in the orderings of Providence
here are many ugly facts which seem to deny it. That is why its asser-
ion here in this chapter of Nahum, in the face of everything that
night seem to deny it, is so remarkable. And verse 15, with which
he prologue closes, quotes the familiar words of Isaiah (52:7).

The magnificent Ode of Nahum in Chapters 2 and 3 was written
n the eve of the destruction of Nineveh, and voices the exultation
not only of Judah but of all the nations that had experienced for a
undred years the horrors of her tyranny. Nineveh herself is now
bout to experience the cruelties she had inflicted upon the peoples

of that ancient world. This impending destruction of Nineveh is depicted by Nahum with a power, a vividness of description, a passion, a graphic attention to detail which carries the reader along on the crest of the poet's inspiration. The rhythm "rumbles and rolls, leaps and flashes, like the horsemen and chariots that he describes." [2] Nahum portrays an Oriental siege, reproduces its horrors and its savagery, its cruelties and mercilessness, in language so realistic that one is able to see it and feel it. First comes the fighting in the suburbs. Then the assault upon the walls. Then the capture of the city and its destruction. And all who receive news of it "shall clap their hands over thee: for upon whom hath not thy wickedness passed continually." As poetry, the Ode of Nahum ranks high in the literature of the Old Testament.

Ethically and religiously, however, it presents problems which must be faced. For one thing, in common with other prophets, there is its coarseness of speech, as found in verses 4–7 of chapter 3. There are, as we all know, certain passages in many of the books of the Old Testament which no one would care to read aloud, which one reads even by himself with some discomfort. The frankness of this language is a stumbling block to many Bible readers. Ugly words, such as these, we say, belong on the lips of the unregenerate rather than on those of religious teachers. What place has language like this on the pages of the Bible? How can a book be called holy which has to be expurgated before it can be read in public or be put into the hands of children? What is the meaning of all this part of an inspired Bible? Allowance must be made, say some, for the crudeness of the age in which these books were written. Their writers shared to a certain extent the vulgar vocabulary of their pagan neighbors. Moreover, if we compare the Bible books with the pagan literature of the same epoch, we find that in contrast to the unspeakable filth and obscenity of the mythologies of the pagan world, the ideas and language of the Bible are lily white and pure as snow. Again, we are justly reminded that there exists a well-marked difference between Oriental and Western habits of thought and language with respect to matters of sex. Hence, what may to us seem to be language that is inexcusably frank to the Oriental seemed perfectly natural; so that what makes us boggle caused him

[2] George Adam Smith, *op. cit.*, "Nahum."

no embarrassment whatever. A vocabulary which affronts us is of the very nature of religion to him.

But beyond all this, it must be said that there is immense moral advantage in the use of ugly words to denote ugly things. Even the most careless readers of the Old Testament cannot fail to notice that there is always deep moral meaning underlying what may seem to be offensive language. Always it is the language that offends, but never the idea underlying the language. And the ideas were kept just, because the language was honest. Language has more to do with ideals than we sometimes imagine. If we fail to call a thing by its right name, there is danger that we will not think of it in the right way. One who does not like the sound of the word "lie" and calls a deliberate untruth a "fib" instead is liable, without knowing it, to weaken in his own mind the sin of falsehood. One who calls a deliberate act of impurity by the word "indiscretion," instead of by its own name, does more than he realizes to break down conviction or standards of personal morality. One who does not like to use the word "drunk" and uses the word "rosy" or "lit" instead is unconsciously preparing for the next breakdown of self-control or manhood. We would do more for the cause of morals by the recovery of an honest vocabulary than we often imagine. The prophets kept Israel straight by calling her infidelities to God by harsh words. And however much such language may jar on our fastidious ears, it did a wholesome work for the people into whose ears it was uttered. And a certain imitation of this part of the Old Testament vocabulary would do a wholesome thing for us. Thus we can echo the words of Henry Ward Beecher: "Let us not be ashamed of the Old Testament. There are parts of the Old Testament that may not belong to polite literature, but they belong to life notwithstanding. I would rather take my child right through the Old Testament from Genesis to the last book in it, and read every bit to him, explaining and unfolding it and having him keep in mind the thread of moral principle that runs through it, than deprive him of familiarity with it." [3]

But besides the coarse language in the Ode of Nahum we are confronted with the main fact that the religious message of this poet-

[3] *Lectures on Preaching. Third Series,* pp. 130-131.

prophet seems to consist solely in a cry of exultation over the fall
Nineveh and a gloating over her emptiness and desolation. Now w
ask, what is the religious value of all this? Why should such a Hym
of Hate and Vengeance be in the Bible at all? Yet, as we all knov
such language is to be found all through the Old Testament. What w
find in Nahum is merely typical of what we find in many other par
of the Old Testament. There are to be found its savage passages, i
vindictive war songs, its stories of brutal warfare, its prophecies o
vengeance upon the enemies of Israel. What are we to do with a
this? What place in a revelation of Grace has the Ode of Deboral
which praises a woman who lured her enemy into her tent and the
slew him with hammer and nail as he lay asleep, her guest? Or wit
the imprecatory psalms: "Break their teeth, O God, in their mouth
(58:6). "Thou shalt break them with a rod of iron; thou shalt das
them in pieces like a potter's vessel" (2:9). "Happy shall he b
that taketh and dasheth thy little ones against the stones" (137:9)
Does not the raucous noise of these curses and maledictions ja
strangely upon the love songs that have cradled our souls to res
What are we to think about the picture which the Book of Nahur
holds up before us of an angry and vindictive God who reserves wrat
and visits death and destruction upon His enemies?

In the first place, we who have been trained in the Christian ide
of God, and in Jesus' teaching that love must extend even to ou
enemies, must remember that we are still in the Old Testament. Th
moral education of God's people was not completed. For the Hebrew
it was as natural to hate one's enemies as to love one's friends. Jesu
put his finger on this moral defect of the ethics of the Old Testamer
when he said: "Ye have heard that it hath been said, Thou shalt lov
thy neighbour, and hate thine enemy. But I say unto you, Love you
enemies." We ought not to expect to find in the Old Testament tha
higher love, broad charity and boundless goodwill of which Jesus i
the perfect exemplar.

But this is not the whole story. There is something more to be saic
The fact is that moral anger is an inseparable part of a true religior
And the Bible does not forget this, whether you and I do or not. Now
to take this specific case, why was it that Nahum hated Nineveh as h

d, that his anger burned at white heat, that his exultation rose to
ric heights at the news of its destruction? Fundamentally, it was be-
use Nineveh had outraged the deepest instincts of humanity.
ahum's anger rose above the level of a personal vindictiveness; even
ove the level of a nationalistic desire for revenge against a power
at had threatened the very existence of the Jewish state. Nahum's
ger—and this may be said to be true of all of the prophets—was
oted in religion. Indifferent as many of them were to the fate of
e Jewish state, they were all profoundly concerned with the fate of
wish religion. And because they believed that the Jewish people were
e custodians of that faith which one day was to be the faith of the
orld, the enemies of the people of God were in very truth the enemies
God Himself.[4] In a word, Israel stood for the Incarnation of Region: their enemies, of irreligion, the consciencelessness of sin. The
al struggle was between faith and paganism, good and evil, right-
usness and sin. And the inveterate antagonism that stretches through
e Old Testament, which reaches from one end of it to the other, is
ither personal nor ultimately racial, political, national, but the fun-
mental antagonism between conscience and sin, between religion
d its opposite. This is the explanation, even if it be not the justifica-
n, of the passionate desire for the discomfiture of their enemies.
ther they must go under or Israel; either they or the people of God
ust be put to everlasting shame and confusion. And forasmuch as
e Old Testament writers were persuaded that the truth of God stood
fell with them, they prayed with a good conscience that they might
e God's vengeance visited on their enemies. The shrieks of rage to
nich we listen, whether in the war songs of Deborah, in the Psalms,
in the voices of Nahum and Obadiah, are in fact the cries of an
traged conscience; the shouts of defiance, and the hurling in the
ce of evil the challenge of an undaunted faith; the cries of victory
e the odes which paean the triumph of righteousness over the hosts
Satan; the description of the desolation of Nineveh is the enuncia-
n of the solemn truth that the wages of sin is death. How true, then,
d righteous altogether appear these denunciations that reverberate
rough the soul of Nahum and make him declare that "the face of

This idea finds further illustration in the Book of Obadiah.

the Lord is against them that do evil, to cut off the remembrance of them from the earth." Surely there is a place for a book like Nahum even in the revelation of Grace. Instead of taking the Book of Nahum out of the Bible, we had better leave it there. We need it. It reminds us that love degenerates into a vague diffusion of kindly feeling unless it is balanced by the capacity of a righteous indignation. A man who is deeply and truly religious is always a man of wrath. Because he loves God and his fellow men, he hates and despises inhumanity, cruelty and wickedness. Every good man sometimes prophesies like Nahum.

We find always in the story of any really good man's life the prophet Nahum embedded in it somewhere. In a brief appreciation in the *Harvard Alumni Bulletin* of Henry Lee Higginson two different friends of his singled out this as one of the distinguishing elements of his character. President Eliot said of him: "He believed in fighting evil, in endeavoring to reduce the amount of evil in the world. When he saw wrong-doing, he wanted to resist and attack it hotly if need be." President Lowell said of him: "Mr. Higginson hated everything that was mean, everything that was iniquitous, and did not hesitate to condemn it with all the force of a very forcible vocabulary." To attack evil hotly, that is Nahum always and everywhere.

"I have in mind a man," writes Professor Cooley in his book *Human Nature and the Social Order* (p. 125), "who is remarkable for an aggressive, tenacious and successful pursuit of the right. He does things which every one agrees ought to be done, but does not do, especially things involving personal antagonism. If one consider how he differs from other conscientious people of equal ability and opportunity, it appears to be largely in having more bile in him. He was a natural friend of animosity, and directs it upon that which is hateful to the general good, thus gratifying his native turn for resentment in a moral and fruitful way. If there were more men like him, it would be of benefit to the moral condition of the country."

Dr. George A. Gordon once declared that there are three tests of a great character: the capacity for a great love; for a great enthusiasm; for a great indignation. Nahum symbolizes the last of these, and it is Nahum who is so often missed in contemporary and conventional

Christianity. We are so good-natured, so fastidious, so complacent, so dainty, so nice. But if we had a tithe of Nahum's passionate love of truth and righteousness we would at times be filled with a passionate hatred of their utter opposite. There is a verse in the New Testament which says "Be ye angry, and sin not." There is such a thing as sinning when we are angry; when that anger is personal; when people wound what we are pleased to call our sensitiveness. But that verse also reminds us that we often sin by not being angry against meanness and wrong and injustice and evil. Alas for any man or woman who, on occasion, cannot speak with the voice of Nahum.

Let us therefore give this old neglected book its rightful place in the revelation of Grace. Let us recover from our superficial ideas and lofty sense of superiority to what is set down there. It is of course only one book in the Bible, and you cannot expect to find the whole of the Bible in any one book of it. It is only one note in the Bible symphony: a deep diapason note—but a note needed to make the whole complete. Leave out this book and the truth for which it stands, and something will be gone that belongs to a true religion.

Take up this book and read it. And when you have read it through ask yourself: Is there anything in my life that compares with that? When last in my life did I feel like that? Can I remember a day when I spoke like that? And you will discover that perhaps we need nothing so much to make us morally sound and thoroughgoing as a recovery for ourselves of the spirit of the old prophet Nahum.

~~~ *Habakkuk* ~~~

I. Introduction

WE KNOW nothing whatever about the man Habakkuk except his name. The three short chapters of his book constitute his sole claim to immortality. The name occurs only here in Scripture. It springs from a verb which means to caress or to embrace. It has a certain symbolic significance in the light of Habakkuk's experience in clinging to God.

The book is undated. But in 1:6 mention is made of the Chaldeans "which shall march through the breadth of the land." Since we know that these campaigns began after 612 B.C. and according to Habakkuk were in full swing, and that "many nations" (2:8) had already been overrun, while Jerusalem was not yet immediately threatened, the date of Habakkuk's prophecy can be placed at approximately 600 B.C. or a few years earlier.

Some scholars have not been satisfied in thus dating the book, and have roamed over the centuries finding other periods for its composition. Thus it has been conjectured that not the Chaldeans but the Assyrians are referred to in 1:2-4 and 6-17, and that the Chaldeans are represented by Habakkuk as raised up to execute vengeance on the Assyrians. With this idea in mind, one group of scholars feels that the book was composed as early as 701 B.C. during the reign of King Hezekiah; while another dates the prophecy about 621-615 B.C. in the years immediately following Josiah's reformation and before the downfall of Nineveh in 612 B.C. Still others find that the chapters are composite and date parts of them in exilic or postexilic times, while some recent scholars by a slight change of the text have advanced the theory that the word for Chaldeans may mean the Greeks. In this case the historical reference will be to the campaigns of Alexander in Asia, and thus the date of the book would be around 300 B.C. But the arguments for this late date are not convincing, and there are grave objections to the other proposed dates, so that with some confidence we may assume that, while there may have been some later additions, and while especially verses 9–20 in chapter 2 may have been expanded in the postexilic age, the body of chapters 1 and 2 belong to the period 612–600 B.C. and quite probably near to the end of the seventh century, 605–600 B.C.

Thus, Zephaniah, Nahum, Habakkuk, form an intimately connected group. Zephaniah belongs to the earlier years of the period before the fall of Nineveh. Nahum follows when Nineveh was about to be destroyed. Habakkuk comes about a decade later. And Jeremiah, who began to prophesy at about the same time as Zephaniah, continues through the whole of this period down to and even after the fall of Jerusalem in 586 B.C.

The conditions within and without the land of Judah when Habakkuk prophesied were nothing short of appalling. When King Josiah was killed at the battle of Megiddo (608 B.C.), he was succeeded after the short three months' reign of Jehoahaz (II Kings 23:31–34, called Shallum in Jer. 22:10–12) by his elder brother Jehoiakim, a selfish, covetous, tyrannical ruler. His was a hardened and reckless character. He opposed the whole prophetic movement, a reaction to which had already set in under Jehoahaz. He murdered the prophet Uriah. All the vices of the time of Manasseh came trooping back again. The story of this may be read in Jeremiah (chaps. 7, 11, 26) who was Jehoiakim's implacable antagonist. The duel between these two men is one of the most grandiose encounters in all history.

The situation outside the land was no less ominous. Nineveh had fallen in 612 B.C. But this event, while it removed an ancient and hated foe, was fraught with the gravest consequences for the little Southern Kingdom. The Chaldeans, under Nabopolassar, with the aid of the Medes, had overthrown the Assyrian Empire and had begun their career of conquest. Under his son, Nebuchadrezzar, they had challenged the supremacy of Egypt. The two nations moved swiftly against each other and the issue was fought out at the battle of Carchemish in the year 605 B.C. The defeat of the Egyptians is referred to in Jeremiah 46:2. Thus the whole of the little buffer state of Judah between these two great antagonists lay at the mercy of the Chaldeans. Fifteen years or so later Jerusalem fell.

Such was the scene within and without that was spread before the eyes of Habakkuk when he began to prophesy.

The first two chapters of the Book of Habakkuk have presented many difficulties to the scholars, and they have rearranged the different sections in order to straighten out certain inconsistencies and to remedy what seems like a disjointed sequence. For one thing, does 1:2–4 refer to internal evil or to external violence? Again, how are we to reconcile 1:5, 6, in which the prophet speaks as if the Chaldeans were about to be raised up, with 1:7–11, in which their operations appear to be well under way and their barbarities familiar to all? Also, would not the sequence be better preserved if the passage about the Chaldeans in 1:5–11 were placed after 2:4 where the connection is very simple?

The scholars are not agreed upon their answers to these questions, and one is free to make his choice. On the whole, the continuity of Habakkuk's thought and the development of his experience seem best preserved by regarding 1:2–4 as referring to internal evils. Surely Habakkuk could not have been unmindful of them. We may assume that the section about the Chaldeans in chapter 1 belongs where it is, and constitutes a first possible solution to Habakkuk's problem, one which he rejects. And upon close examination there appears to be no real contradiction between 1:5, 6 and 1:7–11. The former passage is thrown into the past in dramatic fashion, and represents God as then at work raising up the Chaldeans as His instrument for the punishment of Israel.

With chapter 3, however, the case is different. The whole tone of this chapter differs from chapters 1 and 2. It reads like a psalm, and the musical directions with which it is provided show that it was at some time or other used in the musical service of the Temple. If any of this chapter belongs to Habakkuk, these notations must have been added later. It is difficult to find historical allusions in the chapter which would place it in the time of Habakkuk, and there is little else in the poem that has any bearing on date or authorship. For these reasons it seems unlikely that Habakkuk can have written the whole of it. At the same time we cannot be sure that no part of the chapter belongs to him. A "Prayer of Habakkuk" as a conclusion to chapters 1

[handwritten marginalia at top: "How to determine the author 1. internal evidence / style / 2. vocabulary / 3. vocabulary"]

and 2 seems on psychological or spiritual grounds to be an almost in-evitable epilogue to the experience of the prophet which culminates at the end of chapter 2. The theory is here advanced, therefore, that while much if not most of this chapter belongs to a later date and author we have in it the core of an authentic prayer of Habakkuk. Commentators have always found difficulty in relating verses 17–19 of chapter 3 with the preceding portions of this psalm. Some have even suggested that the poem originally ended with verse 16 and that these verses are an addition. But there is no difficulty whatever in re-lating them to the antecedent spiritual experience of the prophet.

It is commonly affirmed that the subject of the book is a prophecy against the Chaldeans, precisely as the Book of Nahum, with which, it is asserted, it has many affinities, is directed against Nineveh. This is seriously to misunderstand the meaning of the book. We do not have merely the excoriation of an enemy of God's people. Rather, we have the record of the wrestling of a devout mind with the problem of evil as it is presented both by the sins of Judah, on the one hand, and by the ruthlessness and irreligion of the Chaldeans, on the other. The interest of the book lies in the way the problem is presented and in the solution of it at which the prophet arrives.

Thus the significance of Habakkuk in the development of Old Tes-tament religion lies here: that, and almost for the first time, the specu-lative element is present. Habakkuk questions the ways of God. Other prophets had attacked evil, but Habakkuk is the first to raise the prob-lem that evil presents to faith. Other prophets had spoken for God to Israel, but Habakkuk speaks for Israel to God. It is true that Jeremiah had expostulated against what he had felt was the divine injustice (12:1). His emotional nature was hurt because, while he had been working for God, God seems to have deserted him to his enemies. But with Jeremiah this was a personal problem, whereas with Habakkuk it is the problem which the fact of evil presents to every devout soul. In later Old Testament literature, as in Psalm 73, this problem finds increasing emphasis and it comes to its full climax in the Book of Job. But to the mind of Habakkuk it was already present. He believed in God, but the facts of life had bewildered him. Hence he questioned the ways of God in dealing with men. This fact gives the Book of

Habakkuk its present contemporary interest. For never was the question which Habakkuk threw into the face of God more insistently asked than it is today.

As literature, the book ranks high. It is full of force and eloquence. His descriptions of the state of society within and without are graphic and powerful. Habakkuk is master of the old classical style, and thought and expression alike betray the heart of the poet. And if any part of chapter 3 be his, we discover lyrical genius of a high order. For "the grand imagery and rhythmic flow of this ode will bear comparison with some of the best in Hebrew literature." [1] Is it possible that Habakkuk [2] was a Temple prophet and singer and that thus this whole majestic hymn is his?

II. The Prophecy

There is no Old Testament book that is able to do more for the burdened souls of men or to raise them to higher levels of hope and confidence than the brief prophecy of Habakkuk. Yet it is one of the least understood and most neglected of Bible books. We need to recover a true knowledge of it, to read it, love it, use it. For if ever the message of this inspired book was needed, it is needed today.

It is notable because of its literary structure and form. Hardly a book in the Bible is constructed on such simple and majestic lines. These three chapters stand like three august columns, side by side, each complete in itself, unparalleled in their power and appeal. The first chapter states the problem that rests on the prophet's burdened soul. No time is lost. "The burden which Habakkuk the prophet did see." The prophet is the model preacher. He comes at once to grips with his subject. "Why does God do nothing when evil is abroad in the land?" An evident answer is indignantly rejected. What, then, remains? In the second chapter Habakkuk looks for an answer to the question that comes hot from his soul. He sets himself on his watchtower to hear what God will have to say to him. The answer comes. Then is let loose the full force of the prophet's indignation against the pagan power

[1] Hastings' Bible Dictionary, "Habakkuk."
[2] E. A. Leslie, *The Prophets Tell Their Own Story*, p. 204.

that has sought to destroy all that God holds dear. In the third chapter we have a prayer of thanksgiving, of faith, of trust, of the soul from which the burden that has pressed upon it has been removed. Search the Bible through and you will find nothing so matchless in concentrated power as these three chapters of the Book of Habakkuk. Of the outward circumstances of the prophet's life we know nothing. But here was a man with a soul sensitive to evil, yet firm in his faith in an omnipotent God. And this faith he has uttered with a force, an eloquence, a literary power which has caused his words to become a permanent part of the literature of the soul.

Consider these three chapters in order and see what they tell us. For, although written so many centuries ago, they are a veritable tract for the times in which we live.

(1) In the first chapter, then, Habakkuk states his problem, the perennial problem which the fact of evil presents to faith. It is this which endears him to us. He asks the very question that is so often on *our* lips. He wrestles with the problem that staggers us: How can we reconcile faith in God's government of the world with the facts of life as we see them and know them? He brings into the light of open day the doubts that have plagued our souls. At once there is a bond of sympathy between us and this unknown prophet. He was living in evil days, and so are we. How, now, did he work the problem out? How did he vindicate his faith in God in the face of the tragic facts of life and of human experience?

He certainly did not seek to minimize the contradiction by glossing over the evils that disgraced the world in which he lived. No prophet in all Israel pictured these in more vivid terms. In verses of great rush and passion, in sentences direct, pungent, throbbing with spiritual power, Habakkuk describes the terrible conditions that prevailed in his day. Evil is evil, black as night, dark as death. "The law is slacked, and judgment doth never go forth: for the wicked doth compass about the righteous" (1:4). Truth was surely on the scaffold and wrong upon the throne. And Habakkuk utters his protest in passionate words: "O Lord, how long shall I cry, and thou wilt not hear! even cry out unto thee of violence, and thou wilt not save!" (1:2). The contradiction is made as stark as language can make it.

To this angry outburst the Lord replies (1:5-11) that He has not been idle. He has been raising up a nation that will be His instrument to punish Israel for its sins. The Chaldeans will see to it that the wickedness of God's people will get its just deserts. A "bitter and hasty nation," they will "march through the breadth of the land" and make chastisement thorough and complete. Thus God's honor will be vindicated.

This solution of the problem of the evil presented by the recreancy of Judah entirely satisfied Jeremiah. He regarded the Chaldeans in just that light and foretold the destruction of faithless Jerusalem by them (Jer. 36:29-31; 22:22-26, 38:17, 18). But against this idea the soul of Habakkuk revolts. How can these ruthless barbarians be the agents of a holy God? The Chaldeans are even a worse lot than Israel. How can God use so base a crew to further His designs? They are a cruel, conscienceless set of brigands. The tyrants of Judah are saints and angels in comparison. And the people to be punished are white as snow beside these ruthless savages. So, turn his eyes where he will, Habakkuk sees only a mass of evil that shakes his faith in God. And out of his contemplation of it he raises the mighty question of the first chapter of his book. And the question as he puts it is a classic. It is one of the great words of the ages. He speaks for the devout and faithful everywhere who are oppressed not only by the evil that surrounds them from within but also by the evil that threatens them from without. "Thou art of purer eyes than to behold evil, and canst not look on iniquity: wherefore lookest thou upon them that deal treacherously, and holdest thy tongue when the wicked devoureth the man that is more righteous than he?" (1:13) Why do the innocent suffer and the unrighteous prosper? That was Habakkuk's problem, and it is ours.

(2) Let us see, now, what this brave soul does. And this we are told in the second chapter. The Bible, let us remember, never ends in an interrogation point. Always it ends in a period. Bible writers ask questions, but always also they get answers. That is the difference between the Bible and much modern secular literature. Modern writers ask many questions, raise many doubts, project all kinds of difficulties. But they present no answers, offer no solutions. We are left in mental and moral confusion. Not so the Bible. It also asks many questions, asks

every question that tortures the mind of man. But always it ends by giving answers and pointing the way out of doubt and despair. That is one reason why people love their Bibles.

And if people today knew their Bibles better they would not be going around asking questions yet neither expecting nor looking for any answers to the questions they ask. Rather, they would imitate the example of Habakkuk who, after he has flung his passionate question into the face of God, looks to Him for an answer. "I will take my stand upon my watch-towers; station myself upon the rampart and watch to see what he will say unto me, and what answer I get back to my plea" (Am. Trans., 2:1). He feels, that is, that there must be an answer to his problem, and he will wait and listen to see what God will say to him. There is the open and the expectant mind. There is the listening ear. The reason why many people often get no answers to their questions is that they have the seeing eye but do not have the listening ear. They see all the pitfalls, all the obstacles and difficulties, and these are the cause of their questioning doubts. But they do not have an ear attent to the answering voice of God. In order to get God's answers to our problems, we need to pause, wait, listen. Charles Wesley has well expressed this necessary attitude in his hymn, too little known and used:

> Open, Lord, my inward ear
>   And bid my heart rejoice,
> Bid my quiet spirit hear
>   Thy comfortable voice.
>
> From the world of sin and noise
>   And hurry I withdraw,
> For the small and inward voice
>   I wait with humble awe.
>
> Silent am I now and still
>   Dare not in Thy presence move.
> To my waiting soul reveal
>   The secret of Thy love.

We note, then, that Habakkuk sets himself to listen in a watch-tower, away up above the level of daily events, in an altitude removed from the confusing and conflicting happenings of his everyday life. And it will be on some such watchtower to which we ascend above the din of the busy world, in the quiet of the sanctuary in silent hours of meditation that we will wait to hear what God has to say to us. In the Mussulman's devotions, one constant gesture is to put the hands to the ears as if to listen to the messages from the other world. This is the attitude, the posture which our minds assume if we have a standing place above and beyond the stir and confusion and dissipation of this mortal world.

And now, watching and waiting, what does Habakkuk hear? What comes to help him as he seeks to find some clue to his problem? The answers are all compressed in two verses (2:3, 4). But they are pregnant with meaning. First, Habakkuk is told that it is all for an appointed time. Evil is marked for overthrow in the end. "Though it tarry, wait for it; because it will surely come, it will not tarry." Habakkuk is told that he is impatient because he lacks perspective. He cannot see the long unfolding purpose of God, hindered, thwarted, diverted, by the sins of men, yet never halted, always pursuing its course to its destined end. Habakkuk cannot take God's long view of things, who sees through the ages. God's train is never late. It will arrive on schedule time. A time limit is set in the counsels of God to the triumph of evil over good. Whatever else evil is in this world for, it is here to be destroyed. We suffer because we cannot see "how" or "when." But God knows. It is all predetermined. So let us be patient. It will not tarry. It hasteth toward the end. Wait for it, for it shall surely come. That was God's message to Habakkuk, and it is God's message to us.

But that is not all that Habakkuk hears on his watchtower. Next he is given to understand the method, the process by which the evil forces in the world are to be overcome. In a word, they are to be destroyed from within and not from without (2:4a). Evil that seems so mighty has within itself the seeds of destruction. It is incurably diseased. It is not upright, straight, true. In the nature of things it cannot endure. Every unrighteous deed and policy carries within itself the poison of its own destruction. What appears so solid is really hollow with death and decay. Automatic and self-operating laws are at work destroying the grandiose edifices that wickedness has reared. So, Habakkuk, you have nothing to fear. It looks as if evil were mocking the good. It is just the other way. Evil is itself a mockery, a sham. It wears a mask that shall one day fall off and display only the ghastly image of death. What vivid illustrations of this truth have we witnessed in our own day!

In the meantime, what is Habakkuk to do? Well, he is not to sit with folded hands and wait for all this to happen. He has his plain duty, his part to play. In a word, his is to be a life of fidelity. The righteous man shall live a life of faithfulness, of sheer fidelity to daily duty. Such is the plain meaning of these Hebrew words into which, taking them from the Greek, Paul breathed a new meaning. God tells Habakkuk that until the appointed time has been reached, while evil is slowly but surely destroying itself, he himself is to be steady. The summons is from speculation to action, from questioning to conduct, from brooding to duty. God is attending to His business, and Habakkuk must attend to his. Running this universe is not his task. That burden belongs to God. But Habakkuk has his task, and let him faithfully perform it. Thus he will live in moral sincerity and in the moral security that righteous living brings even in the midst of external calamities. That is the way for a righteous man to live in an evil world. Such was God's message to Habakkuk, and it comes with telling force into the life of every man today. We must not spend our time in speculation or allow ourselves to become unnerved by doubt. In the midst of a world that is full of contradiction and bewilderment, we ourselves must stand in the place of our appointment, be steady and faithful in the tasks given us to do, in the sure confidence that in God's own time, when the mists have blown away, all must and will be well with His world.

His lesson learned, Habakkuk, we must imagine, comes down from his watchtower, renewed in faith and strength and courage. Now he no longer fears the Chaldeans, and the thought of what they are doing no longer plagues him. Rather, the soul of the man, hot with indignation at their cruelties and baseness, let itself go in a series of sharp woes, bitter in their denunciation of evildoers, and filled with sure prophetic hope of their ultimate destruction. In the light of what has happened in our poor world today, how contemporary they sound as we have witnessed the inevitable retribution of tyrants who have brought confusion and disaster upon millions of innocent lives: tyrants treacherous and arrogant (vv. 5–6a) who opened their mouths like hell and swept nations into their maws and still are unsatisfied. The nations that they destroyed will rise again and bite them (v. 7), and everything they have stolen will be required of them again with interest (vv. 6b–8). They built their cities with blood and established themselves in iniquity. But one day there will be a new world in which dwelleth righteousness, and the world will be filled with the knowledge of God (vv. 12–14). The tyrants who have humiliated their neighbors shall themselves stagger like drunken men, and their glory shall be turned to shame. They are like a dumb and lifeless image. "There is no breath at all in the midst of it" (vv. 15–19).

And having uttered this terrific denunciation upon the enemies of God, Habakkuk is filled with a sense of the Presence of the Lord above and within His world and utters words which "for many centuries have been the Christian's call to worship, and even yet they throw over our spirits a reverential hush and inspire our hearts to sure confidence in Him who is over all": [3] "The Lord is in His holy temple, let all the earth keep silence before Him." It is interesting that two very familiar quotations from the Old Testament are found in this part of the second chapter of the Book of Habakkuk.

(3) Out of the hushed soul of the prophet there now comes the Prayer which we are able to reconstruct out of the material given us in chapter 3 of his book. And this seems to be such a tender, true, inevitable ending to the whole attitude and dealing of Habakkuk with God. The story, with this in it, reads so true to life. It is like that of a child in relation with his father. The child is disappointed, rebellious at his father's dealings with him which he cannot understand. And so he utters his complaint. He says "Why? Why?" Then his father takes him in his arms and tries to explain as well as he can. And the boy becomes quiet and comforted. Then, persuaded that his father has been good to him and that there have been reasons for what has been denied him, he is sorry that he even mistrusted his father's love, prays that he may be forgiven, and rests contented in the knowledge of his father's love and care.

[3] C. J. Harrell, *The Prophets of Israel*, p. 115.

Just so with the prophet. He has not been given a full answer to his problem, although light has been thrown upon it. Rather, he has attained a state of mind which does not ask for an answer. He has found his comfort not in any explanation of the ways of God. But he has hold of the hand of God and has come into the experience of His loving presence. At this point the experience of Habakkuk closely parallels that of Job, who found in the same way the solution of his problem. "I have heard of thee by the hearing of the ear: but now mine eye seeth thee" (Job 42:5).

Thus in his Prayer the prophet flings himself, as it were, into the arms of God, and breathes this prayer of thanksgiving and of trust. Never again will he misdoubt the providence of God in His dealing with His children, and he utters some of the most eloquent words to be found in Scripture: "Although the fig tree shall not blossom, neither shall fruit be in the vines; the labor of the olive shall fail, and the fields shall yield no meat . . . *yet* I will rejoice in the Lord, I will joy in the God of my salvation" (17, 18). To this glorious conviction has the experience of Habakkuk brought him.

Only such an experience can bring final comfort to our tortured souls in the face of the tragic contradictions of life. It is when the child loses clasp of his father's hand that he wants to know the reasons why his hopes and desires are defeated and denied in a way he cannot understand. When he regains it he is ready to walk on joyfully. We may never reach a full understanding of the ways of God. "It would take an eternity to understand infinity." But it will take but a moment of self-giving now to make the beginning of a friendship with God in which the demand for an answer to our questions will cease in an intimate fellowship with Him which rises above and dips beneath our every doubt. To all burdened souls comes this message out of the Book of Habakkuk. It is not the afflicting thing, no matter how severe it may be, that is bearing us down and wearing us out. Rather, it is our lessened faith in God. Something has separated us, perhaps unconsciously, from Him. It may be the murmur of self-will, the sense of injustice, rebellion against what we feel is undeserved. It may be just a drifting away from the old moorings: an effort to work our own way through the labyrinth and mystery of experience; or the following of other guides than the old teachers of Israel whom we used to trust. Back to God! Back to Him! That is the message of the last chapter of this book of Habakkuk. And if we find our way back to God as the prophet did, then, like him, we will utter our prayer of praise and of trust, and we too will "joy in the God of our salvation."

Haggai

I. Introduction

WE COME now to the postexilic prophets. Haggai and Zechariah were contemporaries. Their books are dated with precision in the text. The prophecies of the former fall between August and December 520 B.C., and those of the latter appeared between November, 520 B.C., and February, 519 B.C., and then again in December, 518 B.C. The general political situation that forms the background to their work is familiar to the Bible reader. It was a critical period in the history of the Jewish people. Cyrus, the king of Persia, had overthrown the Babylonian Empire and established his rule over the Eastern world. The Jews were still in Babylon when he entered it. But soon Cyrus issued an edict permitting their return to Palestine (II Chron. 36:22, 23; Ezra 1:2-4; 1 Es. 2:1-7), and allowing them to take with them the sacred temple vessels which Nebuchadrezzar had carried off to Babylon (Ezra 1:7-11). At first only a small minority of the people "whose spirit God had raised, to go up to build the house of the Lord which is at Jerusalem" (Ezra 1:5) were ready to return under the leadership of Zerubbabel and Joshua the high priest (Ezra 2:2). But small as the returning company was, they were filled with the spirit of joy, of enthusiasm, and of devotion to their country and their God. An arduous and even perilous journey home, which may have taken four months, brought them to their destination (536 B.C.). They set themselves at once to their task of rebuilding the Temple for which Cyrus, who undoubtedly was actuated by religious as well as political motives, had supplied the means (Ezra 6:3, 4).

The first step was to reconstruct the altar (Ezra 3:2), and this was completed seven months after their return. Henceforth the daily sacrifices and the stated feasts were resumed. Thus far all had progressed favorably. But soon serious obstacles were encountered. The Samaritans, indignant at the refusal of the Jews to allow them to co-operate in the work (Ezra 4:1-3), persuaded the Persians (Cyrus having died) to prohibit the rebuilding of the Temple. Only when Darius succeeded to the throne fifteen years later (520 B.C.) could the work be resumed.

It was then that Haggai and Zechariah appeared upon the scene, and by their prophecies sought to reanimate the broken spirit of the Jews, who had come to feel that the completion of the Temple was impossible (Hag. 1:2). To rouse them from their lethargy and from their selfish preoccupation in secular tasks (Hag. 1:4), they devoted their energies, each in his own way. Zerubbabel and Joshua placed themselves at the head of the movement to resume the work. Darius favored the enterprise, forbade any obstacle to be put in their way, and even by royal decree charged the revenues of the province with the cost of the rebuilding. Four years later the Temple was completed (516 B.C. Ezra 6:15).

Further political developments are indicated in Haggai and Zechariah. Darius wore his crown uneasily. Insurrections and revolts in various parts of his empire occurred so frequently during the first two years of his reign that both prophets felt that a world upheaval was imminent (Hag. 2:6–9; Zech. 2:8ff), which might result in the restoration of the Davidic kingdom under Zerubbabel (Hag. 2:23). Possibly Zerubbabel was actually crowned in secrecy; but if so, this may have led to his imprisonment or death. At any rate he seems to have disappeared, and Joshua was substituted for him in the vision of Zechariah (Zech. 6:11). Darius apparently made light of these patriotic aspirations, for he continued to favor the Jews. But the expectations Haggai and Zechariah entertained for the coming glory of the Jewish people were not fulfilled in their day. Not until the time of Nehemiah (444 B.C.) do we witness a genuine revival of the Jewish state.

The Book of Haggai presents no problem to the scholars. It is generally agreed that these thirty-eight verses, divided into two chapters, were written by the man whose name it bears. The name itself may mean "festal" or "festive," and it may have been given him because he was born on one of the feast days of the Jews. Nothing is known about his personal history. His parentage is not told us. There is a tradition that he was born in Babylon during the Exile; that he was of a priestly race and became a member of the Great Synagogue after his return to Jerusalem. He was probably an old man. He may even have been among the number of those few who remembered the splendor of city and temple before the exile (2:3).

The fortunes of the little colony at Jerusalem were at a low ebb when Haggai began his work (1:6; 9–11; 2:16, 17). The land was overrun by Persian armies invading Egypt. A succession of bad seasons followed, the harvests failed, some of the old social abuses reappeared. Religious enthusiasm declined. The leaders of the people failed to rally them, and the great purpose of the Return remained unachieved. Then prophecy came to the rescue of the situation. Haggai came forward and Zechariah was soon beside him—with the divine command to begin at once the rebuilding of the Temple.

It is probable that these two short chapters contain only the outlines of the prophecy of Haggai rather than his full message to the people of his day. At any rate they contain its substance and enable us to understand on what grounds he appealed to them to resume the work of temple building, and the characteristics of his language and style. This has often been described as tame and prosaic. It is true that we find no flights of imagination in his work, no impassioned eloquence or moving poetry. But his simple and severe style was finely adapted to his purpose. "His brief sharp sentences . . . were exactly what the occasion required." He had a stern message to utter, a call to repentance, like that of John the Baptist, and his style conformed to his idea. "There is a ponderous and simple dignity in the emphatic reiteration addressed alike to every class of the community, prince, priest and people: Be strong, cleave, stick fast to the work you have to do . . . Consider your ways." [1]

II. THE PROPHECY

The Book of Haggai is divided into four short prophecies, the first of which is found in chapter 1, the second in 2:1–9, the third in 2:10–19, the fourth in 2:20–23. We will briefly review these, and then seek to understand the meaning of Haggai's prophecies for the days in which we live.

[1] Stanley, *Jewish Church*, III, 101. Quoted in Cambridge Bible, "Haggai," Introduction, p. 22.

1. *Chapter 1. First Prophecy. The Call to Build.*

Here is plain exhortation, interspersed with narrative. It is a practical message suited to the needs of the hour. Haggai did what needed to be done. Prophecy fulfilled its function by supplying the kind of preaching the occasion demanded. Any other kind of preaching at that moment would have been futile. The inspiration of Haggai is seen not in the lofty language and deep ethical thought of his predecessors, but in the accommodation of truth both in form and in content to immediate need. And it cannot be claimed that in laying exclusive emphasis on the rebuilding of the Temple, Haggai reveals himself as an ecclesiastic merely, an institutionalist who has more regard for the externals of religion than for its spiritual meaning. "Without the Temple, the continuity of Israel's religion could not be maintained. The ethical spirit, the regard for each other and God, could prevail over their material interests in no other way than by common devotion to the worship of the God of their fathers." [2] Thus in urging that the Temple be built, Haggai was, in effect, seeking to lay afresh the foundations of the Jewish religion and thus of the Jewish state. "Haggai illustrated at once the sanity and the spiritual essence of prophecy in Israel." In interpreting the bad seasons and harvests as a sign of God's anger at the people for their selfishness, Haggai but echoes a strain in Hebrew thought with which many of the psalms make us familiar: that prosperity and righteousness, adversity and evildoing go hand in hand. It is doubtless a defective interpretation of Providence. Yet it was one which would be sure to impress the Hebrew imagination.

Haggai's straight appeal, we read, went home to the hearts of the people who within three weeks began work on the Temple.

2. *Chapter 2:1–9. Encouragement to the Builders.*

This glowing word of prophecy stands out clear and bright against the sober, somber setting of chapter 1. Without doubt, Haggai was looking for a speedy fulfillment of his expectation of a "shaking of the nations" that should usher in the glories of the Messianic kingdom,

[2] George Adam Smith, *The Twelve Prophets*, "Haggai."

just as the primitive Church in the New Testament expected the Second Coming of Christ in glory in "a little while." This prophecy may, in a Christian interpretation of it, seem to be fulfilled in the great unrest of the world before the advent of Christ. From the earliest times, the passage in verse 7, "The desire of nations," has been interpreted to refer to Christ. The word 'desire' has been personified by the early church fathers and even by Luther himself. Correctly translated in the plural, "the desirable or costly things of the nations," it loses little of its Messianic meaning. One is reminded of the glowing passage in Isaiah 60:9–11.

3. *Chapter 2:10–19. The Contagion of Evil.*

To some it has seemed as if Haggai's "great concern was not the moral and religious wickedness of the people, but adherence to the rules of Levitical purity and the fulfillment of ritual acts." [3] Yet this idea does scant justice to the real motive of Haggai in using this reference to Levitical law. He employs it only as the illustration of a deep ethical principle. The Jews had evidently expected that when they had set about to rebuild the Temple, this act of repentance would result at once in good harvests and prosperity. When this did not happen, they became discouraged again and discontinued work. Haggai reminds them that they have no reason to expect immediate material reward for rightdoing. And here Haggai appeals to old Levitical law. If one touched a clean or holy thing, the cleanness and the holiness of it were not communicated to others. But if a person touched a dead body, not only was he unclean himself, but all who came in contact with him were unclean also. The evil was transmitted by contact more rapidly and effectively than the good. The application seems to be that the feeble attempts of the people to build the Temple were not sufficient to bring them prosperity, whereas their failure to complete it, their contact with this dead purpose had polluted them and thus had had an evil effect upon their fortunes.

This moral principle has wide application in the life alike of the individual and of nations. One may turn from his wickedness and seek

[3] So R. H. Pfeiffer, *Introduction to the Old Testament,* "Haggai," p. 603.

to do the will of God and yet continue to suffer because of a sinful past. The infectious power of evil may persist even after one has undertaken to live a holy life.

4. Chapter 2:20–23. The Messianic Hope.

This prophecy uttered on the same day as the previous one is the climax of Haggai's message to the people. Even in the days of the Exile, Ezekiel had predicted an individual Messiah, a son of the house of David (Ezek. 34:24) whom he calls not king but prince. Haggai now names Zerubbabel as this destined prince who in his person is to preserve the Messianic hope of the Jewish people. For the Christian, this hope culminates in Christ, son of David and descendant of Zerubbabel (Matt. 1:12; Luke 3:27).

Even this brief review of the prophecies of Haggai should be enough to convince us that he is not the second-rate prophet he is often taken to be, uttering an uninspired message in uninspired language; or that the greatest importance of the book, as well as that of Zechariah is "as an historical source . . . the only authentic source that lifts the veil for a moment over the obscure centuries of Jewish history between 561 B.C. and 444 B.C." [4] Although Haggai did not lay emphasis on the great truths of the earlier prophets, nor on the ethical elements in religion, he showed his power to speak directly to the immediate necessities of moment, to persuade his people to address themselves forthwith to their duty, to unfold before them the prospect of a Messianic age, a hope which, if not fulfilled as he expected, kept that hope alive and pointed to its consummation in the advent of Him who is destined to put all things under his feet and to rule as King of kings and Lord of lords.

The Book of Haggai has been sadly neglected by the Bible reader today. He is interested neither in what the prophet has to say nor in the way in which he says it. Here is no lofty idealism, no poetry, no appeal to spiritual imagination. So he passes the book over for what seem to be more inspired books. Now this feeling may be natural,

[4] R. H. Pfeiffer, op. cit., p. 603.

but it is really an undiscerning and superficial judgment of a very useful Bible book. It does not allow sufficiently for the variety of utterance that is one of the fascinations of the Bible. The Bible is not all poetry, it is poetry and prose. Unlike some modern preachers, the Bible preachers do not always talk in the same strain. They knew how to vary their style and to alter their tone. Our Bibles would not be nearly so rich if every book were crowded with lofty ideals and with spiritual visions. It is a relief and aid to our spirits between such flaming books as Zephaniah and Zechariah to find this plain, rugged, homely message of the old man Haggai. We fail also to estimate at its true value simple and unvarnished instruction. We like fire and eloquence and fervor. Even Haggai bursts out in some of this (2:6–9; 21–23). But instruction is important also. It is open to question if our modern preaching would not be more valuable if there were less fire and more plain speaking about the simple, homely virtues and duties of everyday life; if it dealt less in poetical generalities and emphasized more the prosaic performance of neglected tasks. When John the Baptist talked to the Jews, and Savonarola to the Florentines, and Luther to the Germans, and Wesley to the England of his day, there was a good deal of Haggai in what they had to say.

Furthermore, we overlook the importance of the work Haggai accomplished for the cause of Jewish religion. We are not interested, we say, in the putting up of a Temple in old Jerusalem. But we forget the meaning of that Temple as the shrine within which was kept inviolate the faith of the Old Testament. This fact, already mentioned, needs steadily to be borne in mind. Following the days of Haggai and of Zechariah was a terrible stretch of five hundred years before the coming of Christ: a long period during which prophecy all but ceased, and wars rolled over the land as pagan nations strove against each other, this little people apparently at their mercy. During such a time, the faith of the Hebrews could hardly have survived but for the Temple, which stood unshaken over these wrecks of time. What Haggai actually accomplished was not merely to put up a building but rather to preserve the religion out of which in due time the Christian faith was born.

The importance of this book is further revealed in the singular relevancy of Haggai's teaching to the problems of our modern world.

He speaks to us as well as to his own countrymen in stern rebuke for neglecting to build religion into the structure of society, a neglect which is the cause of all of our woes. His message, word for word, can be spoken to men today. You have been concerned, he told the Jews, with accumulating wealth for yourselves, providing yourselves with luxurious homes and meanwhile neglecting to build the Temple, neglecting the cause of religion, neglecting God. No wonder, then, that you have not prospered. Mend your ways. Give less attention to your own selfish interests, and pay more attention to your religious duty. How can you expect to prosper when you do everything for yourselves and nothing for God, when you have left God out of the reckoning? Only when religion prospers will you prosper. Put up a temple to God and you will find things looking up for you.

How modern it all sounds! Is there nothing in this stinging indictment for us in this day to think over? Haggai's preaching may have been in prose, but it was inspired prose. The proof of inspiration is the result it achieves. Haggai's prose in his day succeeded in rousing a whole dull, discouraged people from apathy to the performance of an essential and neglected task. And if that was the inspired message of Haggai in 520 B.C., it is the inspiration we most need in our distracted world today. What have we been doing? Have we been earnestly seeking to build religion into the world? We have been building everything else: bridges and dams, aqueducts and skyscrapers, which are the admiration of the world. We have built temples of finance and industry. But we have lived in ceiled houses while the house of God has gone begging. We have spent five times as much on dispensable luxuries as we have spent on the maintenance of religion at home and abroad. Our civilization from top to bottom has been largely secular. We have left religion out of our business, out of our education, out of our politics. We have not been building religion into the lives of our people or into the life of the nation. We have kept on saying that a man has the right to make as much money as he can and to spend his money as he likes, forgetting that "the silver is mine and the gold is mine, saith the Lord of hosts" (2:8). The right of absolute possession has eaten into men's souls like acid. It has become a sacred belief. And as a result of this, calamity has befallen us, society is in a state of disorder and revolt. What is the use of accumulated wealth if one cannot fulfill the conditions which bring a normal and happy life? So cleverly have we separated religion from business that even now we fail to see that, except business and finance be penetrated by morality, we shall go on perpetuating the glaring contrast between the prosperity of the few and the misery of many. The root trouble, Haggai reminds us, with our modern society is that religion has been left out of it.

Now let us be sensible, says Haggai to us today. How can we expect to prosper except religion prospers also? If we keep on building up the externals of a secular society while the institutions of religion fall apart, is it any wonder if we find ourselves in disorder and distraction? Let us go to work and rebuild religion. To build the temple of religion is to lay the foundations of prosperity everywhere.

And to build religion it is necessary to build the institutions of religion. Religion must be incorporated in a visible Church. It is useless to talk as if religion were one thing and the Church another. In a sense, that is of course true. An individual may be truly religious and at the same time withhold his allegiance from the Church. Yet if the history of religion teaches us anything, it teaches us that nowhere and at no time has religion existed without incorporating itself in institutional forms. "It is a truism that religious institutions tend to degenerate, to become mechanical, to tyrannize. But . . . is it not equally a truism that without the stabilizing and preservative influence of religious institutions, the religion of pure spirit would tend to evaporate . . . or at least would fail to condense in forms of practical spiritual energy?" [5] Religion, that is, if it is to be a real, permanent and effective form of spiritual influence, needs to be embodied in visible form. Group organization is a necessity of human life, and this is as true of the spiritual as of other interests of life. The strange fact is that many people who recognize the need of organization in other relations of life do not admit its importance in religion. Without a visible Church, religion would doubtless remain as a source of private inspiration but it would not be a continuing and constructive force. A visible Temple is as necessary for the preservation of religion as a social force in our day as in the days of Haggai. Without the Church, the Christian religion can

[5] Evelyn Underhill, *The Life of the Spirit and the Life of Today*, p. 159.

achieve nothing as a social dynamic. Therefore, if we believe that this world needs nothing so much as the renovating influence of religion, we must renew our loyalty to the visible Church, and help to rebuild the institutions of religion on which its permanence and effectiveness depend. And that loyalty and support will be given with the frank admission of the limitations and imperfections of the Church, with the recognition that inevitably it will reflect but imperfectly the spiritual ideals to which it witnesses and of which it is the embodiment.

Such is the modern meaning of the message of Haggai to us of today. Equally pertinent is his warning concerning the pervading and contaminating power of evil, the time required for the removal of its poisonous infection. We are in a position today to understand the meaning of this idea as we give ourselves to the task of trying to rebuild the world. We have to face the fact that a fresh enthusiasm and determination to eradicate the evils which have overtaken us will not at once work the change we have at heart. For generations now the life not only of our own nation but of all nations has been made unclean by coming in contact with the dead body of a selfish economic system and a narrow-minded nationalism, which have violated the principles of generosity and brotherhood. And that pollution has gone so deep and spread so far that the new desire for a world in which dwelleth righteousness will not at once be realized. This tragic fact has to be faced. It is the inevitable result of an evil past. We must suffer its consequences for a long time. Here is a truth deeply embedded in human experience of which we are given a vivid realization in the present hour of the world's history. The modern prophet would do well to incorporate this warning by Haggai in what he has to say to people today. You do well to mend your ways and to begin the rebuilding of a new world. But do not deceive yourselves. This will be no easy task. The infection has gone deep and will be eradicated only by long and arduous effort. No swift recovery is possible. Discouragement may inevitably overtake you. Only by steady reliance upon God and the continuous recuperative power of His spirit will the cleansing of the world be achieved and new motives replace those which have brought about our ruin and disaster.

But the final message of Haggai is one of hope. Goodness is more powerful than evil, righteousness than sin. And behind all human effort there is the infinite travail of the soul of God, which will not be satisfied till final victory has been won. Hence the glowing passages in this book of prose in which the old prophet foretells the shaking of the nations, the coming of the Messiah, the crowning of his representative Zerubbabel and the reign of Peace. For the Christian these passages are full of inspiration as the foretelling not only of the coming of the Prince of Peace, but of his final victory. Whatever its literal meaning, the phrase "Desire of Nations" has appealed to the Christian imagination as have few others in the Old Testament as a true description of Christ. It is incorporated in Christian thought and poetry. It finds its place in one of our best-loved Christmas hymns:

> Sages, leave your contemplation,
> Brighter visions beam afar;
> Seek the great Desire of Nations,
> Ye have seen His natal star;
> Come and worship,
> Worship Christ, the New-Born King.

~~ *Zechariah* ~~

I. INTRODUCTION

THE PROPHECIES of Zechariah are contained in the first eight chapters of the book that bears his name. The authenticity of these chapters is unquestioned. 7:1 and 8 are probably editorial, there is at least one gloss (4:12), and there may be a few editorial changes, especially in 6:9-15. Otherwise, the text as it stands represents the authentic prophecy of Zechariah. The last six chapters contain prophecies of a much later date. These may belong to the same unknown author or, more probably, to several writers. They were added to the authentic prophecies of Zechariah by the editor of the Book of the Twelve. It is not our purpose to review these later chapters in detail. A brief discussion of them will follow the exposition of the work of Zechariah himself.

Zechariah belonged to a priestly family (Neh. 12:16), being the son (or grandson) of Iddo. He is mentioned in Ezra 5:1 and 6:14. The name, which means "God remembers" is a familiar one, no less than twenty-nine of that name being found in the Bible. He returned from Babylon to Jerusalem (*c.* 537 B.C.) with the first company of the exiles. And seventeen years later, in 520 B.C. (1:1), he began to prophesy. Like Zephaniah, he was a young man. But while Zephaniah represents the melancholy of youth, Zechariah exhibits its optimism. Indeed, the message of Zechariah is one of the brightest, the clearest, the most hopeful to be found in prophetic literature. His whole activity seems to have been compressed within two years.

Social and political conditions are exactly the same as we find them in Haggai. Darius is king. Numbers of Jews still remain in Babylon. The community at Jerusalem is small and weak, consisting chiefly of young men and men in middle life with a few old folk and some children. The Temple is still to be built, although we may presuppose that some progress has been made. Yet discouragement if not despair was the prevailing popular mood. Zechariah seeks to change this to one of hopefulness by historical retrospect and by glowing Messianic prediction. His faith shines like a clear beacon in the darkness. It is what men see in the night that tests them and proves the strength, the quality, and the fiber of a faith which beholds the realities of God and His enduring power and love.

We need constantly to remember that for the coming of the Messianic era to which all Jews looked forward, the dwelling of Jehovah within the Temple was essential. Already it had been so far completed (8:18ff) that the fasts of the Exile were no longer needed. It remained to carry that work to completion. To that end Haggai and Zechariah worked together.

A reading of these eight chapters of the book of the prophecies of Zechariah reveals an interesting fact. The introduction in chapter 1, verses 1–6, and the 7th and 8th chapters contain simple, straightforward, clear and easily intelligible preaching. In it, the prophet appeals to the lessons of the past, exhorts to faithful living in the present, and paints a bright and beautiful picture of the New Jerusalem that is to be. In reading these chapters one feels oneself to be at home at once. But the last part of the first chapter and the succeeding chapters down to the seventh are of a wholly different nature. They consist of obscure visions, some of them very elaborate, containing strange and fantastic imagery. The combination of these two contrasted types of writing perplexes us. How comes it that one who can write in such clear, ethical fashion can also clothe his ideas in such strange and mysteriously symbolical forms? To at least one scholar, this is proof that "prophecy has loosed itself from its natural soil and developed into a purely literary creation. . . . Zechariah has at his disposal a rich and lively fantasy and his book is highly interesting and in its kind excellent; but it is nevertheless a clear witness of the growing deterioration of prophecy." [1] But may not this union of ethical and apocalyptical prophecy in Zechariah be a witness not to the deterioration but to the completion of prophecy? It is precisely the linking of these two kinds of writing in Zechariah that constitutes the unique significance of his work. A true optimism in his day or in ours would not be possible without both of them. Hence these eight chapters standing just as they

[1] Cornill, *op. cit.*, pp. 152, 153.

are constitute one of the most inclusive statements of faith to be found in prophetical literature.

Zechariah had been brought up in Babylon under the influence of Ezekiel. There he had learned to be true to the teaching of the older prophets that in the acknowledgment of God's providence in the past and in obedience to His Word and Will in the present lies the way into life. "This do, and thou shalt live." But in Babylon he had learned something else. There he had learned the meaning of symbolism and apocalypse as these lie open upon the pages of Ezekiel. The exiles were dreamers. They saw the New Jerusalem arise not only by the work of man but by an act of God. They felt the need of ritual, of purification from sin. The ancient sacrifices were not abolished, but something deeper was needed for the attainment of holiness. Again, the sense of the evil in the world and the evil in themselves had the inevitable effect of the removal of God from the world. He had thus become a transcendent God, and intermediary beings were needed to bridge the gulf between God and man. In Ezekiel we find superhuman mediators (Ezek. 40ff.), although not called angels, who seem to be the spirit of prophecy personified. In Zechariah we have the same idea (1:13, 19; 2:3), but now the process is carried further and angels appear as agents of Jehovah's operation controlling the destinies of nations. From Zechariah's day onward, angels are a prominent feature of Jewish theology. Ritual too was developed during the Exile to an extraordinary degree. Atonement and sanctification were stressed to meet the moral needs of the people. Under these influences, Zechariah grew up. He was himself of a priestly family, was himself a priest. Hence it is not strange that these ideas, as well as the ethical principles of the older prophets should find their illustration in his message to the people of his day. And above all there was the Messianic hope, the hope of a blessed consummation, of ultimate salvation, for deliverance and the restoration of the kingdom of Israel. This expectation existed before the idea of a personal Saviour had taken root in the Hebrew mind, as Zephaniah has shown us. God had made a special covenant with His people, with David and his royal house. The Jews looked back upon the reign of David as the great epoch of national honor. Some descendant of David would restore his kingdom in glory and power (Is.

7:14–16; 9:6–7; 11:1–5). He would be the Anointed One, the King over all, the Messiah, God's true Regent on earth. As the earthly fortunes of the people sank lower and lower, the Messianic hope became clearer and more and more ecstatic. It occupies a central place in the thought of Zechariah.

The idea, often held, that apocalyptical prophecy, visions with symbolic and often fantastic or even, as it seems to us, grotesque imagery is prophecy in decline, a falling away from the high ethical levels of the older prophets, is seen, upon closer examination, to be unwarranted. So long as salvation depended upon obedience to God, upon moral action, upon the acceptance of His Will for His chosen people, prophecy was largely ethical. It dealt with man's duties to God. Its refrain was "What doth the Lord require of thee?" It consisted of exhortations to righteousness, rebuke of evil, denunciation of national sins and promises of national prosperity based on moral obedience to the Law and Will of God. But when the overthrow of Jerusalem had taken place, when the people were confronted with apparently fatal and irreparable disaster, then prophecy, if it was to perform its mission, must change its tone and form to meet the moral emergency and satisfy the spiritual necessities of such a crisis hour in the experience of the people. Now it was not a question of what man should do for God, but of what God could do for man. Now prophecy must speak not of man's duty to God, but of God's duty to man. What moved the heart of the prophet at such an hour was divine intervention and deliverance, salvation by direct act of God. Hence, from the time of the Exile on, prophecy, accommodating itself to the extremity of human need, lifted its voice in an agony of appeal to the Ancient of Days, to bare His arm in the sight of all nations. The scene of prophecy was shifted from earth to heaven. Its pages were filled with the description of the power of God, His resources, His hosts, His anger, His deliverance. Evidently the impression of all this can be conveyed only by the use of highly colored and pictorial language. Symbolism is thus of the very essence of apocalyptical thought. It is, in the main, a grandiose effort of the human mind to portray the mobilization of divine power for the salvation of man. And because this form of prophecy achieved what ethical prophecy at such a time could not have achieved, it cannot be regarded as prophecy in decline. An Apocalypse at the end of the Old Testament era—Daniel—saved the Hebrew faith at an hour of supreme peril. An Apocalypse at the end of the New Testament—Revelation—upheld the Christian faith when threatened by the might of the Roman Empire. Apocalypse is needed as well as ethics. Both are found in the faith of Jesus and of Paul.

Hence the use of apocalyptical prophecy by Zechariah is not a mere "literary device" which shows a falling off in inspiration from the higher standards of the past. It is prophecy of a kind demanded by the exigencies of his time. Zechariah does not rank with the great prophets. Yet his message, both in its ethical passages and in its visions of the future, has its inspired place in the revelation of God's truth to man, and contains important lessons as applicable to our time as to his. He may not have been a great thinker, but he was a noble soul able to see beyond the "sorry scheme of things" in the midst of which he lived the Eternal purpose working out its divine ends for the salvation of men.

II. The Prophecy

In 1:1–6, we find the first of the three plain practical sections in the prophecies of Zechariah, in which he reaffirms the noble teaching of the earlier prophets. These verses read just like a passage from Jeremiah or Deuteronomy. It is a human appeal to profit from the lessons of the past in order to shape the national course for the future. To Zechariah, the older pre-exilic prophets have acquired the same authority that Moses possessed for them. "The history which led to the Exile has become to Israel as classic and sacred as her great days of deliverance from Egypt and the conquest of Canaan." [2] And the lesson that Zechariah deduces from this retrospect of the nation's immediate past is the same lesson which the older prophets sought to bring home to the people from their survey of the past. We hear once more the voice of Jeremiah (25:4–6): "And the Lord hath sent unto you all his servants the prophets . . . but ye have not hearkened, nor inclined your ear to hear. They said, Turn ye again now every one from his evil way . . .

[2] George Adam Smith, *The Book of the Twelve Prophets*, "Zechariah."

and go not after other gods to serve them . . . and I will do you no hurt." In a word, Zechariah's appeal to the past is not to its traditions, to its formulae, to its rites, customs and institutions, but to that Providence which has shaped Israel's history, thwarted only by Israel's moral disobedience. Zechariah holds out to the people of his day that a return to the Lord's Way and Will cannot fail to bring prosperity and peace. Disobedience to the Will of God has brought to pass the judgment of the Exile. Your fathers did not hear nor hearken unto me. So my decreed punishment overtook them and where are they? Be not like your fathers, saith the Lord, but turn to Me that I may turn to you. For God's Word and Will are not dead but live right on. The bodies of the fathers may lie moldering in the grave but God's truth has gone marching on. All through the life and death of men, running like a golden thread through the ebb and flow of human effort and failure, there is the Will of God. "Grass may wither, flower may fade, but the Word of God abideth forever." Such is the eternal lesson of the past, intoned by the older prophets and reiterated here by Zechariah. Israel must link her destinies to that Will if she would live. That is Zechariah's hope out of history and that is the Bible hope. The Bible everywhere sees God at work behind this temporary framework which we call the universe, underneath the mortality and frailty of man. Moral victory is God's victory. We cannot doubt the one if we believe the other. It may be true that in Zechariah we observe an "altered relation of the prophet toward God . . . [that] whilst the older prophets felt themselves to be completely one with God, ever present and living in them, God now grows more and more transcendent, the direct, personal intercourse . . . ceases." [3] But this idea of a transcendent God standing on the field of history has its place in the creation of a final social optimism. And Zechariah is an optimist because he perceives that overruling Will of God.

Such teaching has its evident application to the tragic problems of our modern world. As we, too, survey the past, how true it appears that national calamity and disaster have been due to failure to hearken to the prophets, whether of old or in modern days, who have declared God's Word and Will. Surely His statutes have stood over us, convinced us of our failures, made clear both the cause of our misfortunes and the

[3] Cornill, op. cit., p. 152.

way to our salvation. Our hope today is that we, too, shall turn and say: "God hath dealt with us according to our ways and our doings. If we return to Him, then He will turn to us."

We come next to the visions of Zechariah contained in the last part of chapter 1 and in the following five chapters. Four months had elapsed since Haggai had prophesied that shortly there would be a world up-heaval in which the glory of Zion would be restored. Yet there was still no sign of this and there was a natural popular mood of disappointment. To counteract this, and to encourage the people to resume the work of rebuilding the Temple, the word of the Lord came to Zechariah and he unfolded to the people in this and in the following visions what was the purpose of God for them. These visions—there are eight of them, with an epilogue—may seem to be obscure and even fantastic, yet more closely examined they are seen to contain truths as needed in our day as in the day of Zechariah, truths immediately applicable to the urgent problems of our modern world. "I saw by night, and behold." The inspiration of apocalyptical prophecy lies in this: that when it is night and others can see only clouds and darkness, these seers of God can dis-cover divine powers at work for man's redemption.

1. *The first vision* (*1:1–17*). *The Celestial Scouts.*

The prophet beholds angel horsemen, which have scoured the earth, celestial cavalry scouts with the leader of the troop in front on a red horse. They report: "We have gone to and fro in the earth and behold all the earth sitteth still and is at rest." Yet what an ominous stillness that was. Revolts against Darius were already in progress. This was but a lull in the storm, an unearthly quiet, as it were. Yet these angel scouts bring their word of cheer. God is displeased with the heathen nations that appear to be at their ease. The Lord by His messengers spoke good and comfortable words. Israel has been vexed long enough. Her punish-ment has been sufficient. Days of safety and prosperity are to come. Jerusalem shall yet stand foursquare, and "the Lord shall yet comfort Zion."

This vision had vivid meaning for its time, and for us today there is infinite comfort in the assurance that God's scouts are abroad, going to and fro in our troubled world, keeping watch over all movements and events in time and reporting that all is known, all is overseen by Him who speaks comfortably to our Jerusalem and tells us that our welfare is accomplished, that our iniquity is pardoned, that our cities shall yet overflow with prosperity. Our enemies, we are told, "have exceeded their commission" and themselves deserve punishment. Who today cannot lean upon the truth contained in these inspired words and find rest for his soul?

2. *The second vision* (*1:18-21*). *God's Workmen.*

"And I lifted up mine eyes, and saw." The prophet sees more than can be observed by looking around. He did see the horns on all sides, the military powers so strong and apparently invincible that resistance would seem to be futile. But he sees something more. God's craftsmen are seen at work filing away at the horns. And the time would surely come when the horns would be sawn through and broken, and the power of the enemy would come to nought. This vision, then, speaks of those slow, invisible processes by which evil is gradually destroyed by the irresistible forces of righteousness. God's craftsmen are steadily at work. The evil that seems so firm and immovable is slowly but surely being destroyed. What inspiration lies in that idea! If, when it seems to be moral midnight, we can recapture for ourselves the truth of this vision of our prophet, what hope it will bring us and with what sure patience we can await the downfall of the evil that oppresses us.

3. *The Third Vision* (*chap. 2*). *The Unwalled City.*

Again the prophet lifts up his eyes. This time he sees a man with a measuring rod, surveying Jerusalem, defining its limits, determining the length of its walls. But the young and inexperienced and narrow-minded youth was told that his labor was all in vain. For the City of God has no fixed boundaries, and walls that men have built are not to be her protection. For God Himself is "a wall of fire round about, and will be the glory in the midst of her."

What a prophecy is that! A prophecy of the day when boundaries shall no longer be drawn and defined, when a nation shall not be built about with forts and bastions or need to be protected or defended. Boundary lines shall disappear, and the nations shall join themselves together "to the Lord in that day" and the Lord Himself shall dwell in their midst. Thus the prophet opposes with his idealism the natural instinct of man to defend himself by walls. Jerusalem is not to be a walled town in the future. The fortress idea of the city was not to be perpetuated. A civilization of the unwalled town, that is the prophet's ideal for the future of his people. It is today the ideal for the future of our modern world.

Boundaries, walls, ramparts, security bases, these are the curse of mankind. The walled town represents civilization as it still exists today, a civilization that has been rocked to its center by dreadful wars. Built ostensibly for defence, the wall is always a menace to its neighbors and invites attack. Universal peace and universal brotherhood can never be achieved so long as boundaries are drawn and towns are walled. In the midnight of international jealousies and fears, we are presented in this glowing prophecy of Zechariah's with the vision of a Jerusalem unprotected by force but secure in the presence of her God.

Following the vision there is an appeal to the exiles at Babylon to flee the city before its impending destruction (vv. 6, 7), and a lyrical poem of great beauty which may be an earlier piece appended by Zechariah to describe the glory of the Jerusalem that is to be (vv. 10–13).

4. The fourth vision (chap. 3). Clean Garments.

Joshua the high priest in this vision is the representative of Israel. He stands before God, and Satan (as in Job) appears as his adversary and points at the filthy garments Joshua wore. But the Lord rebukes Satan for accusing the people whom He has saved, as by fire, from destruction at Babylon and sends him away. And the Lord told His angels to take off the filthy garments from Joshua and to clothe him with clean raiment and to put a crown on his head, and the Lord said: "I have caused thine iniquity to pass from thee, and I will give thee a place with my angels." (v. 7.) Then the Messiah will come, the iniquity of the land will be removed. The stone (v. 9) is the symbol of the completed Temple upon which His will will be engraved, and by its sacrifices purity will enter the hearts of His people, and universal peace will descend upon the world. The nature of Israel's iniquity is not defined. It may be partly ethical and partly, as in Haggai, neglect of the Temple and of the worship of Jehovah. But the intent of the whole vision is clear. There can be no prosperity, no ultimate salvation short of the moral and spiritual reformation of the people themselves. Judgment must begin at the house of God. So, in our day, this vision reminds us, there can be no salvation from the evils that oppress us except we ourselves be morally and spiritually re-formed. We look down upon this world, quivering with suffering, soiled with sin, forgetful of God, in its irreligiousness, with its cruelty and inhumanity. We see Satan, our adversary, pointing to these filthy garments and accusing us before God. Then there comes to us this promise of the renewing power of God who will take away the soiled raiment and clothe us with the robe of righteousness and put us once more on the side of the angels. The Church will resume its rightful place of spiritual authority once more having engraven upon it the Will of God. And the reign of the Prince of Peace will be established in the world. Could any teaching more nearly suit our deepest need in the day in which we live?

5. *The Fifth Vision (chap. 4). The Temple Candlestick and the Two Olive Trees.*[4]

An angel wakes the prophet out of his sleep. He is touched by a divine power that brings him out of unconsciousness of spiritual realities to a sharp realization of them. And he sees the Temple in a blaze of light. He beholds a great lamp with seven branches fed from a central bowl higher than itself, which is constantly fed and replenished with oil by two live olive trees. And in the midst of the Temple he sees the two figures of Joshua the high priest and Zerubbabel the civic head of the State, standing together to fulfill the Will of the Lord of the whole earth, who says to them both: "Not by might, not by power, but

[4] The verses in this chapter should be read in the following order: 1-5, 6ᵃ, 10ᵇ-14, omitting 12, 6ᵇ-10ᵃ.

by my Spirit." Church and State are united in the service of God: the Church, a spiritual Church, which relies not upon outward means or material resources but wholly upon the power of spiritual truth; a State, which has lost its reliance on the power of arms and physical force and trusts wholly to spiritual ideas and the power of moral ideals. Before such a union of spiritual forces the mountains of difficulty will be removed, the foundations of peace and blessedness will be laid firm. Even if in its beginnings it appears to be feeble, who shall despise it since the eyes of God behold it with favor? What a vision! What a word for our times: a purified Church and a sanctified State fulfilling together the Word and Will of God.

The sixth verse in this chapter, concise in its eloquence, profound in its meaning, is one of the great, inspired and most quoted words of the Old Testament. Coming as it does in the "Indian summer" of prophecy, it ranks with the greatest uttered by any poet or prophet of the Old Dispensation. It is the message of God to the head of the State in Zechariah's day and in our day. Reliance must be placed not upon military might, diplomacy, political planning, human ingenuity or maneuvering, but ultimately upon the Spirit of God working in and through the mind and will of man. We find here that absence of expectation in human agency and that full trust in God's own direct action which characterise all the prophesying of Zechariah. Zechariah supplies the corrective to the exclusive reliance upon external means and human contrivance which is the tendency in a purely secular statecraft.

6. *The sixth vision* (*5:1–4*). *The Flying Book.*

"And again I lifted up mine eyes." Every time the prophet lifted up his eyes, he saw something more of the power and glory of God. This time he beholds a huge Roll, the dimensions of which are given, flying through the air. On it is written the record of the crimes of the people, especially of thieves and perjurers who preyed upon the poor. It is flying from the land, thus freeing it from social forms of iniquity, just as the previous visions had purged it of individual sins. But the curses for these crimes do not leave the land until the house of every thief and perjurer in it has been destroyed. Here, then, in a single vision, are compressed the two truths: that society must have the curse of its social sins removed if it is to be the community of God, and that judgment will be visited upon those who sin against their neighbors. It may read like a mystic dream, but without this vision of the conscience of God, removing the curse from His children and destroying the work of evil-doers, there is no basis for a true social optimism.

7. *The seventh vision (5:5–11). The Woman and the Vessel.*

Once more the angel bids the prophet to lift up his eyes and this time he sees a huge vessel, round like a barrel. When the circular leaden lid is removed, the prophet sees a woman sitting within the vessel. She is Wickedness personified. The lid is replaced and two flying angels with wings as strong as those of a stork carry the Vessel with Wickedness inside it into the land of Babylon, the abode of evil. And there it is set down.

It is not enough, that is, that evildoers shall be destroyed. The land must be purged of evil itself. The living principle of sin, the power of temptation must be covered up and removed. We have the counterpart of this idea in the Book of Revelation where, after the downfall of the Beast and his followers has been portrayed, we witness the old serpent himself, the *fons et origo* of all evil, cast into the lake of brimstone and fire. So today for a true Social Hope we must believe that not only the crimes that infest our social order shall be removed, we must beyond that believe in the final extirpation of the lure of sin, the very principle of evil. This is the promise contained in this precious vision. "The last enemy that shall be destroyed" is sin, the wages of which is death.

8. *The eighth vision (6:1–8). The Celestial Chariots.*

This vision describes the final impact of the power of God against the enemies which north, south, west, and everywhere else in the world threaten the people of God. Here are celestial troops mobilized and carried swiftly in chariots for the rescue of Israel and the defeat of her worst enemies. Once more the prophet declares that by direct action God will bare His arm in the sight of all nations and bring their devices

to nought. It is not necessary to identify four kingdoms as the destination of the chariots, nor the mountains between which they pass. The
profound truth is here intoned, which we of today need to lay to heart,
that the military forces of the nations of the world are not the powers
that control the destinies of mankind. These are in the keeping of God,
whose invisible troops patrol the earth.

As a kind of Epilogue to the visions, we have described in 6:9–15 a
kind of coronation scene. In imagination, the prophet sees the pagan
powers overthrown. Now Israel may have her king again. A deputation
having arrived from Babylon bearing gifts, Zechariah is ordered to
select enough silver and gold to make a circlet for a crown (not
"crowns") and to place it on the head of Zerubbabel (not "Joshua"
as in v. 11). Then the Messiah shall appear whose outgoings are to the
ends of the earth, Church and State shall work together in perfect
harmony, and all nations shall see it, and Israel, if only she will obey
the Lord, shall know the glory of the Messianic era.

Such are the visions of Zechariah. Can we in darkness behold what
he beheld? Can we lift up our eyes and see beyond and above what are
called current events? Will an angel awaken us out of our sleep? Christianity is the religion for midnight. It was then that it was born, and in
the darkness before dawn in Joseph's tomb it won its final victory. If
in the darkness of our night we can see what Zechariah saw, then,
though terror succeed terror, and woe follow woe, the conviction that
God is, that God reigns, and that events are not left to work themselves
out as chance or accident or lawless force may decree, will bring the
assurance of an eternal Hope into every human heart.

Two chapters in which the prophet resumes the simple prose of
1:2–6 conclude the prophecies of Zechariah. In chapter 7 we are told
that a deputation had arrived to inquire if the people ought to continue
the fasts that had been prescribed in Babylon because of the destruction of the holy city and temple. But now the Temple was being
restored, its rebuilding had been going on for two years, and its services
were being resumed. Zechariah, who now speaks not as priest but as
prophet, with breadth of view, in fresh, young and practical fashion,
tells them that these fasts are no longer needed. Of what good, he says,

are mere fasting and mourning? When the people fasted and mourned during the years of the Exile, was it a real turning unto the Lord? The real thing for you to do is to turn to God in penitence, in thanksgiving and in confidence. Let us forget the fasts, but let us remember God. Let us learn to deal justly every man with his neighbor, to show mercy, to practice brotherliness. This is the true road out of bad times. There is no use in mourning over evil days or in fasting because of misfortunes that lie behind us. The real thing to do is to lay hold of neglected duties, to practice simple virtues, to replace evil-dealing with fairness and honorableness. Lay hold on present tasks, practice the elementary virtues, put into operation the principles that underlie domestic prosperity. This is the way out of misfortune, thus will you retrieve disaster. In all this we hear re-echoed the words of the older prophets.

How plain and straightforward such preaching is, and how much it is needed today. We hear people sighing and lamenting over the state of the world, wringing their hands over conditions in which they find themselves enmeshed. Zechariah says to us today: If you want a different world, be yourselves different men. Practice the simple virtues of justice and brotherliness. Find a common point of understanding with those who differ from you. Be tolerant toward the alien and the foreigner. In the practice of the principles of morality lies the solution of the social problem.

The prophecies of Zechariah close with a tender and idyllic description of the future peace and joy of God's people. Chapter 8 is one of the most beautiful chapters in the Bible. It is an immortal picture of a restored society. It is a bright promise of a new earth in which dwelleth righteousness. "Fine families, unlike the present community with its few children and its men . . . worn out by harassing warfare with enemies and sullen nature; streets rife with children playing and old folk sitting in the sun; the return of exiles, happy harvests and springtime of peace; solid gain of labor for every man." [5] And instead of fasts there will be feasts of joy and thanksgiving and men will turn to the Lord and worship Him and people from all over the world, seeing the prosperity of the people of God, will say: "We will go with you, for we have heard that God is with you."

[5] George Adam Smith, *op. cit.*, "Zechariah."

Such is Zechariah's dream for Jerusalem, for a nation which, in both its civic and its political life, will put justice first and so sow the seeds of peace in its domestic life and in its relations with other nations. This dream was not fulfilled for his people in his day. It has not been fulfilled for our people in our day. But it remains our glowing hope, a hope that will be fulfilled only when we have learned by long and bitter experience to love and to practice truth and love.

Chapters 9–14. The reader of the Book of Zechariah is made aware, when he passes from the eighth to the ninth chapter, of a change of scene and of climate. Instead of the clear historical background of the earlier chapters, he now finds himself in a reeling world of heathen nations of which Zechariah makes no mention and has no knowledge. There is not the faintest allusion to the building of the Temple. It is a new situation in history. The peoples that fill these pages appear only at a later period. The era of peace which Zechariah describes so beautifully has disappeared and the clouds of war fill the skies. The destruction of the heathen is prophesied in such ferocious and bloodthirsty terms that we are unable to associate these with the irenic spirit of the prophet. Apocalypse of a later Jewish type is firmly embedded in these chapters which describe the destruction of Jerusalem and the ensuing Messianic age in language which does not belong to the earlier tradition of prophecy.

For these reasons, and for others, it is impossible to assume that Zechariah is the author of chapters 9–14 of this book. Hence, they have presented a problem to the scholars. How they have attempted to solve it need not detain us. The general conclusion at which they have now arrived, although with variations, is that they were composed by an author or by authors unknown to us, and were put together sometime during the third century, perhaps between 300 and 250 B.C. It is possible that some earlier prophecies were incorporated in this material.

In general these chapters fall into two sections. The first of these includes 9–11, with the addition of 13:7–9, which is misplaced and should be read after 11:17, where it belongs. In chapter 9 we are told of the coming of the Greeks and their subsequent slaughter. In verses

14-15 of chapter 9 we note the apocalyptical means by which the heathen will be destroyed. In chapter 10 sorcerers are condemned and the images (idols) used by them in their magical rites. The anger of the Lord is kindled against the evil leaders (shepherds) of the people, possibly the foreign tyrants. The Lord will change his poor leaderless people into war horses and they will overthrow the heathen. In chapter 11 we have an allegory after the manner of Jeremiah or Ezekiel, in which the prophet personifies the good shepherd who is rejected and murdered by the people. "So they weighed for my hire thirty pieces of silver. . . . And I took the thirty pieces of silver, and cast them to the potter"—a reference that was not overlooked by the New Testament evangelists.

The second section in these chapters (12-14) gives us a series of eschatological pictures of judgment, destruction and final salvation. Here the supernatural and fantastic elements increase steadily. The heathen world is to be destroyed. Only Jerusalem shall be saved and strengthened. A fountain of cleansing shall be opened for her. Idols and unclean spirits and even prophecy shall be done away. For prophecy has now become so degraded that it is inconceivable that another true prophet can arise in the land. And finally the "Day of the Lord" cometh, Jerusalem itself shall be destroyed and half its population shall go into captivity. But after calamity will come salvation. The people will be sanctified, and even the heathen nations which came up against Jerusalem shall go up from year to year to worship the king, the Lord of hosts.

Such, in briefest résumé, is the content of these chapters. The questions remain: How shall we assess them as a whole? What place do they occupy in the Old Testament revelation of God? To some it appears as if this fragment marks "the lowest degradation of the prophetic literature of Israel. The fantasy of the writer positively wades in the blood of the Gentiles . . . The remaining heathen will indeed turn to God, but how shall this conversion show itself? By eating kosher and by going up to Jerusalem to keep the feast of the tabernacles. It is impossible to turn the mind of an Amos, or a Hosea, of an Isaiah or a Jeremiah, into a worse caricature." [6]

6 Cornill, *op cit.*, pp. 167-168.

The careful reader of these chapters will be unable to agree with this wholesale condemnation of this bit of prophetic literature. Doubtless it stands on a far lower plane than that occupied by the Great Prophets, or the Minor Prophets, of Israel. Yet preserved with them, as a precious kernel within the outer husk, are passages of great beauty which are dear to the Christian heart today. In 9:9, 10 we have pictured the coming of the Prince of Peace in words which rightly seemed to the evangelists to describe Christ's triumphal entrance into Jerusalem on the eve of His Passion. And no one will overlook the beauty of vv. 16 and 17 of chapter 9 and verses 8b–12 of chapter 10, which portray in beautiful language the redemption of God's people and may be read with gratitude by all who long for deliverance from the evils that still oppress us. In 12:10 there is a passage of rare beauty, descriptive of the suffering Messiah: "And they shall look upon me whom they have pierced, and they shall mourn for him, as one mourneth for his only son." The opening verse of chapter 13 gives us the image of the fountain of healing where sin and uncleanness shall be washed away. And verse 6 again reminds one of the Passion of our Lord: "What are these wounds in thine hands? Then he shall answer, Those with which I was wounded in the house of my friends." And in chapter 14, which gives us such a lurid picture of judgment, are to be found in verse 7 words which have been of such comfort to suffering souls and are so often repeated in prayer: "At evening time it shall be light."

Ah, no! The Bible *is* the Bible. Its inspiration may not be constant. Yet even in what appear the least inspired portions of it there are these wonderful words of life which illumine even its darkest chapters with the Light that cometh from above.

~~~ *Malachi* ~~~

I. Introduction

THE BOOK of Malachi is undated, but it is not difficult to determine when it was written. The building of the Second Temple (516 B.C.) had been completed. The ritual had evidently been resumed for some time. Also, time enough had elapsed to show that the glowing hopes and promises of prosperity that would be Israel's when the Temple had been erected and Zerubbabel had become high priest had not been fulfilled. When Malachi was written, Judea was under the benevolent rule of the Persians, whose governor (1:8) controlled its affairs. Thus we arrive at a period about half a century later than Zechariah. On the other hand, Malachi appears to know nothing of the reforms instituted by Ezra, who arrived on the scene in 458 B.C. He knows nothing of the new Priestly Code, which was put into operation by Ezra and later by Nehemiah. The "Law" to which Malachi constantly refers is plainly the Deuteronomic Code, which had regulated the religious life of the people since the days of Jeremiah. Thus the Book of Malachi can be dated with a good degree of certainty at about 460 B.C. Scholars are now agreed that originally the book appeared without name of author. It began, just as the prophecies contained in Zechariah 9–11 and 12–14 began, with the words: "The burden of the word of the Lord." A later editor desiring to find a name for the author, who may have concealed his identity because he attacks the priests and the ruling classes, borrowed the word "Malachi" which means "my messenger" from 3:1 and made a proper name of it, adding the words "by Malachi" in the opening verse of the book. The oldest texts do not render "Malachi" as a proper name but as a common noun. We do not know who wrote this book. We know only that he spoke as a messenger from the Lord.

The Book of Malachi has great historical importance, because it gives us the only information we possess about the life of this Jewish community in Jerusalem after the times of Haggai and Zechariah, and preceding the coming of Ezra and Nehemiah. And it is a drab picture that meets the eye. Evidently this was a period of disillusion, of disappointment, of decay. The Temple did not bring the Messianic era. The people were disappointed in all their hopes. Their expectation of a new and glorious era for the nation had not been realized. Zechariah's glowing vision of Zerubbabel as the royal and priestly head of a new kingdom had proved to be illusory. Zerubbabel became a minor satrap of the Persians and then disappeared from the scene altogether. Nor was this all. Internal conditions went from bad to worse. The people had to struggle hard to maintain themselves. Their resources were meagre. A plague of locusts (3:11) and a blight of vineyards had caused great economic distress. "Only a very small part of Jerusalem had been rebuilt. [It was] a wretched, unfortified country-town, not even the shadow of what it had been." [1] The little settlement had not been increased by subsequent migrations from Babylon, and it was constantly harassed by the hostility of its neighbors.

And Jerusalem itself had lost all its importance. It no longer stood in the center of the world's scene. Indeed, the world seemed to have forgotten it. History was in the making, but the Jews had no part in these great events. "We are on the threshold of the period in which the star of empire passed from Asia to Europe." [2] The Roman Republic was founded in 509 B.C. In 490 B.C. the battle of Marathon determined that Europe should not be ruled by Asia. The golden age of Greek culture was at hand. But in all of this drama Jerusalem played no part. How different was all this from the glowing prophecies of Ezekiel, of Isaiah of the Exile, of Haggai and of Zechariah.

No wonder, then, if the hearts of the people were filled with bitterness. For not only had they been forgotten by the world, they seemed also to have been abandoned by God. He had not kept His word with His people. They had rebuilt the Temple, restored the ritual, resumed the sacrifices. But they had reaped none of the promised rewards. Hence a spirit not only of bitterness but of indifference and even of animosity toward God had begun to develop, and this mood had gained possession not only of a majority of the people but even of the priests and of the leaders of the community. Here was a "strange mood, new

[1] Cornill, *The Prophets of Israel,* p. 156.
[2] C. J. Harrell, *The Prophets of Israel,* p. 203.

in Israel." It caused the people to despise the very things they had been accustomed to revere. Through careless indifference and frivolous mockery they sought to disregard the misery of their time. The priests were slovenly in the sacrifices they offered. The people neglected their Temple dues. Immorality became rampant. Life in Jerusalem became sordid and corrupt. Hope had ebbed completely away. Conditions presented the aspect of mud flats at low tide. All this is faithfully described for us in the Book of Malachi. It is indeed the "picture of a dying church." [3]

To such conditions, then, the author of the Book of Malachi addresses himself. The style of the book is unique in the literature of the prophets. Malachi does not attempt the rhetorical development of great principles. Rather, he is applying these principles to the details of life. He is the teacher rather than the preacher. His style is didactic, argumentative, forensic. He states his thesis, and then sets the objection over against it. Then he proceeds to elaborate and prove his truth. He is the schoolman among the prophets. Indeed, in Malachi we can see the beginnings of scholasticism, the method of exposition that afterward became universal in the schools and synagogues of Jerusalem. Yet Malachi was a true prophet. He has a firm grasp on the spiritual principles that underlie a righteous life. He reiterates the old prophetic message of repentance, reform, of judgment between righteous and wicked, of the great and terrible "Day of the Lord" to come. He was prophet enough to see that the root from which all the rest springs is that the religious life of the people was weak, that their spiritual vision was dim, and that this weakened religious life affected their social and moral conditions. The people must return to God (3:7).

The unity of the Book of Malachi has been questioned at two points. It is difficult to believe that 2:11-16 can have come as it now stands from the pen of the writer. Not only do these verses interrupt the connection between verse 9 and verse 17, but they present us with an idea of divorce beyond anything we find elsewhere in the Old Testament.[4] If these verses were not a later insertion, at least they are out

[3] R. H. Pfeiffer, *Introduction to the Old Testament*, p. 615.
[4] It is possible that the passage may be interpreted allegorically of the relation of the people to their God.

of place. Again, the last three verses of chapter 4 are regarded by some scholars as a later insertion by the editor. Yet they are in general agreement with the rest of the book and there seems to be no solid reason for questioning their authenticity as an integral part of the message of Malachi.

The general argument of the book consists of a denunciation of the evils as practiced by priests and laymen, a vindication of the moral character of God, and a message of hope to the faithful, the pious remnant who still cling despairingly to their faith in God.

(1) The book begins (1:2-5) with the assertion that, in spite of all appearance to the contrary, God still loves His people. Proof of this is found in the contrasted attitude of God toward Edom and Israel. The former, the incarnation of worldliness and irreligion, has never merited and has never received the favor of God. But Israel, which has borne in its heart, however faithless this may have been, a true knowledge of God and of its duty toward Him, has always been the object of His enduring and suffering Love. Paul in Romans 9:13 quotes Malachi in referring to this striking spiritual antithesis which ran through the whole history of Israel.

(2) From this, the prophet turns directly to the ways in which the Holiness of God has been affronted by the priests (1:6-14; 2:1-9). They have not scrupled to offer mean and unworthy sacrifices and thus have dishonored God whom as their Father they should have held in reverence. God has been offered gifts so poor that the priests would never have dared to offer them to their Persian governor (1:8). We note here a striking reversal of the attitude of Malachi toward the sacrifices from that of Amos and Isaiah. They would have swept away even the best of sacrifices because these were regarded as a substitute for righteousness. But Malachi condemns his generation for being cheap and stingy in the sacrifices they offer, and thus assumes a different attitude toward the place and meaning of ritual in religion. This tendency, begun in Ezekiel, is continued in Malachi, and comes to its logical climax in the Priestly Code adopted by Ezra and Nehemiah. Malachi is impelled to defend a pure ritual from its profanation. Thus he performed a work that was as needful for his generation as the work of Amos and Isaiah for theirs. But thus also he gave impetus to the later

exaggeration of the purely ceremonial and ecclesiastical ideas, which
later assumed such a sinister supremacy in the religion of the Jews.

(3) From the sins of the priests, the prophet turns to those of the
laity, whom he accuses of various forms of immorality (2:10–16;
3:5–13). They have not hesitated to contract marriages with their
well-to-do, half-heathen neighbors and to divorce their lawful Jewish
wives in order to consummate these unholy alliances; they have practiced fraud and deceit in their relations with each other, have sworn
falsely, deprived the laborer of his just wages, been merciless toward
widows and orphans, and denied the stranger the rights to which he
was entitled. Also, they have failed to pay their Temple tithes and have
robbed God by their niggardly offerings. For all this a curse rests upon
them, which can be removed only by whole-souled repentance, by good
works, by turning again to God who is still ready to bless them.

(4) There remains, however, a remnant of the people who still
fear the Lord. But they are baffled, bewildered, discouraged (2:17;
3:13–14). There is no justice in God's dealings with His people. The
wicked seem to prosper. The Lord seems to take pleasure in them.
"It is vain to serve God." "What profit has come to us from having
been faithful to Him?" We find ourselves in misery and see flaunting
itself before our eyes the good fortune of the proud and arrogant. To
this complaint with which they weary God, comes the answer: "The
Lord will come for judgment, terrible and certain (3:1–5; 4:1–3).
First, He will cleanse the priesthood, then He will purge the people
from their immoralities. But He will be mindful of His own. He will
remember them "that thought upon his name. And they shall be mine
. . . and I will spare them, as a man spareth his own son that serveth
him" (3:16, 17).

Here we have the introduction of the apocalyptic hope. And this
apocalypse, this description of the last judgment is one of the most
beautiful to be found in all Scripture. Its language has been dear ever
since to the Christian heart. It flashes with passion, but also it throbs
with tenderness.

(5) The book closes with an exhortation to remember the Law of
God. Here is an echo of the book of Deuteronomy (7:12; 8:2) which
set before the people the inevitable choice between good and evil, the

blessing and the curse. Their one hope lies in this remembrance of God and of His Law. And before the final judgment, this hope will once more be held before them, not by some new prophet, but by a return of the first prophet, the most powerful personality in all the early history of Israel, who will make a final effort to convert the nation before the Day of Judgment comes.

It is noteworthy that in Malachi we find illustration of every form of prophecy to be found in prophetic literature, and this cannot be said of any other prophet. We have ethics, the call to repentance, the summons to good works and to righteous living. Also, however, we have emphasis upon the meaning and importance of ritual, of ecclesiastical regularity, of sacrament and ceremonial propriety. Again we find, as in Habakkuk, the recognition of the speculative element in Hebrew thought, the questioning skeptical attitude toward God and His dealings with His people. And, finally, there is the apocalyptical idea and the Messianic hope. Thus we find in Malachi, as it were, a résumé of all that the prophets have taught them. In one respect only he differs from all who have preceded him. In Malachi we find no denunciation of the heathen. Rather, we find to our surprise a broad and generous recognition that true religion may be found in them because of their true living; that their sacrifices are acceptable to God; that God's grace is so infinite that it cannot be restricted to the Jews, cannot be exhausted in His chosen people (1:11). In this attitude is revealed all that was deepest and most spiritual in the essential meaning of a faith rooted in the concepts of a righteousness which is as broad as humanity, and in a God of the whole earth whose pity and power extend to all mankind. This truth, before the Old Testament ends, was reinforced by the Book of Jonah, and to it Jesus appealed in His word to the half-heathen woman of Samaria (John 4:21–24) when He lifted religion above the level of place and race and declared that it was rooted in spirit and in truth.

II. The Prophecy

Malachi is no less a book of religion than a book of history. It throws light on the material and social conditions of the Jewish colony before the advent of Ezra and Nehemiah, but it also illumines spiritual truths which are as valid for men today as for those to whom the words of the Messenger were first addressed. This unknown prophet was no creator. He announced no new ideas. Rather, he was a preserver of the past, of the spiritual message of the older prophets, as well as of the later ideas which had their germinating origin in the Exile, and were developed in the postexilic prophecy that preceded him. This is the importance of Malachi in the history of Old Testament religion. In him we find religion still "within the Law." But in him also the Law begins to assume that prominence which later caused it to dominate the spirit of true religion, and separated Jehovah from His people. Malachi preserves the balance between the two. But not for long. The less spiritual and more formal ideas were the easier to hold and these were favored by circumstance. They triumphed in the end. Malachi stands at the beginning of that long and swift decline into the hard and fast legalism of later Judaism which met the uncompromising opposition of Jesus.

The fundamental spiritual message of Malachi is announced at once. "I have loved you," saith the Lord. The persistent sins of the people were to the prophet only a renewed challenge to an unchanging God. It is, that is, of the very essence of the Love of God never to despair, never to lose its redeeming grip on a ruined world. God will have the last word in this eternal struggle between the sinning heart of man and His own pitying and passionate Love. That is a living and energizing Love that will never yield until it creates the love which it seeks. Long before Malachi that eternal truth had been uttered by Hosea and echoed in Jeremiah. In spite of all their record of faithlessness to God since those days, in the face of all their sordid and corrupted life as Malachi saw it, yet again that Fact of the untiring and invincible Love of God is repeated. It needs to be reiterated whenever the soul of man finds itself baffled, bewildered and discouraged by the facts of life as it sees them and knows them in man and in the human society. There is at work a Force mightier than all the forces of evil. "I have loved you," saith the Lord. And, for the Christian, of that Love the Cross is the eternal symbol.

That Love, according to Malachi and according to all Scripture, is both punitive and tender and compassionate. It will come in judgment upon the evil and sweep it and burn it away. The idea of a "Day of Judgment" runs through the Bible from beginning to end. It is part of its fundamental message from Genesis to Revelation. It is incorporated in the religion of Jesus. It forms a part of the Christian language of devotion. "He shall come again to judge the quick and the dead." "We believe that thou shalt come to be our Judge." Faith cannot do without this idea of a final overthrow of evil by an omnipotent Love. It tells us that moral distinctions are never lost; that the victory of Righteousness carries with it the final defeat of all those alien forces which war against God and His holiness. And this victory is not to be won by man alone but by the militant strength of God who shall bare his arm in the sight of all nations. Once more it must be said that this apocalyptical idea is essential to a true faith.

But this Love is revealed also in tenderness and compassion. The Book of Malachi is remarkable for the number of its familiar quotations that have found their way into the permanent language of devotion. The great word of the essential religiousness of the heathen (1:11): "From the rising of the sun even unto the going down of the same my name shall be great among the Gentiles," is read at the Epiphany season as an expression of the inclusive love of God for all mankind. The word: ". . . prove me now herewith . . . if I will not open you the windows of Heaven and pour you out a blessing that there shall not be room enough to receive it" (3:10), has been a beautiful reminder to the human soul of the overflowing grace and refreshing abundance of the spirit of God. The idea of "a book of remembrance" has appealed strongly to the religious imagination, as well as that of the "day when I make up my jewels" (3:16, 17). And no picture of the coming Messiah has brought more of comfort than that of the "Sun of righteousness" who shall "arise with healing in his wings" (4:2). Malachi may have been a plain prose teacher of righteousness, but surely he was gifted with spiritual imagination.

In Malachi we find reiterated the truth of the importance of the institutions of religion, of sacrament, sacrifice and ritual. High value is set on the priesthood, and on the ceremonial forms of religion. At a period when the people ran the grave risk of losing their hold on the ritual and all that it contained for them, Malachi lent his whole influence to maintain its power. Ideals, he asserted, need to be expressed in institutions as well as in words. Great religious truths must create forms which touch the whole life of the community. Men must honor God in His house as well as in their own homes. This is a part of Bible religion both in the Old Testament and in the New. It is also a truth often overlooked or minimized in our own day, one which needs constant repetition and application. It is true that devotion to ritual may be accompanied by a corresponding laxity in morals; that ritual may be a substitute for righteousness. To hold true to the idea that worship in all its forms is not an end in itself, yet always has its importance as an inward impulse urging the soul to the attainment of righteousness, this is the double duty of every truly religious man. Malachi holds to both of these ideas. They meet and mingle in his teaching. And if the balance seems to turn on the side of ritual, that indicates that he was a child of his day in which the outward forms of religion assumed an increasing emphasis because of the conditions of his time. The idea of repentance as we find it in Malachi seems to be limited to the summons to restore ritual to its rightful place and to give it due honor, to pay proper tithes, to offer pure sacrifices. Here is latent the idea of justification by works that assumed such prominence in later Judaism. What redeems Malachi, however, from the accusation of formalism, is his appreciation of the service and sacrifices of those who live beyond the limits of Palestine and outside the cultus of the Jewish religion. On any interpretation of this lofty saying (1:11) it can mean only that a certain priesthood, a fixed ritual, sacrifices and tithes according to the Law, are not essential to true religion. Yet Malachi recognized the presence of a sacrificial system as a central element in religion, and its power as a factor in the religious life of his people.

The message of Malachi to the priests of his time may well be laid to heart by the ministry today. That indictment was on two counts. In the first place, they were slovenly in the sacrifices they offered on God's altar. In the next place, their lips did not keep knowledge and the Law was not in their mouth. The same shortcomings may sometimes be found in the ministry of today. The service of worship often suffers from carelessness and slovenliness upon the part of the minister. He does not exalt this office or offer the sacrifice with the reverence and beauty that belong to it. He does not prepare himself for it with all the consecrated powers of his mind and heart. He is not careful in speech, deportment and outward and inward attitude to be a true instrument for the transmission to the human soul of the divine mysteries of the divine grace. Often the innate reverence and sensitiveness of the worshiper is offended by infelicities, or even vulgarities, of word or manner. People often stay away from church, not because they do not want to worship but because they do. It is their inmost spirit of reverence that rebels against much that they find when they get there, and for which the minister is responsible. The conduct of worship is the highest, the most delicate, and the most difficult of all of the tasks of a true priest of God. To offer anything less than the purest of sacrifices is an offense in our day no less than in the day of Malachi. The Lord has no pleasure in them.

Again, the modern minister often fails because "the law of truth is not in his mouth." Now, the love of truth is a passion with all thoughtful men. Instinctively they listen to discover if the mind of the preacher is a disciplined mind; if it has been informed by the ruling intellectual ideas of the day; if there is evidence of care in statement and quotation; if a true and thorough culture permeates his speech; in a word, if real mentality lies behind all that he says. People do not want sermons that resemble philosophical essays, but neither do they want shallow sentimentality or vague religiosity. They can soon tell whether a preacher's mind is familiar with the best that has been said or thought in the world, and if a trained mind is at work within the warmth and spirituality of the message he utters. "Religion needs all the brains we poor mortals can put into it . . . It is because of the neglect of the intellectual duties of the priest that so much irreligion prevails [and this accounts for the] growing indifference with which the ministry is regarded by thoughtful people." [5]

The accusation that Malachi brings against the laity of his day also has its direct application to conditions existing in the churches in our modern world. It is true that church people are not often guilty of the carnal and fleshly sins condemned by Malachi. Yet divorce is still dis-

[6] Gorge Adam Smith, *op. cit.,* "Malachi."

tressingly common within the Christian community and often for no higher reasons than that which caused men in those days to put away their lawful Jewish wives in order to contract advantageous alliances with their pagan neighbors. Religion in America is discredited by this form of social sin. The Church does well to guard against this evil and to support with all its power and influence the integrity and sanctity of marriage and of family life. Other sins, however, of covetousness, of acquiring wealth by methods that offend the most elementary principles of brotherhood; the sin of inhumanity, of callous indifference to conditions that breed poverty, sickness, misery: these are still a matter of fact in the lives of many church laymen and merit the condemnation of a true social conscience.

And besides all this, the fact must be faced that much of the skepticism with which non-Christians regard organized Christianity is due to the character and performance of the laity in our churches, who sometimes seem to make pretense to all kinds of Christian experience and graces while lacking the fundamental virtues which are admitted and practiced by the non-Christian man. Precisely this brings the whole cause of religion into disrepute with normal healthy men. They see men and women claiming to be Christians, talking about faith and grace, sanctification and regeneration, who yet somehow do not seem to incorporate in their moral make-up certain elementary virtues of simple honesty, courage, generosity and loyalty which every decent man is supposed to possess. So true is this that nothing would do more to rehabilitate Christianity in the general mind of the community and to command its respect than to have the rank and file of church people exhibit the cardinal virtues that underlie all true living, and make these the starting point for a further advance into the higher reaches of the religious experience.

Often it seems to a modern prophet as if there were more real religion outside the Church than within it, that the sacrifices of so-called pagans, incense and a pure offering, were more acceptable in the sight of God than those of His professed followers. Fundamental virtues, a sharpened social conscience, passion for great ideals, appear to be a higher and nobler form of religion than the religiosity of church people with their preoccupation with petty parochial affairs.

Again, the loose way in which many church members wear their plain obligations to the church they have vowed to support is a scandal which enormously weakens its influence. Desultory church attendance, neglect of public worship, failure to identify oneself with the church's work and mission in the world, niggardly gifts, lack of all personal interest and loyalty: these are all ways in which the laity of today rob God of the honor to which He is entitled. It is said that nowadays the work and support of a church is borne by one-third of its congregation; another third looks on; and the remaining third does not know what it is all about. We need in our day, as truly as Malachi urged the need in his day, a revival of interest upon the laity as a whole in the corporate life of the Church. Until the day of that revival comes, Zion will continue to languish.

So pertinent to the days in which we live is the word of the Messenger to priest and layman.

The inspiration of Malachi rests here: he speaks to a dying church; he utters his message when conditions are unspeakably bad. Yet he does not fail to see possibilities of revival and of hope. The Spirit of God can work upon a community as dead in its trespasses and sins as that which he so graphically describes. The "Sun of righteousness" shall yet rise "with healing in his wings." Over and over again in the history of Christianity that divine resurrection has been witnessed. The Church may seem to be dying but it is never dead. For within it lies that animating principle, that inextinguishable spark of life, that voice of some prophet who shall turn the heart of the fathers to the children, and the heart of the children to their fathers, and the heart of fathers and children alike to God. "And all nations shall call you blessed: for ye shall be a delightsome land, saith the Lord of hosts."

~~~~ *Obadiah* ~~~~

I. Introduction

THE BOOK of Obadiah is the shortest book in the Old Testament and one of the shortest in the Bible. It contains but twenty-one verses. We know nothing about the man who wrote it. Obadiah is a common Hebrew name, meaning "The Servant (i.e., worshiper; cf. 'Service' of worship.) of Jehovah." Many others of the same name are mentioned in the Old Testament, no one of whom can have been the author of this book.

Short as it is, it raises many questions with respect to its unity, date and historical allusions. The scholars have wrestled with these problems and have reached very divergent conclusions. It would be tedious to explore all this discussion. A brief summary will be enough to show us what the different opinions have been, and what, on the whole, in the light of the most recent scholarship, the probabilities are with respect to the unity and date of the book.

The traditional view has been that the book is a unity and was written by Obadiah at some period before the Exile. It stands in the Bible just after Amos, possibly because of the reference to Edom in Amos 1:9; 9:12. But this of course gives no clue to its actual date since, as we all know, these books were not arranged in correct chronological order when the Old Testament Canon was formed. The decisive objection to dating Obadiah as a whole before the Exile is the plain reference in verses 11–14 to the destruction of Jerusalem by Nebuchadrezzar, which took place in 586 B.C. Hence these verses, at least, must belong to a period after the Exile. Also, there is grave question whether the whole book can have been written by the same author. In verses 1–7 other nations are God's instruments for the destruction of Edom, whereas in verses 15a, 16–20 all nations alike, including Edom, are under God's condemnation. And even the casual reader will not fail to note the difference between the straight, terse, firm style of verses 1–14, 15b and the less vigorous and apocalyptical language of the later portion of the book. Thus the idea that Obadiah wrote the entire book before the Exile in 586 B.C. is no longer held.

The Book of Obadiah falls into three clearly defined sections. The first of these consists of verses 1-9. An interesting problem is presented here by the close correspondence between portions of these verses and the passage in Jeremiah 49:7-22 (cf. Obad. 1-4 with Jer. 49:14-16; Obad. 5-6, 8, with Jer. 49:9-10a, 7). Did Jeremiah borrow from Obadiah or Obadiah from Jeremiah? Here the predominant opinion is that neither borrowed from the other but that both borrowed from a lost original prophecy against Edom, each using it in his own way. In any event, the parallelism between Jeremiah and Obadiah is not a factor in determining the date of Obadiah, since the material in Jeremiah 49 quite probably belongs in whole or in part to a much later date, and was not written by Jeremiah himself.

Obadiah begins his book, then, by quoting from an early oracle against Edom. He writes, as we have seen, after the Exile. But the question remains, how soon after? This brings us to the second section of the book, 10-14, 15b. This consists of an invective against Edom for its treachery against Judah. This anathema is so hot that it seems as though it must have been written soon after that event in 586 B.C. Thus some scholars hold that Obadiah wrote from Babylon in the early days of the Exile. The difficulty here, however, is that in the preceding verses, 6-9, plain reference is made to an invasion of Edom by its confederates the Arabians who have prevailed against it. But this invasion, as we learn from Malachi 1:4, 5, had not been completed when that book was written in 460 B.C. Thus this appears to be the probable date of Obadiah verses 10-14, 15b. And unless we assume that these verses existed by themselves unrelated to verses 1-9, this must be the date of the whole section. If this be true, we see how deeply indignation against Edom for its betrayal of Judah in the hour of her great need had entered into the heart of her people, that Obadiah, prophesying over a century afterward, should have excoriated Edom in these passionate words.

It is generally agreed that the third section of the book, verses 15a, 16-21, does not belong to the authentic prophecy of Obadiah but was written at a later time. It must antedate Joel (c. 350 B.C.) who quotes from Obadiah verse 17 (cf. Joel 2:32). Thus verses 16-18 may have been written about 400 B.C. And verses 19-21 may be still later because of the reference to the Samaritans on Mount Ephraim.

Thus this book, little as it is, contains material belonging to three different eras in Israel's history, and presents difficult problems, the solution of which is by no means certain.

The Book of Obadiah stands a stern, sad monolith among the books of the Twelve Prophets. It is one of seven books in the Old Testament not quoted in the New, the others being Nahum, Ezra, Nehemiah, Esther, the Song of Solomon, and Ecclesiastes. It is a brief and terrible summation of the indignation of the people of Israel who, when the book was written, had to endure the spectacle of a still undefeated and mocking enemy.

The first mention of Edom in the Old Testament is found in Genesis (25:30) and the last in Malachi (1:2-5), and between the two there is a continuous record of the tragic relations between Israel and her hereditary foe. The word Edom means "red," ascribed in the Genesis narrative, where the name is given to Esau, to the color of the pottage, but probably deriving from the red sandstone cliffs of the land of Edom. It has, too, a sinister moral significance for surely a red trail of hatred and cruelty runs through the history of these two peoples. The land of the Edomites lies southward from the Dead Sea to the head of the Gulf of Akabah. It was a mountainous country, dominated by Mount Seir, rich in material resources. Somehow the people seem early to have acquired a reputation for shrewdness and sagacity (v. 8). It is true that the relations between Edom and Israel were not always strained. At one time Edom, Judah and Israel were all united in an alliance to oppose the Moabites (II Kings 3:9). And in Deuteronomy (2:4-8) the people of Israel were told not to contend with the Edomites who are their brethren; and again (Deut. 23:7) they are admonished not to "abhor an Edomite; for he is thy brother." This, however, may be regarded as a counsel of perfection which hardly reflected the popular consciousness. For from the day of the quarrel between Jacob and Esau down to the end of Old Testament history the record is one of almost unbroken hostility. Saul fought against Edom (I Sam.

14:47); David conquered Edom and put garrisons into it (II Sam. 8:14); Joash slew Edom (II Kings 14:7). Yet in spite of these occasional conquests Edom maintained itself and was viewed by Israel with jealousy and suspicion (Amos 1:11; 9:12). Few antipathies in history have been more prolonged or more bitter. The event, however, that fanned into a flame of white heat the hatred of Judah for Edom was the treachery of Edom at the hour of Judah's greatest need. When Nebuchadrezzar threatened Jerusalem with destruction, Judah appealed to Edom for help and some refugees sought for safety in Edom (Obad. 14). But not only did Edom turn a deaf ear to these appeals, but she actually utilized this moment of Judah's helplessness to seize a portion of Jewish territory (Ez. 36:5). That act of treachery aroused the deepest anger and resentment in the heart of the Jewish nation. That was a sin which Judah never forgave. How passionate was the hatred thus aroused can be realized from the reading of such passages as Psalm 137:7, Lamentations 4:21; Ezekiel 25:12-14, 35:1-15; Isaiah 34:5-6; 63:1-6; Joel 3:19; Malachi 1:3-5. Of this hatred, defiance and malediction the Book of Obadiah is the climax. As for the later history of Edom, its final downfall was not complete until after the days of the Maccabees. Judas Maccabeus drove them from the South of Judah in 164 B.C. and John Hyrcanus in 109 B.C. conquered their country and compelled them to adopt Judaism.

II. THE PROPHECY

The reader of the Book of Obadiah inevitably wonders why this short hot prophecy is in the Bible at all. The whole of it is fiery denunciation and nothing more. Not a word of grace can be found in these twenty-one verses. If Obadiah was inspired at all, it appears that he was inspired with wrath alone. The book consists of a shriek of rage, a shout of defiance, a cry of victory. Now what has this quintessence of hatred to do in the Bible? What place has it in a revelation of love? How strangely its intense nationalistic spirit contrasts with that of the Isaiah of the Exile, who looked upon the sufferings of Israel to be for the healing of the nations.

Yet the book, just as it is, found its place in the Bible. And the only reason for this must be that its essential message has its place in the spiritual experience of God's people. For it was not only by chance, neither was it by arbitrary decision of ecclesiastical authority, but by proved spiritual worth and meaning that the books of Old and New Testaments alike found their place in the Sacred Canon. Thus, if we do not understand a book, the trouble does not lie in the book, it lies in ourselves. Get behind this book, understand the conditions that produced it, and we will find in it the inspiration that we need when baffled and discouraged on our moral battle fields.

It is a defiance of Edom. And Edom, as we have seen, was the most inveterate of all the foes of Israel. The hostility between the two peoples had stretched over the long period of a thousand years, and it was the more intense because they were blood relatives. A man's worst foes are those of his own household. Why this should be so presents a curious psychological problem. Perhaps the secret of it is to be found in the fact that what men hold most sacred, if it becomes a matter of dispute, is that for which they will most desperately fight. A modern writer has pointed to the strange and at first sight almost inexplicable fact that Mr. Gladstone was far more tolerant toward freethinkers like Mr. Morley, who became his best friend and biographer, than for Dissenters who were much closer to him in matters of religious opinion. It was precisely at the point where he divided most sharply from his coreligionists that he found it most difficult to compromise. Be this as it may, blood feuds, family quarrels, civil wars, religious strife: these are the cruelest and the most bitter of which we have any knowledge.

And this was a family feud. The origin of this age-long tragedy lay in the unhappy relations of two brothers, Jacob and Esau. When Jacob defrauded his brother of his birthright, he set in motion an antagonism which was destined to endure right down to the threshold of the Christian era. The two brothers may have become reconciled. Not so their sons. When Jacob and Esau separated upon the plain beyond Penuel (Gen. 33), we read that Esau returned that day on his way to Seir, the mountain fastness that became the abode of the generations of Esau, "who is Edom" (Gen. 36:1). And from that day, the descendants of Jacob and of Esau became deadly enemies. The two peoples from then on "scorned, hated and scourged" each other.

That tragic story has many a counterpart in our modern world. Families have been divided for generations by a misunderstanding, a quarrel, an act of injustice, which may have been petty in itself but has had woeful consequences. The story of Jacob and Esau points a solemn warning to all who are tempted by irritation, by anger, by a sense of injustice, to open a rift in family relationships which may never be healed.

All through Hebrew history, then, lay the Edomites near-by, secure in their mountain refuge. And never did a bandit people have a more strategic location. Mount Seir was a purple range that is said to present the finest rock scenery in the world. Eagles and hawks screamed about these mountain fastnesses. The villages represented nothing so much as wildfowls' nests. The houses were human eyries perched upon high shelves of rock. There dwelt the Edomites. And they kept a watchful, implacable eye upon their foe, the Israelites, in the plains beneath. Outnumbered, they never engaged in open warfare. But they made forays when the Israelites were off their guard or were fighting more formidable enemies. And it had been impossible to dislodge them. They were incapable of inflicting great damage at any one time. But the Israelites knew that at any hour they might make one of their hateful assaults, carry off a flock of sheep, or ruin a harvest of wheat. "How it kept the people on the strain all the while! The moment that a Jew stepped across the border, the Edomites were on him. The moment a flock or a beast of his had wandered too far, the enemy had seized him. There was no rest, no safety. The constant dread, the nightmare of Jewish history, is this Edom lying there upon the border, like a lion crouched to spring." [1] Thus, of all the enemies of Israel, the Edomites, descendants of Esau, were alike the most persistent and the most pestilential.

Just what caused this denunciation of Edom to spring from the ho heart of Obadiah we cannot know. Possibly it was the attack on Edom

---

[1] "The Conqueror of Edom" by Phillips Brooks in Vol. I of his sermons. The reade is referred to it for an eloquent interpretation of the essential message of the Boo of Obadiah.

y the Arabians that caused him to exult. Once more, at any rate, the
ge-long hatred of Israel for Edom finds expression in this outburst, in
hich Edom's vilest treachery toward Israel is remembered and anathe-
atized. Shaking his fist, as it were, at the Edomites, the prophet cries:
Thou that dwellest in the clefts of the rock . . . that saith in his
eart, Who shall bring me down to the ground? . . . Thence I will
ring thee down, saith the Lord."

It would be doing an injustice, however, alike to the soul of Obadiah
d to the soul of Israel as a whole, to assume that a nationalistic
ndictiveness alone accounts for the hatred of Edom. It is true that
cial antagonism had a large part in the Hebrew attitude toward other
ations. Only in the loftiest passages in the later prophecies of the Old
estament do we approximate the teaching of Jesus that, since God
the Father of all, all men are brethren. Even in the thought of
eremiah, the most spiritual of the prophets, vindictiveness toward the
emies of Israel, without hint of love or forgiveness, finds its place.

Yet it remains true, as we have seen in our study of the Book of
ahum, that the antagonism between Israel and paganism went deeper
an race or nationality. It was essentially the antagonism between region, of which the Hebrew people were the custodians, and the irre-
gion of their neighbors; the antagonism of conscience against sin.
nly so can we find a moral meaning not only in this short, hot prophecy
f the Book of Obadiah, but in the many imprecatory passages to be
und elsewhere in the Old Testament. It is all summed up in the
ord of the Psalmist: "Ye that love the Lord, hate evil." The Hebrews
ere the symbol of the fear of the Lord. The nations symbolized the
ct of evil. And between the two there could be no compromise. It was
arfare to the end. It meant the fundamental opposition between good
d evil, light and darkness, life and death.

All this comes to a head in the relations between Hebrew and
domite. From the beginning there was this contrast between Jacob
d Esau. The one, with all his faults, kept in touch with God. The
her, with all his lazy good nature, and "no consciousness of his birth-
ght, no faith in the future, no capacity for vision: dead to the unseen
d clamoring only for the satisfaction of his appetites." [2] And this
George Adam Smith, *The Twelve Minor Prophets*, "Obadiah."

essential materialism became the outstanding characteristic of th
Edomites. They were a worldly, conscienceless and bitter people, livin;
for food, spoil, plunder and vengeance, with no national conscience
no religious ideal, whereas the Israelites, with all their weakness an(
dereliction from duty, had never lost their vision of God, of spiritua
ideals, of national destiny. Thus the antagonism which the Israelite fel
for Edom in Obadiah's day was not exclusively racial or national, bu
also the fundamental antagonism between faith and worldliness, con
science and sin.

It is so that we must interpret the seemingly savage and bitter word
of this prophet in order to comprehend their eternal moral meaning
Here we see the never-ending conflict between truth and falsehood
right and wrong, God and Satan. The shriek of rage is the outburst o
every soul in which conscience is not dead, that once more sin has ha(
dominion over him; its shout of defiance is the undismayed challeng(
which that soul hurls back in the face of its taunting sin; its cry o
triumph is that which shall roll over the battlefield when help shal
come from Mount Zion and the Saviour "from Edom, with dye(
garments from Bozrah . . . travelling in the greatness of hi
strength," shall bring at last the victory.

Thus interpreted, the Book of Obadiah has lasting inspiration fo
tired and often defeated souls of men in face of the inveterate foes tha
war against their peace and purity. Israel facing Edom, that is the pic
ture of every one of us, confronted by his well-remembered and stil
unsubdued and mocking temptations and sins. With us, too, it is a1
old antagonism. It has its long history. We too can go back througl
the years and almost put our finger on how it all got started. And, Go(
knows, we have campaigned and fought against these Edomites of ours
Sometimes we have won a victory; sometimes we have suffered a defeat
One thing we know: they have never been dislodged. When we have
been off our guard, they have made a swift descent upon us. When w(
have been weak and weary, they have taken a treacherous and mear
advantage of us. Other foes may have been overcome. But never thes(
Edomites of ours. There they remain where we cannot reach them, bu
whence they can reach us. Israel still facing Edom after many centuries

You and I, after all the years, still facing our besetting and unconquered sins.

Right here lies the moral value of the Book of Obadiah. Hardly a book in the Bible which will do for us now as much as this little neglected book. We can face these evils in the spirit of this undaunted soul and cry: "Thou that dwellest in the clefts of the rock, whose habitation is high, that saith in his heart, Who shall bring me down to the ground? . . . Though thou set thy nest among the stars, thence will I bring thee down, saith the Lord."

For the social worker also, for the one who confronts the evils that still degrade and disgrace the life of humanity, and wars against them, this book supplies undying faith and courage. How deeply entrenched these evils are. How impregnable and inexpugnable they seem to be. Generations have sought to dislodge them. Yet they remain mocking every effort to subdue them. Sometimes a temporary victory is won. Follows lassitude, an ebb of idealism, a loss of vision and courage. And back they come again and the battle has to be joined all over again. Is any permanent victory possible? Will the Edomites ever be dislodged? Or is history to be in our modern world but a repetition of the ceaseless, never-ending, inconclusive struggle between the Israel and the Edom of old? Into such a mood comes the ringing defiance, the hot challenge, the confident faith of Obadiah. Edom shall be laid low: "Shall I not in that day even destroy the wise men out of Edom, and understanding out of the mount of Esau?" The Book of Obadiah points the worker for social righteousness to a far-off, it may be, but to a sure victory. Three thousand years ago there was a temple in Babylon which men thought would last forever. Today it is level with the sand. Sooner or later, God takes hold of every entrenched evil in this world and breaks it down. History has justified the faith of Obadiah. The people of Edom were at last dragged down from their mountain fastness, humiliated and broken. The modern visitor to Mount Seir finds nothing but a few ruined temples in which the jackals of the desert make their home. And if it be said that the material hopes of the Jews were involved in the same ruin, yet it remains true that the glory of Israel has not departed from the world. But what has Edom left of herself?

Besides this confident prediction of the Doom of Edom, so essenti
to the warring soul, the Book of Obadiah tells us what are these mor
qualities necessary to moral victory. First, there is undying hatred (
Edom. We must keep within us this hot anger against personal an
social sin. No matter how often Israel had been worsted, she nev
came to terms with Edom, never compromised, never laid down arm
There is nothing but detestation and loathing for the foe. And s
it must be with us. Only when hatred of sin is hot and unending is ther
the hope and promise of salvation. "Our greatest glory," wrote Steven
son, "is not in never failing, but in rising every time we fail. We ma
fail a thousand times, but so long as we are ashamed of our failures, s
long as we do not hopelessly acquiesce in them, so long as we do n
make parade of our other virtues to cover up our well-known fault
we are in the pilgrim road."

Again, in this little book we find the spirit of defiance unbroke
For long centuries the Israelites had been campaigning against th
Edomites. Yet when this book was written, the brave heart of its auth
had not weakened. The soul of Israel spoke through him and hurle
hot words of defiance in the face of her malicious and treacherous fo
Here is no sign of discouragement, no trace of hopelessness. The spir
of struggle is still there. This world would be better off than it
today if the militant soul of this unknown prophet were the spiritua
property of God's people. "Unconditional surrender." These wer
the only terms Obadiah offered to Edom, and the only ones a Christia
will offer his enemy. No compromise, no negotiated peace, no parley.
only warfare to the end. Against the spirit of defeatism the book o
Obadiah is a sure antidote.

Finally, we note the source of the confident faith of Obadiah in th
ultimate destruction of the Edomites. It is the Lord God who sha
bring them down. The habitation of the Edomites might be high, bu
the Lord was higher still. They might set their nests among the star
But there was one "who made the seven stars. The Lord is his name.
They might exalt themselves like the eagle. But the Lord shall laugl
and have them in derision. The Edomites might defy the power of th
Israelites to dislodge them, but they had still to reckon with th
militant spirit of the Almighty.

This faith in God as the conqueror of Edom was set forth by the great Prophet of the Exile long before the time of Obadiah, but that faith had never grown dim. "Who is this that cometh from Edom, with dyed garments from Bozrah . . . travelling in the greatness of his strength?" And the answer came. "I that speak in righteousness, mighty to save. . . . I looked, and there was none to help . . . therefore mine own arm brought salvation." Yet only by blood. Evil incarnate, of which the Edomites were the symbol, was to be overcome and put away only by the sacrificial Love of God for His people. The vision of the Messiah, who should thus achieve victory over Israel's most inveterate foes, finds its fulfillment for the Christian in the Saviour of men who by his own sacrifice of himself has put away the sin of the world. Because God in His mercy saw that man of himself could not dislodge the Edomites, He sent His Son to tread His enemies under his feet.

Never do men so deeply realize their need of Christ's salvation as when they face the Edomites. We may raise ourselves above the great disappointments of life. We may weather by wisdom the gales of misfortune and disaster. But what staggers our faith and defies our courage is the Edomite. There he sits watching us with malicious and malignant eye. Try as we will, we cannot be rid of him. Sin continues to crouch at the door ready to spring out at us at any moment. The mood of moral despair threatens to overtake us in face of the Edomites. In such a mood there comes to our rescue the inspired prophecy of Obadiah, who, lifting up his eyes to the heights where the Edomites still mock him, cries out: "Thou that dwellest in the clefts of the rock, whose habitation is high, that saith in his heart, Who shall bring me down to the ground? Though thou exalt thyself as the eagle, and though thou set thy nest among the stars, thence will I bring thee down, saith the Lord."

～～ Joel ～～

I. Introduction

WE HAVE no information about Joel, except that he was the son of Pethuel, whoever he may have been. The name "Joel" probably means "The Lord is God." It was not an uncommon name (cf. I Sam. 8:2; Ezra 10:43; I Chron. 4:35, etc.). We are not told where Joel lived although Jerusalem, or its near neighborhood, was probably the scene of his labors. The book is undated. And the scholars have had much difficulty in seeking to determine when it was written. The suggested dates run all the way from 800 to 350 B.C. It is interesting to observe how the experts have sought to solve this problem. The significant fact is that neither Assyria nor Babylon is anywhere mentioned in the book. Assyria assumed the dimensions of a world power about 760 B.C., and the Babylonian Empire had fallen by 537 B.C. Thus the book of Joel must have been written before 760 B.C., or after 537 B.C. Otherwise it is inconceivable that the one empire or the other should not have been mentioned by the prophet. Of these alternatives, scholarship at first preferred the earlier date for the following reasons: Joel's book comes early in the order of the prophets; his vague pictures of the "Day of the Lord" and his fear of the interruptions of the daily sacrifices reflect the simplicity of the earlier religion of Israel; his vindictive attitude toward the heathen nations is akin to that of Deborah and David; the ravages of the locusts would appall a purely agricultural community like that of Israel in the eighth century; the absence of any mention of a king and the prominence of the priests fits in with conditions that prevailed when Jehoash (or Joash) was still too young to be king (837-798 B.C.) and Jehoiada the priest was regent (II Kings 12); the many parallels between Amos and Joel show that Amos quoted Joel.

These arguments, however, do little more than to indicate the possibility of an early date for Joel. And later scholarship has gravitated almost unanimously to a later date, not only after the Exile, but after the work of Ezra and of Nehemiah (458–444 B.C.). The Exile appears to be in the past (3:2). No great power is threatening Israel; her enemies are malignant near-by neighbors; the Greeks (3:6) are not mentioned by any Hebrew writer before the Exile; we know that Syrian slaves (3:6, 8) were sold in Greece in the fifth and fourth centuries. The absence of any mention of a king, the prominence of priests, the religious temper, emphasis on daily sacrifices and the ritual of the Temple: all this points to the late date, as does the apocalyptical coloring of the book. The fact that Joel is placed early in the order of the prophetical books has no weight. And the literary parallels between Amos and Joel (cf. Joel 3:16 and Amos 1:2; Joel 3:18; Amos 9:14) can mean equally well that Joel quoted from Amos as vice versa. All this and more seems to warrant Cornill's assertion that "few results of Old Testament research are as surely determined and as firmly established as that the book of Joel dates from the century between Ezra and Alexander the Great," [1] i.e., about 350 B.C. It is one of the very latest books in the Old Testament.

Few scholars seriously question the unity of the Book of Joel. The fact that the first chapter is distinctly historical while other portions are apocalyptical does not invalidate Joel's authorship of the whole book. It is true that chapter 3 introduces ideas and interests far different from those in the preceding chapters, with which it has little connection.[2] Yet this may be explained by assuming that this prophecy was written at a later time and under different circumstances. The entire book we may consider to be the work of Joel, the son of Pethuel.

Joel occupies an important place in the history of the religion of Israel. He marks the definite transition from the spiritual religion of the earlier prophets into the legalism of later Judaism. This development had already made great headway. The narrowing Judaizing tendency under Ezra and Nehemiah, whose concern lay solely in the rebuilding of city and Temple, had inevitably resulted in a conception of religion as a punctilious observance of its rites and ceremonies. For the first time in prophecy, we find in Joel no censure for civic or

[1] *The Prophets of Israel*, p. 164.
[2] This has led some critics to maintain that Joel's work is confined to chapters 1 and 2 and that in these some interpolations are to be found.

national sins, "that distinctive note . . . which in all the older prophets without exception from Amos to Malachi was the chief concern of the prophets." [3] This tendency toward legalism continued uninterruptedly into New Testament times.

The occasion of Joel's prophecy was a terrible invasion of locusts, to a description of which the first chapter and the first part of the second chapter of his book are devoted. This disaster was so terrible and complete, joined as it was with a severe drought, that it seemed to the prophet to be an omen of the immediate emergence of the "Day of the Lord." The reading of this half of the Book of Joel inevitably projects the question, Were these real locusts, or is it all allegory and are hostile armies symbolized by these insects? One wonders if the prophet would have connected a scourge of locusts, however severe, with "so ultimate a crisis as the 'Day of the Lord.' " A careful study of Joel's language, however, points unmistakably to the conclusion that real locusts are meant. His language is too realistic and too accurate to known facts to admit of any other solution. It is true that in the second chapter the imagination of the prophet is given full play and the locusts are described in highly poetical and rhetorical fashion and are clothed with supernatural powers. This has led some to differentiate between the locusts of chapter 1 and those of 2:1-11, and to call the latter apocalyptical "monsters . . . similar to the mythical locusts in Rev. 9:3-11 which are described more elaborately." [4] It is true that the poetical imagination of the prophet here rises to a point beyond the limits of experience into the sphere of apocalyptical dreams. Yet, with this admitted, the description of the locusts in chapter 2 is truer to fact than might at first appear, and that these are to be identified with the locusts of chapter 1 appears from 2:25. Thus Joel's locusts are neither allegorical nor wholly apocalyptical, but real locusts. In both passages he is describing an actual calamity wrought by them on the land of Israel.

In order to understand how Joel could feel that such a disaster in the sphere of nature could be a precursor of the "Day of the Lord,"

[3] Cornill, *op. cit.,* p. 164.
[4] So R. H. Pfeiffer, *Introduction to the Old Testament,* p. 574.

we need to remind ourselves what such a calamity was like. We have never had experience of it. If we had, we would understand Joel better. The destruction wrought is such as to be barely imaginable by those who have not witnessed it. Locusts appear to be created for a scourge with strength incredible for so small a creature. Their sawlike teeth are admirably calculated to destroy herbage of any kind. Their numbers are astounding, the whole face of the sky being blackened by them when they appear. The noise of their approach is remarkable— a rushing sound occasioned by the flight of so many millions of them. They charge with the directness, swiftness and precision of horsemen. Indeed, there is a strange resemblance between the head of a locust and that of the horse. They prepare for attack like an army, arranged in order for the fray. Nothing can stop them and all opposition of man to resist their progress is in vain. Neither weapons, fires or ditches filled with water are of any avail. Nothing escapes them. The whole vegetable produce disappears. Not a leaf, shrub or blade of grass is left. They crawl over everything, climb walls, enter into the inmost recesses of homes, consume everything with wonderful expedition. When they eat, the sound is like the crackling of a prairie fire. The devastation left in their wake is complete.

Mr. James Bryce has described an invasion of locusts which he witnessed in South Africa: "It is a strange sight, beautiful if you can forget the destruction it brings with it. The whole air to twelve or even eighteen feet above the ground is filled with the insects . . . When you see them against a cloud, they are like the dense flakes of a driving snowstorm. You feel as if you had never before realized immensity in numbers . . . They come on in fresh clouds appalling in their power of collective devastation . . . The roads were covered with them, all marching in regular lines, like armies of soldiers with their leaders in front . . . Though our men broke their ranks for a moment, they closed [in] again and continued their march . . . They are the incarnation of hunger. No voracity is like theirs whose million separate appetites nothing is too minute to escape. For eighty or ninety miles they [will] devour every green herb, leaf and blade of grass so that the bare ground appears as if burned; and the fields finished they invade towns, swarm into barns and homes alike in search of stores, and leave them stripped of hay, straw, wool, linen, leather. They flood through windows and lattices. Nothing can keep them out." [5]

If to the horror of such a calamity is added the terrible effects of a drought plainly indicated in 1:19, 20, there is reason in Joel's ominous prediction that these calamities portend a day of judgment from the Lord. The fact that the locusts came from the north (2:20) accentuates this idea, for the northland was to Israel always typical of doom (cf. Jer. 1:14; Ezek. 38:15, 39:2).

Theologically, many of the ideas of Joel are to be found in the older prophets. Calamities are the fruit of sin. Punishment can be escaped only by repentance. If this be sincere, it will obtain divine favor and restitution. And judgment will be visited upon the heathen nations. On the other hand, Joel differentiates himself sharply from earlier prophecy in that the sins of Israel are not described, deplored and condemned. And he lays an emphasis upon the importance of ritual and the continuity of the daily sacrifices, which is not only foreign to ethical prophecy but is actually condemned by it as insincere and an evasion through formalism of moral duty and living (cf. Is. 1:11–15; Amos 5:21; Hos. 6:6). Also, the limitation of God's grace to Israel and the wholesale condemnation of the heathen nations is in contrast to the broad universalism of Amos (9:7), of Malachi (1:11), and of Second Isaiah (49:6).

It is surprising how much of the imagery and thought of Joel appear in other Bible books. His description of the "Day of the Lord" (2:10) has colored the picture of the day of judgment to be found in the Gospels (Matt. 24:29; Mark 13:24; Luke 21:25) and in Revelation (6:12). His idea of the Harvest (3:13) is reproduced in Matt. 13:39 and Revelation 14:19. The fountain (3:18) is found in Revelation 22:1. And Joel's summons to fasting and to repentance

---

[5] Quoted by George Adam Smith, *The Book of the Twelve Prophets,* "Joel." The reader will find much additional material about locusts and their invasions in the excursus to Driver's commentaries on Amos and Joel in the Cambridge Bible series. In our own day similar invasions took place in Mexico and other parts of Central America and as late as 1929 in Argentina. In 1878 locusts wrought such havoc in the United States that a commission was appointed to report on the best means of combating it.

(2:12-14) and his promise of the outpouring of the Spirit (2:28-29) are classical passages taken up by the New Testament and used by the Church ever since.

The Book of Joel is easily and clearly divided into three sections. The first includes chapter 1 and chapter 2:1-17. Here we have the description of the plague. The style is clear, strong, vivid. The description is true to life, and as the prophet advances, his imagination is tinged with supernatural ideas that lend a lurid color to the terrible picture. "For the day of the Lord is at hand" (1:15), "a day of darkness and of gloominess, a day of clouds and of thick darkness" (2:2). "The earth shall quake before them; the heavens shall tremble: the sun and the moon shall be dark, and the stars shall withdraw their shining" (2:10), "for the day of the Lord is great and very terrible; and who can abide it?" (2:11). In the face of this imminent judgment, the people are called upon to repent (2:12-17), to turn unto the Lord with fasting and weeping, with true penitence. They are to rend their hearts and not their garments. A solemn assembly of the people must be held, in which the priests for the people shall invoke the help and deliverance of God.

Between the seventeenth and eighteenth verses of this second chapter, we must imagine that a considerable period of time has elapsed. The people have repented. Their prayers have been heard, deliverance has come. Thus opens the second section of the book. Then the Lord became solicitous for His land and had pity on His people: "Behold, I will send you corn, and wine, and oil, and ye shall be satisfied therewith" (2:19): Then follows a beautiful picture of national prosperity and plenty. "And ye shall know that I am in the midst of Israel, and that I am the Lord your God . . . and my people shall never be ashamed" (2:27). But physical benefits are not all that the people shall receive. There will follow upon material prosperity a dispensation of the Spirit, an outpouring of the Spirit of God which shall cause even the youth of the land to have visions of God, and to become His heralds and the messengers of His grace.

The third section of the book is found in chapter 3. The heathen nations of the world are to be herded together in the valley of Jehoshaphat, and the Lord will sit to judge all the nations from every side.

Multitudes will be gathered in this valley, where final settlement with them will be made. "Egypt shall be a desolation, and Edom shall be a desolate wilderness, for the violence against the children of Judah. . . . But Judah shall dwell for ever, and Jerusalem from generation to generation . . . for the Lord dwelleth in Zion" (3:19–21).

II. The Prophecy

At first sight, the occasion and the message of the prophecy of Joel might seem to be remote from the interests of our modern world. More closely examined, however, we discover that the book deals with problems with which we are wrestling today.

The first of these concerns the relation between calamities in the sphere of nature and the moral life of man. Joel, doubtless, shared in that idea which is so prominent in the Old Testament, that calamity of any kind, either in the social or in the individual life of man, is proof of sin. Thus this overwhelming catastrophe, for which directly the people were in no wise responsible, is viewed as a divine judgment, as coming from God, and thus calling for immediate and thorough repentance. No actual sins are mentioned, no concrete virtues are enjoined: the "Day of the Lord" is so imminent that there is no time for anything except to make the people feel that the hand of the Lord has been laid upon them, that this visitation was an act of God calling for repentance and a return to Him whom they had forgotten. Today we do not consider that adversity, especially in the field of natural phenomena, earthquakes, hurricanes, droughts and floods, are a sign of wrongdoing on the part of people so afflicted. Yet whenever there is such a manifestation of the malignant forces of nature, the effect inevitably is to draw men nearer to God in the consciousness of their own helplessness, in supplication for deliverance in their need. We live on from day to day in comparative safety. We forget that our dependence for that safety lies in the hand of Him who "hath his way in the whirlwind and in the storm, and the clouds are the dust of his feet." And when these tempestuous powers break loose and wreak their fury on helpless humanity, then man, made aware that he has been at their mercy all along and that only a beneficent Providence has

protected him from them, turns to God in recognition that only He has
saved him hitherto, only He can save him now. Rarely has there been
a great catastrophe like that described in Joel that there has not been
also, as in Joel, a day of humiliation, of supplication and of prayer.

Beyond this, it should be said that there is a plain connection which
needs to be remembered between some disasters in the sphere of nature,
and national sin. A direct cause of floods has been the destruction of
forests by cupidity and unrestrained selfishness. Famines are the result
of the neglect or exhaustion of the soil. Waste and extravagance have
produced crises in the distribution of fuel. Nature takes revenge upon
us for abuses due to sin. Not all calamities can be dissociated from moral
delinquency. Our whole national policy of the conservation of natural
resources is an act of repentance for sins of the past. Public attention
is now being called to the vast property that is constantly vanishing for
lack of care and foresight, and facts are being gathered about waste
and its prevention. Experts in forestry are telling us the worth of wasted
timber. Experts in engineering remind us that we waste more coal than
we mine. Experts in agriculture have been explaining how the soil can
be enriched by care and irrigation. Experts in medicine have shown how
many plagues can be banished by modern methods of combating them.
And social experts have pointed to the possibility of redeeming whole
areas of human life by abolishing unsanitary tenements, unwholesome
conditions of labor, and providing possible protection in dangerous occupations.

Looking back on the whole story and bearing in mind that the wholesale loss of life among the underprivileged people both at home and
abroad has been due in part to human greed and in part to failure to
provide the means of preventing famines and floods, who shall say
that this piercing summons of Joel to repentance in the face of disaster
does not have its immediate application to conditions in our modern
world?

Akin to this is the relation between economic justice and the cause of
religion. After the people had repented, according to Joel, there followed an era of prosperity. The rain came down in its season. The barns
were full of wheat. All the harm done by the locusts was repaired by the
healing powers of nature. There was plenty of food for everyone to

eat. The people praised the Lord and were satisfied. Verse 25 of chapter 2 describing this idyllic era of prosperity is one of the unforgettable verses of the Bible: "I will restore to you the years that the locust hath eaten." It speaks of the marvelous recuperative powers of nature. The land may be scorched and withered by drought or fire or by the ruthless hand of man. To the eye, every living thing may be destroyed. Yet in time nature will heal its wounds and cover a scene of desolation with the garment of its loveliness. Even more deeply the verse tells us of the healing power of God in a human soul. It, too, may be seared and blackened by sin until there may appear to be no sign of life in it. But the grace of God can touch hidden roots of holiness, unseen and unsuspected capacities of goodness and can restore once more into the likeness of God the years that the locusts of sin have eaten. In these immortal words of the prophet is enshrined the eternal promise of the possible redemption and regeneration of every human soul. And as of men's lives, so of the lives of nations and peoples of the earth. At bottom there is goodness there, innate goodness capable of high and noble living, more goodness by far than cruelty and hatred. And after the years that the locusts have eaten, after the calamities and woes that selfishness and sin have wrought, after the locusts have done their worst with the soul of a nation, there is the promise of the regenerative power of God who, upon repentance and turning to Him, will restore it to its true and rightful destiny. There lies the ground of our social hope.

And "afterward" (v. 28), when the people thus lived without poverty, destitution and misery, there came an outpouring of spiritual blessings. Religion came to life. There was a revival in men, young and old, of their spiritual natures. The Spirit of God had its free access and way in the hearts of "all flesh." Thus the connection is made plain between the outward conditions in which men live and their response to the religious appeal. We cannot expect religion to thrive among the masses of the people so long as they are oppressed by unjust social conditions. The first step toward the revival of a true religion is the creation of a just social order. What is often called the eclipse of faith is largely due to a harsh, unjust and unnatural foreshortening of life. The children of Israel, we read, "hearkened not unto Moses for anguish of spirit, and for cruel bondage" (Ex. 6:9). And because of an identical slavery today, many men do not hearken to any Moses who speaks of God and religion. So long as men and women have to struggle so hard to keep body and soul together that they have neither the leisure nor the desire to concern themselves with the higher things of the Spirit; so long as they migrate from one place to another in search of employment, are without any sense of social security, feel resentment against an economic system that condemns them and their families to poverty in a land of plenty, so long will they turn a deaf ear to the appeals of organized religion, which all too often appears to them to be in league with the forces that oppress them. We shall never have an Age of Faith until we have an age of social justice. Not until men are liberated from economic servitude will they also be liberated from skepticism and doubt concerning the spiritual realities of life. Preachers may preach and evangelists may exhort, but there will be, because there can be, no general response to the voice of God. It is idle to expect men to be hungry for God so long as they are hungry for bread. This again is the message of Joel to us of today.

The outpouring of the Spirit was to be upon Israel only. By "all flesh" (2:28) is meant all of God's people, for the heathen are to be destroyed. We have here an evident limitation of God's spirit to exclusive application to Israel. Without doubt, this idea appears at first to be narrow and provincial. The prophet Joel has been called just that. Yet it is not difficult to detect a divine purpose within this seeming limitation of His grace. His people must be thoroughly evangelized before the world could be evangelized. His spirit must have free entrance into all classes and flow freely through the whole body of His people, before they in turn would be prepared to be His evangelists to the ends of the earth. "In the earlier stages of all religions it is impossible to be both extensive and intensive." [6] This truth receives striking illustration in the word of Jesus: "I am not sent but unto the lost sheep of the house of Israel" (Matt. 15:24). Why should Jesus, according to his own words, have confined his work to the Jews? From the beginning, religion for him was a thing of the Spirit that knew no frontiers and his gospel was for all mankind. He was indeed the

[6] George Adam Smith, *op. cit.*

Saviour of all men and knew that he was. But how best could he perform that universal mission? By concentrating his attention on the few, not by seeking to reach the many. He would firmly plant the Truth that he had come to reveal in the hearts of a handful of men whom he had chosen to be his disciples, and then by them and through them that Truth would find its way to the ends of the earth, as indeed it did. Just so in Joel this seeming limitation of the divine grace to Israel is seen in the broad perspective of her mission to be not an exclusive appropriation of God's spirit, but a divine preparation for the diffusion of that spirit throughout the world.

A third message from Joel has its immediate application to our modern needs. As we have seen, we find in his book the progressive crystallization of spiritual truth in the visible forms and institutions of religion. The most serious effect, to Joel's thinking, of the plague of the locusts was the interruption of the daily sacrifices and offerings, a discontinuing of those offices which, to his mind and to the contemporary Jewish mind, represented the continuance of religion itself. This interruption of the ritual was more of a calamity to Joel than it would have been to the older prophets. Jeremiah attaches no importance to it. But after the Exile, in Haggai and in Zechariah, and after them in Ezra and Nehemiah, extraordinary emphasis was laid upon the daily ritual, and this steadily increased as time went on. And the possible disaster of a break in this ritual actually overtook it in the days of Joel. And for him this was another proof that the great and terrible "Day of the Lord" had come. This emphasis on its institutional forms is commonly interpreted as a deterioration of religion in Israel. And indeed, in the extreme lengths to which it was later carried, this is true. But Haggai and Ezra and Joel were doing a work which needed to be done if Old Testament religion was to be preserved in the world unto the coming of Jesus Christ. Once more we are reminded that it needed to be incorporated within a firm, visible and indestructible structure, if it was to endure the ordeals that awaited it. Heathenism threatened it on every side. And even more dangerous than the direct attacks made upon it was the slow, pervasive and apparently irresistible penetration of Greek culture which infected and overcame the whole Eastern world with the exception only of the Jewish people. The divine deposit of spiritual truth was protected and preserved within the firm confines of the Law, the inviolable external defence of the truth enshrined within it.

From this we again learn the lesson, too often forgotten, that spiritual truth, if it is to survive in a still pagan world cannot do without the institutions of religion. If the history of religion has taught us anything, it has surely taught us that always and everywhere it inevitably incorporates itself in outward and visible forms. The action and reaction of these two aspects of religion constitutes its history. First comes religion as spiritual truth. Then that truth is embodied in external form. This in its turn tends to become externalism only, and is broken up by a fresh assertion of a truly spiritual religion. Both are necessary if religion is to survive. What would have become of the idealism of the older prophets without the later emphasis on law and ritual as we find it in Joel? Or of the religion of Jesus without the early Church? Or of the fervor of the Wesleys without its incorporation in Methodism? Religion, if it is to be a permanent and effective form of spiritual influence, needs to be embodied in visible form. It demands some incarnation.

Today we are witnessing a popular revolt against the institutions of religion. The most radical dissenters insist that the Church as an institution is a positive hindrance to Christianity. The question is asked in all seriousness, "Can Christianity tolerate the Church?" There is no mistaking the fact that "the general modern judgment is adverse to institutionalism in religion . . . The sense that religion involves the [acceptance] of the rules and disciplines of an organized society . . . that church-going and formal corporate worship are a normal and necessary part of a [truly religious] life, has weakened and actually ceased in multitudes of thoughtful people." [7] And to this absence of a thoroughgoing persuasion of the worth and value of the Church to the individual may be traced every weakness in the cause of religion as a practical spiritual energy operating in the world of affairs today.

Our generation needs a thoroughgoing re-education in the values of the Church as an institution, a positive persuasion of the necessity of the Church both for society and for the individual. Those who take religion seriously need to be reminded that the advocates of a personal, spiritual religion and the advocates of corporate religion are both right. Isaiah

[7] Evelyn Underhill: *The Life of the Spirit and the Life of Today,* pp. 186-187.

was right, but Joel was right also. Solitary vision and experience of God and the incorporation of this in visible form are both needed in the actual normal life both of the world and of the individual. Thus again, Joel has a message for the days in which we live.

The last chapter of the Book of Joel brings us one more truth which our day needs to lay to heart. It is indeed a lurid picture that is there presented. The heathen nations are to be gathered into a dark and dismal valley. The atrocities they have committed are excoriated. They are told to prepare for battle, for the Lord is to meet them with judgment. The day has come for His final settlement with the enemies of Israel. They are to be destroyed and Judah is to know her final redemption from the foes who have persecuted her.

In all this it should be said that Joel is but repeating the solemn refrain which has echoed all through the prophets from the time of Amos onward. With one voice they pronounce the doom that awaits those nations which have flouted not only the Word and Will of God, but also the very instincts of humanity itself. In varying degree this general anathema is nationalistic in its spirit of vengeance. Yet beneath it all, as we have repeatedly seen, there has lain the ultimate antagonism between religion and irreligion, righteousness and evil, truth and falsehood. Israel, in spite of every sin and infidelity, has yet been the symbol of the one; and the heathen nations have been the incarnation of the other. Thus, reading beneath what seems to be the wholly vindictive and ruthless utterance of this terrible chapter, we discover its nethermost message to be the final judgment of God upon those peoples who have opposed every principle and truth to which His Being witnesses. However powerful they may have been, they shall go down to ruin in the end. A dramatic and grandiose illustration of this truth has been given us in the days in which we live. In these tragic days we behold once great and proud nations being judged by an omnipotent Righteousness, precisely as described by Joel and for the same reason. Between Joel and our day how many multitudes have found themselves in the same valley of decision? And before the mind and conscience of every nation today stands the same solemn truth. Is it in very truth a heathen nation: heathen in its policies; heathen in its intentions; heathen in its motives and ambitions? Then, however proud it may seem to be, however great in possessions and power, one day it shall fall into ruins and go down into dust in the valley of God's final judgment. Never perhaps did the ominous truth of this dark final chapter of Joel need more solemn reiteration than in the day in which we live. In the end, only truth, only righteousness, shall prevail. Whoever opposes these is headed for final destruction. Joel's picture of this judgment comes nearer that of the Day of Final Judgment than any other in Scripture before we come to the seventh chapter of Daniel. And it is a day which comes to both individuals and nations in ways they do not expect. The Lord's face is set against falsehood, tyranny and cruelty everywhere. The true antithesis is not between Israel and the nations, but between those of any nation who fear God and those who do not.

Such then are the modern messages of the Book of Joel, the son of Pethuel.

~~~~ *Jonah* ~~~~

I. Introduction

IF THESE Twelve Minor Prophets were arranged in our Bibles in chronological order, the book of Jonah would probably follow directly after the Book of Joel. Thus after the third chapter of Joel we would pass at once to the first chapter of Jonah. And what a contrast is presented by these two chapters! In Joel 3 we find unmitigated condemnation of the heathen. In Jonah we are given a message of grace and love, more lofty and universal than is found elsewhere in the Old Testament. Thus are sounded one after the other the two dominant notes of the Bible: justice and mercy.

In II Kings 14:25 mention is made of a servant of the Lord by the name of Jonah who predicted the conquests of King Jeroboam II. All that we know of him is that he was the son of Amittai and that he lived in Gathhepher. He was evidently a strong nationalist, an intense patriot, who supported by his prophecies the campaigns of Jeroboam.

If the Jonah mentioned in II Kings is the author of this book, its date comes very early, for Jeroboam's reign was from 785 to 744 B.C. An examination of the contents of the book, however, precludes such an early date. It seems most likely that Jonah made use of Joel (cf. 3:5 with Joel 1:13, 14; 3:9 with Joel 2:14; 4:2b with Joel 2:13), the late date of which has been established. In the narrative in II Kings no mention is made of a trip by the prophet to Nineveh, which had ceased to exist in 612 B.C. The language of the book has nothing in common with that of the earlier prophets. And above all, it is impossible to imagine that such a message of God's loving-kindness to Israel's worst enemies should have been written so early in Israel's history. Nowhere, it must be noted, does the book claim to have been written by Jonah himself, nor does it offer any proof that it came from an eyewitness of the events described. For all these reasons we can safely assume a very late date for the book. Jonah is probably the last of the Old Testament prophets except Daniel. We can date it about 300 B.C.

166

Thus the author of this book, possibly because the historical Jonah was such an intense nationalist, took this name as the hero of his tale. And the question is, how are we to understand it? There seem to be three possibilities. The first is that it is a true story, the literal history of what happened to a prophet living late in Israel's history, who concealed his identity under the name of Jonah. The difficulties in the way of such an interpretation of the book are apparent. To take this story literally is to reduce it to absurdity. Aside from the swallowing of Jonah by the fish there are other difficulties such as the fantastic description of a three days' journey to Nineveh and of the wholesale conversion of the Ninevites. Also, it is noticeable that all details and precise data are lacking which we would have a right to expect in a literal narrative. And there is "the abrupt close of the story at the very moment when its moral is obvious. The truth is pushed to the front, not the facts. We sin against the spirit of the book in trying to take it as real history." [1] As for Jesus' reference to Jonah (Matt. 12:40), it is enough to say that this does not authenticate the literal truth of the story. Jesus placed himself at the level of his contemporaries and used for his own purposes the traditions and customs of his people.

Another possible interpretation of the book is that it was a story pure and simple. "It is fiction—a short story with a moral—like the book of Ruth . . . or the stories about Daniel. . . . is a perfectly good short story—with a beginning, a middle, and an end. . . . The author of the story utilized ancient myths and folk tales . . . [and] out of such miscellaneous materials . . . composed a charming story intended to teach the lesson . . . that Jehovah's loving-kindness and compassion are not restricted to the Jews but extended to the heathen as well." [2]

The difficulty here is in finding a place for the book, upon such an interpretation of it, among the prophets. Why was it inserted in the list of those men who were commissioned to declare a message of God to His people? The parallel found in the insertion in Isaiah (36-39) of narrative material taken in part from the Book of II Kings (18:13ff.) is not convincing. For this was an insertion in a prophetic book, but Jonah is a book by itself. And again we confront the abrupt close of

---

[1] George Adam Smith, *The Twelve Prophets,* "Jonah."
[2] So R. H. Pfeiffer, *Introduction to the Old Testament,* pp. 587-588.

the book when the truth it intended to teach was uppermost in the author's mind. Surely a short story writer would have contrived a different ending from that.

We arrive therefore at a third interpretation of the book, which seems to give us the deepest insight into the author's purpose and authenticates its right to be included among the prophetic books of the Old Testament. It is neither literal history nor a short story pure and simple, but an allegory, similar to the parables of Jesus. By Jonah is meant the people of Israel who had been disobedient to the Word and Will of God that they should carry His message to the other nations of the world, even to their worst enemies. Nineveh was chosen to represent the whole heathen world, because Nineveh was the very incarnation of Israel's hate. This idea was repugnant to them, and instead of obedience they sought to flee from God's presence and embarked upon a stormy and treacherous sea. The stormy sea was always the symbol in the Hebrew mind of strange and unholy adventure. It was a symbol, too, of that tossing heathen world which was always ready to engulf Israel. Now, the popular mythology of the time had pictured the sea as filled with monsters, leviathans, dragons. When, therefore, the prophet in our story wished to tell of the misfortunes that befell the people of God who had been disobedient to His commandment, he employed these ideas. A great monster of the sea swallowed them up and later disgorged them. In this pictorial language was described the disaster of the Babylonian exile and the subsequent return of the people to Jerusalem. If one will read carefully the many passages in the Old Testament in which the sea and its monsters rage against Jehovah, the conclusion will seem inevitable that by the "great fish" is meant the heathen power which for a time engulfed Israel, but was compelled later to disgorge her. There is a passage in Jeremiah (51:34, 44, 45) which seems to point conclusively to this interpretation of the Book of Jonah. Jeremiah explicitly describes the Exile of Israel in the precise language of Jonah: "Nebuchadrezzar the king of Babylon hath devoured me . . . he hath swallowed me up like a dragon, he hath filled his belly." But Jehovah answers: "I will punish Bel in Babylon, and I will bring forth out of his mouth that which he hath swallowed up . . . My people, go ye out from the midst of her."

Here, then, we have a real prophetic message, a message from God to His people. But this message is cast into the form of a parable. Jonah is the only one of the prophets by whom the form of a narrative is used. The other prophets introduced personal elements, but in Jonah there is absence of any prophetic discourse, and that is true of Jonah alone. Precisely as Jesus taught in parables and brought spiritual truth to the people in his parables of the Prodigal Son and the Good Samaritan, so this inspired prophet of the Old Testament taught the people of his day the great humanitarian truth that the mercy of God extends to all men everywhere, even to those who had been Israel's most bitter foes. Their disobedience had brought disaster upon them. Let them now fulfill their true mission to the world and make the great discovery that all men are susceptible to the Spirit of God, capable of repentance, able to embrace His mercy. The purpose of this prophecy was to enforce this truth upon the reluctant mind of Israel. How reluctant that mind was is represented by Jonah's bitter disappointment when Jehovah, instead of destroying Nineveh, spared it and caused its people to repent and turn to Him. The rebuke (4:10) to Jonah is the prophet's protest against this narrow and vindictive attitude on the part of the Jewish people. "In our effort to appreciate the wonderful truth of the book, we labor under the disadvantage of our sense of humour. We miss the sublime spirit by attention to detail." [3] Yet if we can dismiss all that, understanding that those features which seem grotesque may be traced to the popular poetry of the prophet's time, we cannot fail to be moved by the truth it contains, which lifts the book to the highest level of Old Testament prophecy and brings it nearest to the New Testament.

The unity of this little book has been questioned. By some it is felt that the prayer or psalm contained in chapter 2 is a later interpolation, and is not an integral part of the book. If the book is regarded simply as a story, the reasons for this would seem to be plausible, since this is not a prayer to be saved out of the fish but a psalm of thanksgiving for having been saved from drowning. If, however, this psalm is taken to represent the emotions of the Hebrew people during their years of exile, it is seen to be entirely appropriate. It consists of passages taken from the Psalter, yet it has "features all its own. It is not a string of quotations

[3] George Adam Smith, *op. cit.*

but a living unity. We have the book of Jonah as it came from its author." [4]

II. THE PROPHECY

"An involuntary smile passes over one's features at the mention of the name of Jonah. For the popular conception sees nothing in this book but a silly tale, exciting us to derision. Whenever shallow humor prompts people to hold the Old Testament up to ridicule, Balaam's ass and Jonah's whale infallibly take precedence. I have read the book of Jonah at least a hundred times, and I will publicly avow, for I am not ashamed of my weakness, that I cannot even now take up this marvellous book . . . without the tears rising to my eyes, and my heart beating higher. This apparently trivial book is one of the deepest and grandest that was ever written." [5] So writes one of the profoundest students of the Old Testament. One of the first things a serious-minded reader of the Bible should do is to rescue this book from the bathos of ridicule into which it has fallen. "The tragedy of the book of Jonah," as George Adam Smith has said, "is this: that a book which is made the means of one of the sublimest revelations of truth in the Old Testament should be known to most only for its connection with a whale."

Closely examined, also, this inspired book is seen to contain a marvelous message not only for its time, but for our times as well. At first sight it might seem as if there could be no possible connection between the Book of Jonah and the days in which we live. No book apparently could be more remote from present-day events and the insistent problems of our modern world. On the contrary, no book in the Old Testament bears so directly upon them and teaches us truth that it is so imperative we should learn as the book of the prophet of Jonah.

The book, as we have seen, is a protest against the narrow, nationalistic, vindictive attitude of the Jewish people toward the heathen nations, caused by their intense revulsion against the crimes of heathendom. This "had filled Israel's eyes too full of fever to see her duty." Jonah turned away, because he felt that God meant good to the Nine-

---

[4] George Adam Smith, *op. cit.*
[5] Cornill, *The Prophets of Israel*, p. 170.

vites. To the nationalist mind this was so abhorrent that he turned his back upon it and fled. The story of the shipwreck is told with consummate art. How noble was the attitude of those heathen sailors. Jonah felt his kinship with them in this moment of their common necessity. In those sailors Jonah saw already the heathen turned to the fear of the Lord and offered up his own life to secure for them the saving mercies of God.

Yet even after his deliverance Jonah was reluctant to go to Nineveh. The old hatreds die hard. And when he went, he did not preach God's mercy but declared: "Yet forty days and Nineveh shall be overthrown." To his consternation, this preaching caused immediate repentance and a turning to God upon the part of the whole people. And this angered Jonah, who neither desired nor expected any such thing. Follows the fourth and concluding chapter with its touching teaching of the gourd, the withering of which had vexed Jonah. "Then said the Lord, Thou hast had pity on the gourd . . . And should not I spare Nineveh, that great city?" "More simply, as something quite self-evident and therefore more sublimely and touchingly, the truth was never spoken in the Old Testament, that God, as Creator of the whole earth, must also be the God and Father of the entire world, in whose loving, kind, and fatherly heart all men are equal, before whom there is no difference of nation and confession, but only men, whom He has created in His own image." [6]

Thus the Book of Jonah gives expression to the loftiest and most spiritual ideals that had ever entered into the consciousness of the Hebrew people. Applied to our own time, the Book of Jonah rebukes the narrow spirit of nationalism, of racial hatreds, of contempt for alien peoples, of human antagonisms whenever and wherever found. Thus it is a veritable tract for the times, a message that pierces to the very heart of all the problems that vex our modern world. Who, then, is Jonah? Jonah is not only Israel, he is every modern nation with exclusive regard for its own interests, selfish ideas of its own glory, with nothing but fear of or hatred for other nations, with complete disregard for the underprivileged peoples of the world, exploited at will. The whole of our modern history is a striking illustration of the attitude of

[6] Cornill, *op. cit.,* p. 173.

Jonah toward Nineveh. Let one read such a book as Haskins' *History of Modern Europe*. It tells in the opening chapters in simple and graphic style of the kind of government Europe had one hundred years ago; of how no nation thought of the welfare of its own underprivileged people, nor thought of consideration or honor in its relation to other States. From the time of Frederick the Great down to the day of Disraeli one can find no single episode that was not filled with deceit, treachery, self-seeking; not one impulse of brotherhood or generosity. Such has been the history of our modern nations. And to what shipwreck has such diplomacy brought us, to what inconceivable disasters. Disobedience to the plain commandment of God in the relation of nation to nation has indeed cast us on a stormy sea of troubles.

"And the word of the Lord came unto Jonah the second time." It comes a second time unto the nations of the world today. We are told once more that there can be no peace or stability in our modern world except it rest upon the principle of the essential brotherhood and equality of all human beings. Peace is founded upon justice. There can be no peace in a world where one nation feels itself wronged by another nation or one class by another class. Not until tyranny and oppression are abolished everywhere, trade restrictions, caste, dishonesty and political trickery, can we expect order and stability. We must get rid of the idea of racial superiority, of a master race. Unless the united policies of the great nations are built upon law, brotherhood and justice, humanity will again revolt. If peace is to be stable it must be built not upon the dictation of a conquering race but rather upon the united will of all nations, small and great alike, based upon the common desire to achieve justice. And by justice is meant the protection of human rights and of the individual man. In the areas of the world where problems of colonial government must be faced and settled, this principle of the essential equality of human beings—which is the fundamental message of the Book of Jonah—"cuts like a two-edged sword every alien rule based upon the exploitation of another race, contains the seeds of unrest and revolution and makes against international stability and lasting peace. The age of imperialism is ended. The only possible basis for an enduring civilization is equality of human rights, irrespective of race, creed or color. This applies to every country and to every race, white, yellow, brown or black." [7]

This is the Book of Jonah, with its broad humanitarian teaching, down to date. Jonah has been called "The Pioneer Internationalist." [8] And so he was. In an era of seething international hatreds, he advanced the idea of the deeper brotherhood that unites all mankind in the fellowship of a human family. This inspired prophet tells us today what we need to learn as surely as the Hebrew people of old, that God cares, not for Israel alone, not for America alone, but for people, all peoples everywhere, for all men, for the multitudes, for humanity. And nothing short of the learning, the believing, the practice of this truth can save our modern world from irretrievable disaster.

In the discovery by Jonah of his essential kinship with those heathen sailors we find the solution of the race problem that disturbs our domestic peace. Between Jonah and those aliens there was the spirit only of brotherhood and toleration. Here we find no hint of superiority of Jew over Gentile, no race inferiority of Gentile to Jew, but only common humanity, equally noble on both sides, equally generous. Here we find conceded to all alike the great common virtues that belong to humanity as such. Here is the frank recognition of the Spirit of God in all mankind, the possession of which sets all men on the same level and rebukes the sinister ideas of race prejudice, racial superiority, and all other attitudes of mind which disgrace and endanger the social order in which we live.

Nor can we overlook the message at the end of the book, the conversion of Nineveh, which eloquently depicts the susceptibility of conscience everywhere to the call of God, its capacity for repentance. Upon that universal fact the hope of the world is based. For if Nineveh, that incarnation of evil, that symbol of all that is unrighteous, if Nineveh could turn to God, then any, then all. And never did we need to learn this truth more than in the days in which we live. We are tempted to believe that there are peoples in the world who are hopelessly depraved and unregenerate, whose conscience has been so perverted that

[7] Francis B. Sayre, *The Years Ahead.*
[8] John Wright Buckham, *Advance,* May 1, 1940.

they cannot and will not choose the right, who understand no message save that of force, who never will listen or respond to any summons to a spiritual life of brotherhood with other peoples and nations. Hence they must be dealt with accordingly. We must not expect from them any inward regeneration of national purpose. They must be controlled from without. They never will be reborn from within.

Against any such idea comes this glowing message from the book of Jonah. It tells us that "under every form and character of human life, beneath all needs and all habits, . . . more native to man than sin itself, lies the power of the human heart to turn. . . . It lies in every heart, needing indeed some dream of Divine mercy to rouse it; but when roused, neither ignorance of God, nor pride, nor long obduracy of evil may withstand it." [9] In this capacity for repentance, Israel and Nineveh were one. And Nineveh, however remote it might seem from God, was still susceptible to the touch of His spirit, was still capable of being renewed in His likeness. This has been the hope that has animated the missionary who has gone to coarse, cannibal tribes, submerged populations, with the word of grace. And this faith has reaped its rich rewards.

Always in our relations with other nations of the world, however obdurate, recalcitrant, vicious and inhuman they may have been, this nethermost capacity for inner repentance and renewal must be borne in mind. External control, punishment for evil that has been done, restraint and vigilant oversight, these may be immediate necessities. But unless behind and beneath all of them there is the belief that nobler motives can be evoked, that the evil can be forsworn, that better ways can be learned, that the currents of the national life can be turned into new channels, in a word, that even Nineveh can repent, we shall never have arrived at a true and final method of reaching the hearts of those nations which have disturbed and disrupted the life of our modern world.

Jonah himself needed to repent, and he did repent. And his repentance at last taught him to believe and even to rejoice in the repentance of Nineveh. We need to repent, for we have all fallen short of our duty to God and man. And the experience of national repentance,

[9] George Adam Smith, *op. cit.*

if it be deep and thorough, will lead us also to believe in the possibility of the repentance of any modern Nineveh.

We call them the Twelve Minor Prophets. But surely they have taught us major lessons. We have thought of these as obscure books, whose value lies chiefly in their exhibition of the conditions in their own day and are thus of importance only to the students of ancient history. But now these men stand out, when truly understood, as preachers whose messages come home to us in a world so different from theirs in many ways, yet needing today the very same truths if it would escape judgment and endure "in truth and in righteousness."

~~~ *Appendix: Exegesis of the Text* ~~~

AMOS

Chapter 1 v. 1 *saw,* i.e., to behold in prophetic vision (cf. Is. 2:1, 13:1; Mic. 1:1; Hab. 1:1) ; *Israel,* i.e., the N. Kingdom; *earthquake:* a not infrequent calamity in Palestine. The one referred to here must have been of unusual severity, for it was long remembered (see Zech. 14:5). v. 2. *will roar* (cf. Joel 3:16; Jer. 25:30). The temple on Zion was conceived as the earthly abode of Jehovah; *habitations* = pastures. The term is a pastoral one. *mourn,* i.e., in consternation. v. 3. *three transgressions and four:* the numbers are typical only, used to assist the imagination. The meaning is that the measure of guilt is not only full but more than full; *threshed Gilead:* the specific sin of the Syrians is the cruelty of their wars against the trans-Jordan Israelites (cf. II Kings 8:12, 10:32ff., 13:7). v. 4, *fire,* i.e., a flame of war. *Ben-hadad,* possibly the then ruler of the Syrians. v. 5. *bar,* i.e the bars of iron or bronze by which the gates were secured; *inhabitant:* see R.V. marg., "him that sitteth enthroned." *Aven:* the reference is uncertain. It may refer to Baalbek (Heliopolis LXX) and to the worship of the sun in an ancient temple there. Hence we may translate "cut off him that is enthroned on its idolatrous plains." *Eden,* or Beth-Eden, is another uncertain locality. It may have been a summer residence of the kings of Damascus. *Kir:* see chap. 9:7, the original home of the Syrians to which they shall return. v. 6. *Gaza,* i.e., the Philistines, whose four cities are named; *the whole captivity,* i.e., the whole population, sold as slaves to the Edomites. vv. 7. 8. *fire, inhabitant:* see vv. 4, 5. v. 9. *Tyre,* i.e., the Phoenician towns. Amos does not restrict his censure to wrongs done against Israel (see 2:1). v. 11. *Edom:* The Edomites and Israelites were blood brothers (Deut. 2:4, 23:7; Obad. 10–14) ; *anger did tear:* for the figure see Job 16:9; *kept his wrath,* i.e., nourished and cherished it. v. 12. *Temen:* a district in the northern or western part of Edom, synonymous with Edom (Jer. 49:7; Obad. 9; Hab. 3:3) ; *Bozrah:* a town of Edom and an important place (Jer. 49:13; Is. 34:6, 63:1). v. 13. *The Ammonites:* occupied a district east of the Jordan, whose capital was Rabbab (v. 14), the only Ammonite city mentioned in the O.T. (II Sam. 11:1; Jer. 49:2, 3; 25:5, etc). v. 15. This verse is borrowed by Jeremiah (49:3) with slight changes.

Chapter 2. v. 1. The Moabites occupied the fertile district east of the

Dead Sea. *Burnt the bones:* a mark of unrelenting hate and vindictiveness. v. 2. *Kerioth:* possibly the capital of Moab (Jer. 48:41). v. 3. *the judge,* probably as in Mic. 5:1 another designation of the king. v. 4. *despised,* i.e., rejected; *their lies,* i.e., their unreal gods. v. 5. cf. Jer. 17:27b. vv. 6, 7a. *sold the righteous,* etc.: judges accepted bribes to pronounce the innocent guilty, and hardhearted creditors sold into slavery those who could not pay even for a pair of sandals, trampled to the dust of the earth the heads of the poor and thwarted the purposes of those helpless to protect themselves. vv. 7b, 8. The reference here is to temple prostitution, a revolting practice found in many Semitic religions, and followed in defiance of Jehovah's will by the carnally minded Israelites. v. 8. *clothes laid to pledge,* i.e., garments pawned by the poor which creditors have failed to return (see. Ex. 22: 26ff.) ; *wine of the condemned:* they use the fines which they have extorted to purchase wine for the sacrificial feasts. v. 9. They thus sin against the Lord who had saved them from the mighty Amorites and bestowed further favors upon them. v. 12. They had tempted the Nazarites to break their vow. v. 13. *I am pressed:* better, "I will press you." So R.V. v. 14. *flight:* rather "place of flight," refuge (cf. Jer. 25:35; Job 11:20 [see R.V. marg.]; Ps. 142:4); *strengthen his force,* i.e., command his powers.

Chapter 3. vv. 3–8. The meaning of these verses is that, just as every event in nature implies the operation of some cause adequate to produce it, so if the prophet has uttered this condemnation, it is because there has been a sufficient cause impelling him to do so. v. 4. *cry,* rather, "growl," with satisfaction. v. 6. *evil in a city* etc: calamity according to the Hebrews, presupposed an act of God. v. 7. *surely,* etc.: The sense is, For the Lord does nothing without revealing His purpose to His prophets. v. 9. *Ashdod-Egypt:* the Philistines and the Egyptians are called to witness that the sins of Israel deserve punishment; *publish* = proclaim. v. 11. *an adversary* = distress. v. 12. *taketh out,* better, "rescueth" (so R.V.); *in the corner of a bed,* i.e., in the cushioned corner of a divan. *Damascus:* evidently the text is at fault, the rendering may be "and on the damask [R.V. silken cushions] of a couch." v. 14. *Bethel:* the principal sanctuary of the Northern Kingdom; *horns of the altar,* which provided safety for those who laid hold of them (I Kings 1:50, 51; 2:28). v. 15. *great houses:* rather "many houses" (so R.V. marg.).

Chapter 4. v. 1. *Bashan:* a fertile plain east of the Jordan, well known as a pasture ground. The women of Samaria are here called "kine of Bashan" because of their luxurious and animal existence; *masters* = lords, husbands. v. 2. *he will take you:* rather, ye shall be taken. v. 3. *at the breaches,* i.e., through the broken walls of captured Samaria; *ye shall cast them* etc. The text is corrupt and its precise meaning is unknown. The idea is that they shall be cast into exile in some locality of which the word "palace" is a mistranslation. v. 4. is of course in irony: *Gilgal,* a well-known site of idolatrous worship (cf. 5:5, Hos. 4:15, 9:15, 12:11); *every morning,* instead of once a year; *every three days,* instead of every three years (Deut. 14:28, 26:12). v. 5. *this liketh you,* i.e., this is like you. v. 6. *cleanness of teeth:* a striking description of a famine. v. 8. The water supply of one city would not suffice for so many; *wander* = totter. v. 11. *Sodom and Gomorrah* (see Gen. 19:24, 25, 28).

Chapter 5. v. 1. *lamentation* = a dirge in the form of a literary composition. v. 5. *Beer-sheba,* in the extreme south of Judah. v. 6. *house of Joseph,* i.e., the Northern Kingdom. v. 7. *wormwood:* always the symbol for something bitter (cf. Jer. 9:15; Prov. 5:4; Rev. 8:11); *leave off:* lit. "lay down," i.e., dethrone. v. 8. *calleth for the waters* (see 9:6). The reference is probably to long-continued rains. v. 9. "that causeth devastation to flash forth upon the strong so that devastation cometh upon the fortress" (cf. R.V.). v. 10. The prophet reverts to the subject of v. 7: "They are heedless to the claims of justice." For "reprover in the gate" of justice, cf. Isa. 29:21. The "reprover" is the one who seeks to convict the wrongdoer. v. 11. *burdens* = exactions. v. 18. *The Day of the Lord:* an ancient idea originally signifying a Day of Victory. It is here used by Amos for the first time meaning a Day of Judgment and in this sense finds constant repetition in the later prophets (see Is. 2:12–21, 13:6–10; Zeph. 1:7, 14–16; Joel 2:1ff.); *to what end,* etc. = "what good will it do you?" v. 25. *have ye offered* = "did you bring" —calling for a negative answer. Sacrifice is no indispensable element of the people's religion. v. 26. You and your idols will go into exile. The details in this verse are obscure. *Moloch-Sakkuth,* the Assyrian god of war; *Chiun* is the Assyrian name for the planet Saturn. The middle part of the verse does not seem to be in order. The reference in 26b is to star worship.

Chapter 6. v. 1. *Zion,* i.e., Judah (cf. 2:4–5); *trust* = are secure (R.V.). *chief of the nations,* etc., i.e., the nobles of Samaria who held it to be the first of the nations. To them the people came for justice. v. 2. The cities named Calneh and Hamath in northern Syria down to Gath on the Philistine border in the south are no more prosperous than is the kingdom of Israel. Thus hath the Lord blessed His people who repay Him with indifference and neglect (vv. 3–6). v. 6. *affliction,* i.e., the wound, the disease of the body politic. v. 10. *uncle,* i.e., his father and brother are supposed to be dead; *burneth:* the ordinary process of burial is imagined to be impossible; *by the sides* = in the innermost parts (so R.V.); *with thee,* i.e., "alive"; *we may not mention,* i.e., lest some fresh judgment should be invoked. v. 12. To turn justice into injustice and so transform righteousness into its opposite is as irrational as horses running over jagged rocks or an attempt to plow there. v. 13. *thing of nought,* i.e., in what has no reality; *taken to us horns,* i.e., become strong. v. 14. *but =* for; *river of the wilderness,* i.e., the whole territory through which the Jordan flows.

Chapter 7. v. 1. *formed =* was forming; *the king's mowings:* a tribute levied by the kings of Israel as fodder for their horses (cf. I Kings 18:5). v. 2. *by whom =* how. The nation is too weak to endure this calamity. v. 4. *contend by fire:* the Lord arraigns His people and summons fire as His accusing agent; *the great deep:* the subterranean waters (Gen. 7:11). v. 7. *upon =* beside (so R.V.). v. 8. *set a plumbline,* i.e., apply a crucial moral test; *pass by =* pardon. v. 9. *Isaac,* only here and in v. 16 is this term used as a synonym for Israel. v. 12. *seer:* this word is probably used on account of the visions related by Amos. v. 14. *no prophet,* i.e., did not belong to the school of the prophets (I Kings 20:35; II Kings 2:3, 5, 7, 15); *son,* i.e., a member of a prophetic guild. v. 17. *shall be a harlot,* i.e., treated as a harlot when Samaria is conquered (cf. Is. 13:16; Zech, 14:2); *line,* i.e., a measuring line (cf. II. Kings 21:13); *polluted land:* a foreign land was regarded as unclean, because Jehovah could not be worshiped there.

Chapter 8. v. 1. *summer fruit,* i.e., Israel is ripe for judgment. v. 2. *pass by =* pardon as in 7:8. v. 3. There will be no time for decent burial; *with silence =* 'hush!' as in 6:10. v. 4. *swallow up =* "pant after," i.e., eager to destroy. v. 5. *new moon,* observed as a popular holiday when trade must be suspended; *ephah, shekel,* i.e., short measure and weighed scales (see Lev. 19:35-36; Deut. 25:13-15). v. 6. The poor in the end must sell themselves as slaves because they owe money or even a pair of sandals (cf. 2:6). The rich in their avarice sell wheat diluted with worthless grain. v. 7. *excellency of Jacob:* the words may refer to Jehovah Himself (cf. I Sam. 15:29) or they may be used ironically of Israel. v. 8. The reference is to the rising and sinking of the river Nile. v. 10. *feasts =* pilgrimages, and *lamentation* a composed dirge (cf. 5:1); *baldness:* the shaving of the head as a sign of mourning. v. 11. *words,* better the word, i.e., the Word of the Lord. The people will seek in vain for prophetic counsel. v. 12. *wandering =* tottering as in 4:8. v. 14. The reference is to the calf set up in Dan (I Kings 12:29); *the manner of Beer-sheba:* the text is obscure. The idea may be that the well-marked and frequented road to Beer-sheba, since it was permanent, was regarded as something to be sworn by (see G. A. Smith, *Amos*).

Chapter 9. v. 1. *standing =* stationed at as in 7:7. v. 6. *troop =* vault.

The sky is a solid vault, its extremities resting on the earth; *calleth for:* repeated from 5:8b; long-continued rains. v. 7. Israel on the basis of moral standards is no more to Jehovah than other nations. His providence has guided them also. *Caphtor* is probably Crete (see Deut. 2:23; Jer. 47:4); *Kir:* see 1:5. v. 9. The people (of both kingdoms) are to be sifted. No good grain will fall upon the ground and be lost. v. 10. *prevent* = come in front of. v. 12. The empire of David is to be restored to its former limits; *called by my name,* i.e., in token of conquest and so of ownership. v. 13. No sooner will the ground be plowed than the corn will be ready for the reaper, and the grapes will be ready as soon as they are sown.

HOSEA

Chapter 1. v. 4. *Jezreel* (see II Kings 9:30). v. 6. *Lo-ruhama:* the name means "unpitied." v. 9. *Lo-ammi* means "not my people." vv. 10–11. These verses, difficult to connect with the context, are a later insertion.

Chapter 2. v. 1. The names are changed by a glossator to mean their direct opposites, in harmony with 1:10–11, which are not Hosea's. v. 6. *hedge up thy way:* the figure is that of a traveler who finds his way barred by a thorn hedge which he is unable to break through (cf. Job. 3:23, 19:8; Lam. 3:7, 9). The reality signified is some irretrievable disaster. v. 7. i.e., prayers and sacrifices at idolatrous shrines will have no efficacy. v. 8. *did not know:* better, "took no notice that it was I who," etc. v. 13. *visit upon her* = "not fail to notice" the days in which she worshiped Jehovah in degraded ways. *earrings and jewels:* rather, nose rings and necklaces. v. 14. *allure,* i.e., I will put into her heart to return while she is yet in exile (wilderness). v. 15. *Achor* (see Josh. 7:26) v. 16. *Ishi* = my husband. v. 17. *remembered:* better, mentioned. v. 21. *hear:* rather, respond. In this and the following verses we have a picture of the harmony between the physical and spiritual spheres. The prophet adopts the Semitic idea that the deities were the productive powers of nature. Thus, *Jezreel* (v. 22) (= Israel) calls upon its plants to germinate; they call upon the earth, the earth beseeches the heavens for rain, the heavens call upon the Lord who responds in faithful love. v. 23. *earth* = land.

Chapter 3. The narrative is resumed from 1:9. Gomer had left her husband and fallen into the depth of misery. v. 1. *beloved of her friend,* etc.: rather, beloved of a paramour and an adulteress; *flagons of wine:* rather, cakes of (dried) grapes, considered a luxury (see I Sam. 25:18; Is. 16:7). v. 2.

As nearly as can be reckoned, the total price paid for Gomer was about twenty dollars. v. 3. *abide:* rather, sit still, i.e., lead a quiet secluded life. v. 4. *image,* i.e., a consecrated pillar, the distinguishing mark of holy places; *Ephod:* the sleeveless coat of the high priest (cf. Ex. 28:6–12; Judg. 8:24–27), probably both in Judges and here the word is used for an image of Jehovah overlaid with gold and silver; *teraphim:* household gods (cf. Gen. 21:19, 34; I Sam. 19:13, 16), regarded as the protectors of domestic happiness. This passage reveals (a) the extent of popular idolatry in Northern Israel and (b) the unorthodox worship of Jehovah. v. 5. *David their king:* not the Messiah but the family or dynasty of David. *Latter days* = days to come. This verse does not belong to Hosea.

Chapter 4. v. 1. The Northern Kingdom only is addressed. In v. 15 the prophet turns to Judah. v. 2. *by swearing,* etc. = there is nothing but (false) swearing, etc.; *break out,* i.e., into acts of violence: one deed of blood follows another. v. 4 is obscure. Its general meaning seems to be that it is useless for anyone to seek to reprove the people since they will not listen to the priests whose counsel they resist. v. 5. *the prophet,* i.e., the lower class of prophets who prophesied for gain (cf. Mic. 3:11); *thy mother,* i.e., the stock from which they sprang, the caste or clan. v. 6. *thy children,* i.e., members of the priestly caste. v. 7. "The more they increased, the more," etc. v. 8. "They [the priests] eat up the sin offering of my people." "They greedily devoured what the people had brought to atone for their sins." v. 11. A proverb or adage. v. 12. *stocks* = wood, the name Hosea gives to images of Jehovah; *staff:* probably the diviner's wand (see Ez. 21:21). v. 13. *shall commit:* rather, do commit. v. 14. The burden of guilt rested upon their elders who set a wicked example; *separated with:* rather, they themselves go aside with consecrated prostitutes. v. 15. *Gilgal:* one of the chief centers of idolatrous worship in Northern Israel (cf. Am. 4:4; 5:5); *Beth-aven:* the word means "house of wickedness," a sarcastic substitute for Bethel (house of God); *nor swear:* deprecating the use of a solemn oath in sacrilegious ways (cf. Am. 8:14). v. 16. Rather, is stubborn like a stubborn heifer (cf. Jer. 31:18; Deut. 32:15); *feed them like a lamb,* etc.: an incredulous exclamation, "This being so, should the Lord feed them in a large meadow?" v. 17. *Ephraim:* as elsewhere, the Northern kingdom, i.e., of the house of Joseph. v. 18. *their drink is sour:* a mistranslation. The meaning is: When their carousal is over, they indulge in lewdness; *her rulers,* etc.: the words as they stand make no sense. The probable translation is: "The rulers love infamy. The wind hath wrapped them up in its wings and they shall be ashamed of their sacrifices" (so R.V.). The figure of the wind describes the suddenness and violence with which Israel will be carried away into captivity (cf. Is. 57:13).

Chapter 5. v. 1. *Mizpah* and *Tabor:* mentioned probably because of especially idolatrous worship there. v. 2. *and the revolters,* etc.: an obscure passage. A possible rendering is: and the apostates are gone deep in corruption (cf. 9:9), but I am a restraint to them all (Am. Trans.). v. 4. *they will not frame,* etc.: better, their doings will not suffer them to turn unto their God. v. 5. *the pride of Israel:* here used as a title of Jehovah who testifies against Israel. v. 7. *a month:* the time for punishment has arrived; each new moon will bring it nearer. v. 8. *Gibeah* and *Ramah:* both towns were situated on heights well adapted for signals of alarm; *after thee:* rather, behind thee. The cry of warning is to be sent from Bethel to Benjamin over the border in Judah. v. 9. *rebuke* = punishment; *tribes of Israel,* i.e., both Northern and Southern Kingdoms. v. 10. *remove the bound,* i.e., the landmarks the removal of which brought a curse on the offender (cf. Deut. 19:14; 27:17). v. 11. *judgment,* i.e., the judgment of God; *the commandment:* an amended reading makes this mean: he would go after vanity, i.e., after idols (cf. Ps. 31:6; Jer. 18:15). v. 12. *therefore I will be:* better, as for me I am; *as a moth:* denoting a gradual inward corruption. v. 13. *King Jareb:* the name means "fighting king" and some Assyrian ruler is given this nickname, possibly Tiglath-pileser III to whom the epithet would accurately apply. v. 14. *I, even I:* "The axe may be human but the hand that wields it is divine" (cf. Is. 10:15).

Chapter 6. The first three verses of this chapter are closely connected with the preceding verses of chap. 5. v. 2 (cf. Ez. 37:1–10). v. 3. *then shall we know:* render, "Yea, let us know, let us be zealous to know." These verses describe a facile and hasty repentance from which a full confession of sin was absent. The answer of Jehovah in the following verse shows that this cannot satisfy Him. v. 5. *thy judgments:* read, "my judgments"; *mercy and not sacrifice,* i.e. mercy rather than sacrifice (cf. Is. 1:11–20; Mic. 6:6–8; Matt. 9:13, 12:7). v. 7. *like men* = like other men, i.e., ordinary common man, as in Ps. 82:7; Job 31:33. v. 8. *polluted with blood:* rather, tracked with bloody footprints. v. 10. Jehovah is the speaker; *set a harvest* = a harvest is appointed for thee. The concluding words of v. 11 should be attached to v. 1 of chapter 7.

Chapter 7. v. 1. *for they commit:* rather, how they commit. v. 2. *heart* = self; they feel no pricks of conscience. v. 4. Passion subsides only to rise again. v. 5. *in the day,* probably birthday; *made him sick:* rather, (the princes) are become sick; *stretched out* = entered into close relations with;

scorners = proud, lawless men (Ps. 1:1). v. 6. "For their inward part is like an oven, their heart burneth in them"; *baker:* better, their anger. v. 9. *strangers have devoured,* i.e., by tribute and invasion. v. 10. *Pride of Israel.* i.e., Jehovah, as in 5:5. v. 12a. *when* = as soon as. v. 12b. The punishment will be according to that announced to the people. v. 13. *though I have redeemed:* rather, I indeed would redeem. v. 14. Instead of quiet communion of the heart, there are howls of rage and despair; *assemble:* the reading is doubtful. It may mean "cut themselves," a forbidden sign of mourning (see Deut. 14.1; Lev. 19:28). v. 16: *deceitful bow,* i.e., one which shoots the arrow in the wrong direction; *rage of their tongue,* i.e., insolence.

Chapter 8. v. 1. *house of the Lord* (cf. 9:15). The land of Canaan is the abode of the Lord. v. 2. In the hour of punishment Israel will plead her unique relation to Jehovah. v. 4. The schism of the theocratic community was Israel's great offense. v. 5. *calf,* i.e., a small golden bull symbolic of Jehovah; *hath cast thee off:* a better rendering is, "Thy calf . . . is loathsome." v. 6. *was it also:* better, was this also. v. 8. *now shall they be,* etc.: rather, now are they become among the nations. v. 9. "The point of the comparison is obstinacy." v. 10. The verse is obscure. The meaning may be that, although Israel may obtain temporary success in its dealings with foreign nations, the Lord will frustrate these endeavors; *king of princes* may refer to Tiglath-pileser III of Assyria; by *burden* may be meant heavy tribute (II Kings 15:20). v. 11. Sacrifice without repentance but increases the load of national guilt. v. 12. *a strange thing,* i.e., as something that did not concern them. v. 13. Their sacrifices are a mere form, a secular feast. The people are threatened with captivity by Egypt as well as by Assyria. v. 14. *temples* = palaces, a symbol of worldliness and tyranny.

Chapter 9. v. 1. *loved a reward,* etc., i.e., loved a harlot's hire. Israel, a harlot, is bound to the Baalim to whom the blessings of the harvest were falsely ascribed. v. 4. *bread of mourners:* everything connected with the dead body was regarded as unclean; *bread for their soul:* the meaning is that their bread shall satisfy their appetite, but not their soul with the sense of divine favor. v. 6. *because of destruction:* rather, from the devastation. They have left their ruined country; *the pleasant places:* rather, their precious things of silver. v. 7. *the prophet is a fool:* introductory words such as "who say in their pride" must have dropped out of the text. v. 8. *the watchman is with my God:* the prophet refers to himself. He is helped by his God and ensnares those who would lay a trap for him (cf. Is. 29:21) because of their hatred and hostility. v. 9. *Gibeah* (cf. Judg. 19:12–16). v. 10. *Baal-peor* = Beth-peor (cf. Deut. 3:29). v. 11. *from the birth,* etc., i.e., there shall be no birth, nor being with child, nor conception. v. 12. As for children already born, they will soon perish. v. 13. The passage is obscure. Tyre seems to be entirely out of the picture. A different text yields the sense: "As I foresaw, Ephraim's sons must become a prey; Ephraim must bring out his sons to the slaughter" (Am. Trans.).

Chapter 10. v. 1. rather, Israel was a luxuriant vine which brought forth fruit freely. v. 2. *divided:* better, slippery or deceitful; *be found faulty:* rather, be dealt with as guilty. v. 3. *we have no king,* i.e., the king shall not be able to deliver them; *do to us:* rather, do for us. v. 4. *spoken words:* mere words, i.e., falsehoods; *thus judgment,* etc.: the seeds of sin shall produce judgment upon the people as abundant as the poppy of the fields. "The plant in question cannot be identified with precision." v. 5. *Beth-aven:* a contemptuous name for Bethel (4:15): far from delivering them, the "calves" shall cause their worshipers to fear; *departed from it:* i.e., gone into exile. v. 6. *of his own counsel:* i.e., of trusting in idols as protectors. v. 7. *foam:* rather, a piece of driftwood. v. 8. *Aven* = Beth-aven. v. 9. "From the days of Gibeah, you have sinned, O Israel. Then they said that war would not overtake them in Gibeah" (Am. Trans.). v. 10. "When I desire, I will chastise them, and they shall be bound for their two iniquities," i.e., revolt against Jehovah and against David their king. The word "furrows" yields no sense. v. 11. *passed over upon,* i.e., spared. [But now] I will make her to draw. v. 14. *Shalman spoiled Beth-arbel:* no one knows who Shalman (some Assyrian) was. Beth-arbel an unidentified locality in the Northern Kingdom, possibly Pella, east of the Jordan. Some recent event is here referred to of which we have no knowledge.

Chapter 11. v. 2. "The more they [i.e., Moses and the prophets] called them the more they departed from them" (cf. Is. 6:9, 10; Jer. 7:25, 26). v. 3. *taking them by their arms:* rather, I took them up in my arms. v. 4. *cords of a man,* i.e., such as a man can bear; *on their jaws:* rather, but lift up the yoke over their neck. v. 5. *he shall not return:* this is inconsistent with 8:13, 9:3, 6, 11:11. The sense required is, "He shall return"; *refused to return,* i.e., to Jehovah. v. 7. *though they called:* rather, and if they (the prophets) called them upwards, not one striveth to arise. v. 8. *Admah Zeboim:* cities of the plain that were overthrown (cf. Gen. 19:29; Deut. 29:23); *my repentings:* "a close rendering would be, 'I am wholly overcome with sympathy.'" v. 9. *I will not enter:* this yields no sense; probably the right rendering is: "I will not come to destroy the city." v. 11. *tremble,* i.e., thrill with eagerness. v. 12. *but Judah ruleth:* rather, and Judah still seeks after God and is faithful to the Holy One.

Chapter 12. v. 1. *the east wind,* a parching, destructive wind (cf. 13:15; Job. 15:2, 27:21) ; *oil,* a precious product (cf. Deut. 8:8; Ez. 16:19). v. 4. *with us:* rather, with him. v. 5. *memorial* = his name (cf. Ex. 3:15). v. 7. *he is:* i.e., Canaan, a synonym for a degenerate Israel. Another rendering of the latter part of this verse would yield the meaning: "[but] all his profits will not suffice" (to expiate his guilt). v. 9. *and I:* rather, "for I" who am as ready to help as to punish. v. 10. *similitudes* = parables. v. 11. If Gilead is (given to) idolatry, the Gileadites shall become mere vanity; their altars shall be as stone-heaps gathered from the field. v. 12. *served for a wife* (cf. Gen. 29:18–20; 31:38–41). v. 14. *therefore shall he leave:* rather, and his bloodshed will be cast, i.e., Jehovah will bring sudden retribution upon him; *his reproach,* i.e., the insult to Jehovah in Israel's idolatry.

Chapter 13. v. 1. The meaning is in doubt and the text may be corrupt. A possible sense of the words is: "when Ephraim spoke, there was awe and he rose to an exalted position" (cf. Gen. 49:22, 26) ; *offended in Baal:* sinned by identifying the Canaanitish Baal with Jehovah. v. 2b. *They say of them,* etc.: the passage is difficult, it may mean: "To such, they say, sacrifice. Men kissing calves!" (Am. Trans.) v. 6. *according to their pasture:* rather, when they fed, they waxed full, and in their plenty forgot God. v. 9. This verse may be rendered: "This is thy destruction, O Israel, that to me thy helper (thou hast been faithless)." v. 11. The reference is to the elevation of Jeroboam I and his successors. v. 12. *bound up* = tied up as in a bag (cf. Job. 21:17) ; *sin is hid:* rather, laid by in store, as in Job. 21:19. v. 13. Israel is first the travailing woman, and next the child whose birth is imperiled by its weakness (cf. Isa. 37:3). v. 14. *O death,* etc. Render, "Where are thy plagues, O Sheol? where thy pestilence, O death?" *repentance is hid:* this may mean that the Lord will not go back on his word, or it may be a resumption of the threat of judgment as a preface to what follows. v. 15. *He shall spoil:* "he" is Jehovah whom the east wind figures, or the enemy, the agent of Jehovah.

Chapter 14. v. 2. *words,* i.e., penitent words uttered from the heart; *take away:* rather, forgive; *render the calves of our lips,* i.e., pay the fruit of our lips, praise and thanksgiving (cf. Is. 57:19). v. 5. *roots as Lebanon:* a reference to the cedar trees at Lebanon (cf. Ps. 80:10). v. 7. *they that dwell,* etc.: render, "once more shall they that dwell under his shadow bring corn to life"; *the scent thereof:* rather, his (Israel's) renown. v. 8. *I have heard him,* etc.: rather, I respond and look on him.

MICAH

Chapter 1. which he saw: an early synonym for "to prophesy." Hence, *seer* (I Sam. 9:9) and *vision* (Is. 1:1; Obad. 1:1). v. 2. *people,* rather, peoples (R.V.) ; *temple:* temple of heaven is meant. v. 5. *Jacob:* when first used in this verse the term denotes the whole of the nation. The second time, however, it means only the Ten Tribes (sometimes called "Ephraim" but oftener "Israel"); *high places,* i.e., the sin. v. 6. *as a heap,* etc.: I will turn Samaria into a ruin of fields on which vineyards will be planted; *discover =* lay bare; v. 7. *hires:* the images and rich votive offerings; *shall return,* i.e., shall again become. v. 8. For *dragons* read "jackals" and for *owls,* "ostriches" as in R.V. v. 9. *he is come:* read "it is come," or "it hath reached." v. 10. *at Gath,* alluding to II Sam. 1:20. Its power has gone but its name was still a symbol of bitter hostility; *weep not at all,* an alternate reading is preferable: "weep bitterly." Most of the towns mentioned in this passage were in Micah's near neighborhood and there is a play upon the words which cannot be reproduced in translation. v. 11. The verse is obscure. Perhaps the sense is that Zaanan is deterred from flight because the sound of lamentation from Beth-ezel has filled it with despair, and has taken away its confidence (standing) ; Am. Trans. translates: "Beth-ezel is taken from its foundations, from the site where it stood." v. 12. Either "waiteth anxiously for good" (R.V.) or "is in travail" (R.V. marg.). v. 14. *presents,* i.e., parting gifts: say good-bye to; *lie =* snare. v. 15. *heir =* conqueror who shall possess the land: Sargon and the Assyrians; *he shall come,* rather, the glory of Israel shall come even unto Adullam, i.e., take refuge in a cave. v. 16 *poll thee,* viz., tear out thy hair; *delicate children:* "the children of thy delight" (so R.V.) ; *are gone* should be "will go." The Exile is in the future.

Chapter 2. v. 3. *family,* i.e., the nation, the Northern and Southern King-doms alike, the whole family (Am. 3:1) ; *necks:* the "evil" is a foreign yoke (Jer. 27:12). v. 4. *parable,* a taunting song; *he hath changed,* etc.: the idea is that the promised land has been transferred to the heathen; *turning away,* rather, (as in R.V.) "to the rebellious" (i.e., their conquerors). v. 5 alludes to the original distribution of Canaan by lot (Josh. 14:2). v. 6. False prophets protest that Micah should not keep harping upon such things; *that they shall not take shame:* "shame will not overtake us" (Am. Trans.). v. 7 is best understood as the words of the false prophets who seek to lull the people into a false sense of security. v. 8. Micah's reply: *even of late:* rather, but of late; *pull off the robe from the garment,* i.e., appropriate the more valuable upper garment, possibly as "a remorseless use of the rights of a creditor." v. 9. *women,* i.e., unprotected widows; *my glory:* the privilege which belonged to every one of God's people. v. 10. As a just retribution, Canaan was no longer to be to them a land of rest (cf. Deut. 12:9; Ps. 95:11). The land is polluted by the sins of the people. v. 11. The false prophet who, walking in the spirit (or wind) of falsehood promises prosperity, he would be the prophet of the people. vv. 12 and 13 are so abrupt in their transition that it is evident either that they are misplaced or most probably that they belong to a later editor. v. 12. *O Jacob:* the whole of the nation is meant; *Bozrah:* the sheep will be gathered even from Edom. v. 13. "one of that breaketh through" (a human leader) is gone up before them; they have broken through their barriers, and have passed out of the gate of their prison.

Chapter 3. vv. 2, 3. A figurative expression: "who act like cannibals." Between verses 3 and 4 there may have been a clause missing in the transcription, describing a "Day of the Lord"; v. 5. *bite with their teeth:* an idea in harmony with the preceding image of cannibalism; they declare war against anyone who does not fill their mouths; or, the idea may be that if these false prophets are not richly fed for preaching peace, then they will change their tune and speak of war. vv. 6ff. are addressed to the rulers; their land will be overwhelmed and there shall be no open vision; the false prophets will be put to shame. v. 12. Quoted by Jeremiah (26:17-19).

Chapter 4. v. 1. *in the last days:* rather, in the days to come; *in the top of the mountains,* i.e., on the highest mountain. v. 2. Jerusalem is to become the metropolis of the world (Is. 11:10, 60:3; Jer. 3:17; Zech. 2:11). v. 3. *among many people:* rather, between many peoples (R.V.); *beat their swords* (cf. Is. 2:4, Hos. 2:18; Zech. 9:10); in Joel 3:10 we have the same figure reversed. v. 5. *will walk:* rather, walk (R.V. marg.). v. 7. "I will treat Israel in spite of her feeble condition as the remnant to which the Messianic promises belong." v. 8. *tower of the flock,* i.e., Jerusalem; *the first dominion,* i.e., the whole united kingdom of Israel. v. 9 refers to the coming capture of Jerusalem and of its king; *counselor:* a synonym of king. v. 10. *shalt go to Babylon:* these words must be a later insertion, since it was a century afterwards that the Babylonians captured Jerusalem; at this time Babylon was a province of Assyria. v. 11. *now also:* rather, and now; *many nations,* i.e., the Assyrians; *look upon:* namely, in contempt; *thresh:* a figurative expression for "conquer" (cf. Is. 41:15; Jer. 51:33). v. 13. *people:* rather, peoples (R.V.).

Chapter 5. v. 1. "Assyria may marshal her hosts, may lay siege against the holy city, may violate the person of the king, but from insignificant Bethlehem a royal Deliverer shall arise." v. 2. *Ephratah* (a fuller form of Ephrath) was another name for Bethlehem (I Sam. 17:12; Ruth 1:2); *thousands* is another name for a family or clan (cf. Num. 1:16; Josh. 22:14, 21). v. 3. Because the deliverance of Israel is to be of the Lord, she will first be given over into the hands of her foes; *then* = and or until. v. 5. *shepherds,* viz., princes; *seven* is the perfect number; *eight,* that is, more than enough. v. 6. *Nimrod* (cf. Gen. 10:8). v. 7. *people:* read "peoples." v. 9. *thine hand shall be,* or, as in R.V., "let thine hand be," so also in next clause. vv. 10-15. The holy city is to be purged of its implements of war and of its idolatries. v. 11. *cities,* i.e., as centers of luxury and of immorality; v. 12. *soothsayers,* i.e., sorcerers. v. 14. *groves:* rather, Asherim (R.V.; cf. Ex. 34:13); Asherah was a sensual Canaanitish goddess whose symbol was a wooden pillar or tree. v. 15. *Such as they have not heard:* rather, who have not hearkened and been obedient.

Chapter 6. v. 2. *strong:* rather, enduring (so R.V.). v. 5. *from Shittim to Gilgal:* the grammatical connection is not clear. Some words may have dropped out. The R.V. inserts "remember." The miraculous crossing of the Jordan from Shittim, the last station on its other side, to Gilgal, the first in the land of Canaan, may be the reference here. v. 8 (cf. Deut. 10:12). v. 9. *and the man of wisdom,* etc.: a better rendering is: "wisdom is it to fear thy name." v. 10. "Does the oppressor go on heaping up his loot?" v. 11. *shall I count them?* A different rendering puts this in the third person, "Canst thou (O Jerusalem) be pure?" v. 14. *thy casting down* = emptiness or humiliation (R.V.); *shalt take hold,* i.e., shalt seek to remove thy goods, but shalt not be able to take them away in safety.

Chapter 7. v. 3. The text is very obscure. It may mean: "Their hands are only for evil to do it skillfully"; the sense of the following clause is that the prince asks the judge to shut his eyes to some act of violence and the judge is ready to do so for a reward; *so they wrap it up,* i.e., weave their infamous schemes. v. 7. *therefore I:* rather, but as for me, I. v. 11. "Here the soliloquy of repentant Israel ceases and a prophetic announcement begins"; *in the day that:* rather, A day will come for rebuilding thy walls; *decree:* rather, boundary (so R.V. marg.). v. 12. *he shall come:* rather, men shall come; *fortified cities:* rather, and from the cities of Egypt; *even to the river,* i.e., the Euphrates. v. 14. An abrupt transition. The prophet makes supplication for the salvation of the people; the pastures of *Bashan* were famous, and Gilead was noted for its cattle (Num. 32:1; Jer. 50:19). v. 15. Here is the divine answer to the prophet's plea; *unto him,* viz., unto the people. v. 16. *They shall lay their hand upon their mouth,* a mark of reverence (cf. Job. 21:5; Is. 52:15); v. 17 *they shall move,* etc.: "like crawling things of the earth they shall come trembling out of their close places" (R.V.).

ZEPHANIAH

The text of Zephaniah has presented difficulties to the scholars. It is difficult to know at times whether or not we have the true reading. There have been evident insertions, and there are words and grammatical constructions which are unusual, some of which appear only in later writers.

Chapter 1. v. 2. *from off the land,* i.e., the face of the earth; man and beast alike shall be swept away. v. 3 (cf. Hos. 4:3; Ez. 38:19). *Stumbling-blocks* (cf. Ez. 14:3, 4, 7); the sense is obscure, it may mean ruins, or, as in Ezekiel, idols; possibly the meaning is "I will cause the wicked to stumble." Some scholars omit the phrase, which seems out of harmony with the rest of the verse. v. 4. The universal judgment is now focused upon Judah. The words *from this place* indicate that the prophet lived in Jerusalem. *Baal* is a general term indicating any false worship of Jehovah; *Chemarims,* means false and idolatrous priests (cf. Hos. 10:5; II Kings 23:5), while the *priests* refer to the degenerate priests of Jehovah. v. 5. *host of heaven,* i.e., the heavenly bodies, sun, moon and stars; *Malcam:* probably Molech, a heathen god: a generic term for heathen gods in general. The people swear indiscriminately to Jehovah and to heathen gods. v. 7. *Day of the Lord* (see Am. 5:18); *a sacrifice:* Israel is slain for the sacrifice, and the guests to eat the sacrificial meal (i.e., the foes of Israel) are invited and receive the ceremonial sanctification (cf. I Sam. 16:5; Is. 13:3). v. 8. *princes and the king's children* (i.e., sons): their condemnation by the prophet is especially noteworthy since Zephaniah himself came of royal blood. Josiah and his sons are not referred to. v. 9. The threshold was considered a dangerous part of the house as the abode of some demon (cf. I Sam. 5:5). v. 10. *second* [*quarter*]: probably an addition or suburb of the city where the aristocracy may have lived; *crashing,* i.e., a shriek. v. 11. *Maktesh:* the word occurs nowhere else as a proper name; it denotes a depression or valley within the city that lay exposed to attack; *merchant people,* i.e., people of Canaan (so R.V.): not the Canaanites as a whole but specifically merchants or traders (cf. Prov. 31:24, R. V. [marg]; Zech. 14:21). v. 12. *settled on their lees,* i.e., men who have lived at ease and are sunk in apathy, who feel that the Lord is indifferent to moral distinctions. v. 14 (cf. Is. 13:6; Joel 2:2, 11, 31; Mal. 4:5). v. 18. *the whole land,* rather the whole earth (cf. 3:8).

Chapter 2. v. 1. The sense is obscure. The verb *gather* may possibly have the meaning to turn pale, to be ashamed, and this would agree very well with the next clause. v. 3. Only a remnant of the people shall escape destruction and they only if they turn to the Lord with all their hearts. vv. 4–15. This passage appears to be written in the elegiac measure; in some verses the rhythm is broken and imperfect. v. 4. *Gaza and Ashkelon, Ashdod and Ekron:* well-known cities of the Philistines; a fifth, Gath, no longer existed at this time; *at the noonday* (cf. Jer. 15:8): the idea may be a sudden or open attack. v. 5. *Cherethites* = Philistines (cf. I Sam. 30:14). v. 6. The text is not clear. By *cottages* may be meant *caves* (so R.V. marg.): the idea is that all that will be left of the land of the Philistines will be pastures for cattle. v. 7. A remnant of the people shall have its prosperity restored. The phrase *turn away their captivity* is used figuratively (cf. Job. 42:10; Am. 9:14; Hos. 6:11). vv. 8–11. Probably a later insertion. v. 8. The Lord has heard the taunts of Moab and the insulting words of the Ammonites, wherewith they have vaunted themselves against the territory of Israel. v. 9. The idea is of utter barrenness. v. 11. By a demonstration of His power, the Lord will show how impotent other gods are, and the nations will turn from them and worship Him. v. 14. *beasts of the nations;* i.e., every beast of the field; *upper lintels,* i.e., *chapiters* (R.V.): the carved tops of the pillars that now lie in the dust. *"Their voice shall sing":* The word *voice* should probably be changed to mean "owl": "The owl shall hoot in the window"; *desolation:* with difference of one letter, the word means raven or buzzard, doubtless the meaning here; *uncover the cedarwork* = rase to the foundations.

Chapter 3 v. 2. "She has listened to no voice." v. 3. *gnaw not the bones till the morrow:* the sense is uncertain; possibly, eat everything in sight. v. 5. They do all this evil undeterred by the fact that the righteous Lord is in their midst. v. 8. *until* = for: for the day that I arise *to testify,* a better reading than "to the prey." v. 9. The sense is: "I will turn their unclean lips into a purified speech." v. 10. Am. Trans. translates: "From beyond the rivers of Ethiopia, to the farthest regions of the north, they shall bring offerings unto me." vv. 9 and 10 interrupt the sense and are probably a later insertion. v. 11 connects logically with v. 8. v. 15. *The King of Israel:* i.e., the Lord of Israel (cf. Is. 41:21). v. 16. *be slack,* i.e., hang down in terror or helplessness. v. 18. This verse is obscure. The sense may be: "The scattered of thy congregation have I gathered, upon whom reproach hath lain."

<h1 style="text-align:center">NAHUM</h1>

Chapter 1. v. 1. *burden* = oracle or prophecy (cf. Is. 13:1, 14:28, 15:1, etc.) ; *vision,* i.e., prophetic intuition, a general term for prophecy. v. 2. *reserveth:* this idea is denied in Jer. 3:5 and is forbidden to man in Lev. 19:18; but the difference in circumstances must be noted. v. 7. *stronghold* (cf. Jer. 16:19; Zech. 9:12). v. 8. *an utter end,* as in Jer. 4:27, 5:18, 30:11, who uses the same expression in reverse; the ruin which now confronts Nineveh will be once for all. v. 10. The sense is not clear. The text is corrupt. For *thorns,* cf. II Sam. 23:6ff.; Is. 33:12. Am. Trans. translates: "They are thorns cut down and dried out; they will be consumed like dry stubble." v. 11. Sennacherib is meant. v. 12. The text is difficult. The sense is: "When many days are fulfilled, they shall be cut off and pass away." v. 14. "I will make thy grave a disgrace for thou art of small account."

Chapter 2. v. 2. This verse follows naturally after 1:15, and is misplaced. v. 3. *with flaming torches,* i.e., flame like torches; *fir-trees* (R.V. spears) *are shaken:* better, "The horses will quiver." v. 4. *broad ways,* i.e., plains in suburbs. v. 5. The Assyrian king summons his nobles for the defense of the city. They *stumble,* i.e., they are badly disciplined. v. 6. The enemy inundates Nineveh from the river Tigris. v. 7. *Huzzab* = the queen or mistress of the palace; *tabering,* i.e., beating upon their breasts. v. 8. The vast population of Nineveh shall melt away like water escaping from a tank. v. 11. Nineveh is called a den of lions.

Chapter 3. v. 1. *robbery* = booty. v. 4. *whoredoms:* the word is used to describe a beguiling friendship by which Nineveh has lured nations to their ruin; *witchcrafts,* i.e., spells or sorceries. v. 5. refers to the practice of exposing a woman convicted of unchastity (cf. Ez. 16:37; Hos. 2:3) ; *discover* = uncover. v. 6. *make thee vile,* i.e., treat you with contempt. v. 8. *No,* the city of No-Amon, called Thebes by the Greeks, the capital of Upper Egypt; by the *sea* is meant the waters of the river Nile. v. 9. *Put and Lubim:* peoples of North Africa; Nineveh is to share the fate of Thebes. v. 11. Am. Trans.: "You, too, shall seek refuge from the foe." v. 13. *gates,* i.e., mountain passes. v. 17. *crowned captains:* the sense is uncertain; the words may denote princes and nobles, or watchers and scribes. v. 18. *shepherds,* i.e., rulers. v. 19. *bruit,* i.e., report.

HABAKKUK

Chapter 1. v. 1. *burden,* i.e., the truth or revelation. v. 2. *violence:* the word means wrong or injury whether or not accompanied by force. v. 3. *shew me,* i.e., cause me to see; *grievance* means trouble or mischief. v. 4. *slacked,* that is, paralyzed and ineffectual; *judgment,* etc.: see R.V. marg. "goeth not forth to victory"; *wrong judgment,* etc., i.e., judgment goeth forth perverted (R.V.). v. 6. The prophet writing some twenty-five years later throws himself dramatically back into the past; *hasty,* i.e., impetuous, driven by violent impulse. v. 7. The Chaldeans are superior and autocratic and assume supremacy and sovereignty (dignity). v. 9. The striving of their faces is forward, "set eagerly as the east wind." v. 11. "Then he changes like the wind and sweeps onward in his guilt." v. 12. It is necessary to suppose the lapse of some time between verses 11 and 12. The Chaldeans have now become an imminent threat to the Jews. v. 12. *shall not die:* it cannot be God's purpose that His people shall be destroyed. v. 13. *treacherously,* i.e., ruthlessly. v. 16. He worships the means by which he takes his captives. v. 17. "Shall he keep on emptying his net and never cease slaying the nations?"

Chapter 2. v. 1. *What I shall answer,* etc.: the words should be transposed: "What answer I shall get concerning my complaint" (R.V.). v. 3. The vision is a witness that the time is appointed and that the end is determined. v. 4. *faith* = faithfulness. v. 5. The text is faulty. There is no point in the mention of wine. The sense is that the treacherous and faithless man comes to nought, even the arrogant and restless man who is insatiable and avaricious. v. 6. Here begins a series of five woes pronounced against the Chaldeans: *all these,* i.e., the nations they have overrun; *ladeth himself with thick clay* (R.V. "pledges"), i.e., loads himself with debts that one day they shall be compelled to pay. v. 7. These creditors will rise up suddenly and strike back. v. 10. "Devised disgrace for your own household . . . so forfeiting your own life" (Am. Trans.). v. 11. The very materials which the enemy has used to build his nest shall cry out against him. v. 13. The possessions which the enemy has labored to acquire are all destined for the fire. He wears himself out for nothing. v. 14. A new world shall be built on the ruins of the old. v. 15. The contemptuous treatment of helpless nations by their conqueror is represented under the figure of making men drunk and then exposing them to shame; *puttest thy bottle,* i.e., makest him to drink from the cup. v. 16. "filled with shame and not with glory; drink thyself and be disgraced."

v. 17. Lebanon was the haunt of beasts (cf. Is. 40:16); *which made them afraid* = shall terrify or break thee; the ravage and terror carried into Lebanon shall come back in destruction on the Chaldean.

Chapter 3. v. 2. *afraid,* i.e., am filled with awe; *in the midst of the years,* i.e., at this late hour. v. 3. *Teman* is a district lying to the northwest of Edom (cf. Ez. 25:13); *Paran:* a mountainous region north of Sinai, the scene of the divine manifestation. v. 4. *hiding* = hiding place. v. 6. *measured the earth:* by a slight emendation these words may mean "he made the earth to rock"; *were scattered,* i.e., shattered; *his ways,* etc. = these be his ways from of old. v. 7. *Cushan:* the country of the Midianites. v. 9. A description of the redemption of the Exodus from Egypt: *the oaths of the tribes:* the meaning is unknown; Am. Trans. translates: "Thou didst fill thy quivers full of arrows." v. 13. *woundest,* etc.: "Thou didst smite off the head from the house of the wicked" (R.V. marg.) ; *neck:* possibly, rock. v. 16. The second part of this verse is very obscure; it seems to have no connection with what has preceded; Am. Trans. translates: "I will wait for the day of trouble to come upon the people that oppress us."

HAGGAI

Chapter 1. v. 1. *Zerubbabel:* In I Chron. 3:19 he is called the son of Pedaiah, probably a younger brother of Shealtiel, who had no sons of his own; hence Zerubbabel became the heir, "son," of Shealtiel; he was the recognized head of the Jews in Babylon (Ezra 3:8) and bears a leading part in the history of the Return. v. 4. see R.V.: "Is it time for you, yourselves"; *ceiled* = covered or boarded inside: this was a luxury even in kings' houses (Jer. 22:14). v. 6. The description refers to the whole period in which the rebuilding of the Temple has been neglected. v. 8. *mountain* = "hill country" (R.V. marg.), where timber was to be found; *I will be glorified* = show my glory (see 2:9). v. 9. *ye run* = "while ye run" (R.V.) to adorn your own houses. v. 10. Not only is there a drought of rain, but even dew is shut off; the copious dews in Palestine were often a welcome substitute for rain. v. 13. *messenger:* Haggai is the only prophet who uses this title of himself. The Hebrew word is "malachi," the anonymous title of the author of that book.

Chapter 2. v. 3. *in comparison of it:* these words should be omitted as in R.V. v. 5. *my spirit remaineth:* read, "and my spirit abode" as in R.V. (cf. Is. 63:11; Zech. 4:6.) v. 6. *saith the Lord of hosts:* this expression is a marked characteristic of the prophecies of Haggai and "Malachi." It is found here four times in as many verses, and is a solemn and reiterated assurance of the power and resources of God; *yet once,* etc., i.e., "Yet a little while and I will shake." v. 7. *desire:* the following verb is in the plural, and thus desire must be rendered "the desirable or costly things of all nations"; The meaning is that the treasures of the world belong to God and are at His disposal (cf. Is. 60:5-7, 11, 13, 17, 61:6). v. 9. Read as in R.V.: "The latter glory of this house." v. 12. *holy flesh,* i.e., flesh that has been offered in sacrifice to God (cf. Jer. 11:15). v. 14. *there,* i.e., on the altar built on their return from Babylon (Ezra 3:3). v. 15. The sense is: "Consider this from now on: Since the time when no building of the Temple went on, how have you fared?" v. 16. *since those days were,* i.e., through all that time (R.V.). v. 17. Two diseases of the corn (cf. Deut. 28:22; Am. 4:9). Haggai adds *hail* as destructive of the vines (Ps. 78:47). v. 20. *again* = the second time (so R.V.). v. 22. *heathen:* read, "nations" (R.V.) as in v. 7; *shall come down,* i.e., be brought low (Cf. Is. 34:7). These wars and the overthrow of the pagan nations refer doubtless to the revolts that occurred during the reign of Darius and threatened the destruction of the Persian Empire. v. 23. *signet,* i.e., signet ring, the symbol of authority (cf. Ecclus. 49:11, a plain reference to this passage in Haggai).

ZECHARIAH

Chapter 1. v. 1. *son of Berechiah:* in Ezra 5:1 and Neh. 12:16 he is called the son (not the grandson as here) of Iddo. v. 4. *former prophets:* the reference is not to any particular prophet or prophets, but to all who had preceded; *have cried:* better, "cried" as in R.V. v. 6. The sense is: "did not my words and my statutes finally overtake your fathers till they turned?"; *returned:* better, "turned," as in R.V. v. 8. *myrtle trees:* said to be indigenous to Palestine (cf. Neh. 8:15); *in the bottom,* i.e., in the depths of the valley, possibly here the Valley of the Kedron; *speckled:* R.V., "sorrel." v. 9. *the angel that talked with me,* the uniform title of the angel throughout the visions. v. 10. *the man,* i.e., the rider on the red horse (cf. v. 8); he also is the angel of the Lord in v. 11. v. 12. *threescore and ten years* (cf. Jer. 25:11). "Why art thou still angry with us now that the appointed time of our punishment has passed?" v. 15. *at ease:* as described in v. 11. (cf. Ps. 123:4); v. 16. *a line,* i.e., a measuring line to mark out the rebuilding of the city; it had been measured before for destruction (II Kings 21:13; Lam. 2:8). v. 18.

The horn is a symbol of honor (I Sam. 2:1; Job 16:15) and of power (Jer. 48:25; Am. 6:13; Dan. 7:21). Here the latter is meant. By the number *four* may be signified that enemies encompass Israel on all sides of the compass. v. 19. The whole Jewish people is included in this prediction. v. 20. *carpenters* (R.V., "smiths") : the word is used for workers in both wood and metals (Is. 44:12, 13; II Sam. 5:11).

Chapter 2. v. 1. *a man,* i.e., a servant or apprentice. v. 4. *towns without walls,* i.e., as open, unwalled country villages (cf. Ez. 38:11; Deut. 3:5; Esth. 9:19). v. 6. *come forth:* to be omitted (so R.V.) ; *land of the north,* i.e., Babylonia. v. 8. *after the glory:* rather, after glory, possibly, to manifest my glory. Am. Trans. translates: "hereafter he will send me forth with honor"; *apple of his eye* (cf. Deut. 32:10; Ps. 17:8). v. 11. *be joined,* rather, join themselves to (so R.V.).

Chapter 3. v. 1. *Satan:* appears only in the O.T. in I Chron 21:1; Ps. 109:6, here, and in Job; *resist* = to be his adversary (so R.V.). v. 2. *a brand,* etc. (cf. Am. 4:11). v. 4. *that stood before him,* i.e., attendant angels; *change of raiment:* in R.V., "rich apparel." v. 5. *I said:* Zechariah as onlooker makes this suggestion. v. 6. *protested* = solemnly affirmed. v. 7. *places to walk,* i.e., a place of access (R.V.) to God. v. 8. *sit* = that are accustomed to sit; *men wondered at,* i.e., men which are a sign (R.V.), i.e., "men of good omen" (Am. Trans.) (cf. Ez. 12:6, 24:24, 27); *branch* (cf. Jer. 23:5, 33:15). v. 9. *seven:* the perfect number; *eyes:* denoting perfect watchfulness and care; *in one day:* possibly here the Day of Atonement is meant; to the Christian it can mean only "on the day when Jesus died."

Chapter 4. v. 2. *a bowl:* better, its bowl, or reservoir: the meaning of this is contained in v. 6; no human agency is needed; the bowl yields a ceaseless supply of oil; *seven pipes:* "there are seven pipes to each of the lamps" (R.V.) : the perfect number seven denotes the plentifulness of the supply, fed by the two olive trees (vv. 11, 12) each of which had a fruit-bearing branch which emptied the oil by a golden tube into the oil bowl of the candlesticks. v. 7. *great mountain* (cf. Is. 40:4, 49:11) : the obstacles of the power of their captors and the resistance of the people first to return and then to persevere in the building of the Temple. v. 10. *those* = these, as in R.V.; the seven lights are the seven eyes of God. v. 12 is a gloss which interrupts the context.

Chapter 5. v. 3. *earth:* read, "land" (R.V.) : the land of Judah is meant; *stealeth:* this commandment and that in v. 4 are singled out perhaps because they were the most prevalent sins among the Jews; *on this side,* etc.: the R.V. translates: "On the one side, on the other side," i.e., the roll was written on both sides. v. 4. *remain* (R.V., "abide") till the house has been destroyed. v. 5. *went forth* = came forth. v. 6. *ephah:* the largest vessel in use among the Jews, round in shape: its actual size is here exaggerated to suit the prophet's purpose; *resemblance,* etc.: the sense is: this ephah and all that you shall witness is the presentation of what shall happen to the wickedness of the land. v. 7. *talent* = lid. v. 11. *to build it a house,* i.e., to put it where it belongs, to bring it to its proper habitation; *Shinar:* a name given in the O.T. to Babylonia (cf. Gen. 10:10; Is. 11:11).

Chapter 6. v. 1. "And again I lifted up mine eyes" (R.V.) : it is not necessary to identify four kingdoms as the destination of the chariots, nor the two mountains between which they pass; *of brass,* i.e., even the mightiest powers have their course determined by God's immutable will. v. 3. *grisled and bay:* rather, "spotted and strong" (R.V. marg.). v. 5. *spirits* = winds (so R.V.). v. 7. the bay horses seek to have a roving commission to cover the earth, and this is granted them. vv. 10, 11. The text is somewhat involved. It should read: "Take of the captivity . . . and come thou thyself to take it in person into the house of Josiah to which they have come from Babylon and take silver and gold," etc. v. 11. For *crowns* read "crown," and for *Joshua* read "Zerubbabel." v. 12. *out of his place,* i.e., he shall branch forth from his place (cf. Is. 11:1). v. 13. You are building the outer temple, but the building of the true temple is reserved for him. v. 14. *Helem,* probably a copyist's error for Heldai (v. 10), and Hen is another name for this reputed son of Zephaniah who previously has been called Josiah. Nothing is known of him. The LXX does not treat these and the others mentioned as proper names. The text is obscure.

Chapter 7. v. 1. *fourth year,* i.e., nearly two years after the visions. v. 2. "Now they of Bethel had sent" (so R.V.) ; *pray before,* i.e., to implore the favor of (cf. Ps. 45:12). v. 3. *fifth month* (cf. II Kings 25:8, 9; Jer. 52:12, 13). v. 5. *seventh month:* an additional fast kept during the Exile to commemorate the final calamity at Jerusalem (cf. II Kings 25). v. 8. No interval of time is implied. v. 9. *judgment* = justice. v. 11 (cf. Neh. 9:29; Hos. 4:16). v. 12. *in his spirit:* rather, by his spirit (R.V.). v. 14 (cf. Deut. 28:33; Jer. 16:13).

Chapter 8. v. 1. *again* = and. v. 2. *I was* = I am (so R.V.). v. 6. *in these days* = in those days (R.V.) ; so also in v. 10. v. 7. "The things that are impossible with men are possible with God." v. 9. *by the mouth:* rather, from the mouth (R.V.). v. 12. Read, "there shall be the seed of peace." v. 16. The judgment of peace is righteous judgment which alone secures peace. v. 19. On the tenth month the siege of Jerusalem had begun (II Kings 25:1;

Jer. 39:1) and on the fourth month it surrendered (Jer. 39:2, 3, 52:6, 7). Hence the fasts.

MALACHI

Chapter 1. v. 1. *burden,* i.e. a divine announcement or oracle (cf. Nah. 1:1; Hab. 1:1; Zech. 9:1). v. 2. *wherein:* these short, pointed questions are a characteristic of Malachi's style. v. 3. See R.V.: "I made his mountains a desolation and gave his heritage to the jackals of the wilderness." v. 4. *impoverished* = beaten down, laid prostrate: the desolation of Edom here referred to was caused by an invasion of Arabian tribesmen; *return and build:* since there is no evidence that the Edomites at this time were driven from their land, this should be rendered "rebuild." v. 5. *from the border* = beyond the borders. v. 6. *fear:* rather, reverence. v. 7. *bread* = food. v. 8. *if* = when; *accept thy person,* i.e., receive it graciously. v. 9. *beseech,* i.e., propitiate; *by your means,* etc., i.e., "when things like this have come from your hands, can He respect you?" v. 10. "O that there were one among you that would close the doors [of the Temple], that you might not kindle mine altar in vain?" (Am. Trans.) v. 11. *shall be:* rather, is, as in R.V. v. 12. After allowing unworthy sacrifices to be offered, the priests complained that they were inadequately remunerated, that their allotted portion was "contemptible," and that the service of the sanctuary was but weariness. v. 13. *snuffed* = sniff: in the present tense; *brought* = bring; *torn* = mangled, from having been taken by violence (see R.V.). v. 14. He vows it, but sacrifices in its stead a damaged and miserable beast; *dreadful,* i.e., feared.

Chapter 2. v. 3. *corrupt* = rebuke; *feasts* = sacrifices (so R.V.); *one shall take you,* i.e., "ye shall be taken" (R.V.) or "I will carry you away from beside me" (Am. Trans.). v. 4. *my covenant* (cf. Num. 25:12, 13). v. 9. *in the law,* i.e., they did not interpret the law impartially. v. 11. *of a strange god,* i.e., of a heathen race. v. 15. The sense is obscure: "Not one did this who had a remnant of spirituality." v. 16b. "So take heed to your spiritual life and be not faithless."

Chapter 3. v. 9. *have robbed* = are robbing. v. 10. *all the tithes:* better, "the whole tithe" (so R.V.). v. 11. the *devourer* doubtless refers to the locust. v. 15. Now we see the haughty prospering, evildoers are eminent, and those who have defied God have escaped punishment.

Chapter 4. v. 4. *The Law of Moses* refers to the Deuteronomic Code. This was later succeeded by the Priestly Code under Ezra and Nehemiah, the influence of which is discernible in the prophet Joel, whose book follows.

v. 5. *Elijah* (cf. Matt. 17:10; Mark 9:11; John 1:21). In Matt 11:10, 14 and 17:12–13, the messenger is identified with John the Baptist, who was to come "in the spirit and power of Elijah" (Luke 1:17).

OBADIAH

v. 3. By *rock* is meant *Seir,* the Edomite capital; in Greek, "Petra." v. 4. *nest among the stars* (cf. Num. 24:21) ; *I will bring thee down* (see Am. 9:2). v. 5. Insert the word "only" before *till.* They will not stop when they have had enough but will go on to ravage the land. v. 7. *they that eat thy bread* is a gloss: read simply, "They lay a snare for thee." v. 9. *Teman* (cf. Gen. 36:11; Am. 1:11–12): an important district in Edom, and so used of Edom itself. v. 11. The phrase *stoodest on the other side,* i.e., without intervening, is found in II Sam. 18:13 (R.V.), II Kings 2:7; *cast lots* (cf. Joel 3:3). v. 12. *shouldest not have looked,* i.e., with pleasure. v. 14. *crossway,* i.e., clearing. v. 15. The two clauses should be transposed: the latter refers to what precedes, the former to what follows. For the following verses cf. Joel 3:1–3. v. 18. *the house of Joseph:* the Northern Israelites are included in this promise of redemption. vv. 20 and 21 are probably corrupt. The general sense is that the exiles of the Northern Kingdom will be settled in the north, and those of the Southern Kingdom in the south. *Zarephath* (see I Kings 17:9): in the north of Palestine near Sidon; *Sepharad:* a district in North Asia Minor, here used of Babylonia in general.

JOEL

Chapter 1. v. 4. Successive swarms of locusts appearing in the same year and in following years are indicated by four names which are listed in a different order in 2:25. They may describe different species of locusts, less probably the locust in the different stages of its development. vv. 5ff; all classes are to unite in lamenting this calamity which brings destitution to them all. v. 5. *howl,* i.e., in wild and desperate grief. So in vv. 11, 13 (cf. Am. 8:3). v. 6. *nation,* i.e., an army (cf. Prov. 30:24–26) ; v. 11. *be ye ashamed* = show your disappointment. v. 13. The sacrifices are no longer possible. v. 15. *Day of the Lord:* see Am. 5:18; Zeph. 1:7, 14; Is. 13:6. v. 16. *meat,* i.e., food. v. 17. The grains shrivel (R.V. marg.) as the result of the drought. The text is uncertain. Am. Trans. translates: "the mules stamp at their stalls." v. 18. *are perplexed:* wandering about in quest of food. v. 20. *rivers.* i.e., channels (cf. Is. 8:7; Ps. 18:15).

Chapter 2. v. 2 (cf. Zeph. 1:15). The masses of locusts obscure the sun. *As the morning,* etc.: "The figure is of dawn . . . struggling with a mass of cloud and mist and expresses the gleams of white which so often break through a locust cloud" (G. A. Smith). But Am. Trans. translates: "Like blackness spread over the mountains," which is better suited to the context. v. 3. *a fire devoureth before them,* etc., i.e., the country over which the locusts have passed is as bare as if scorched by fire. v. 4. *as horsemen:* both because of their speed and because of the resemblance between the head of a locust and the head of a horse. v. 5. *like the noise of chariots* (cf. Rev. 9:9); *like the noise of flame:* the reference here is to the sound made by the locusts while feeding. v. 6. "At their presence the peoples are in anguish: all faces are waxed pale" (R.V.). v. 8. *when they fall upon the sword:* "they plunge through the missiles unbroken" (G. A. Smith); weapons are powerless to arrest their progress. vv. 10, 11. Supernatural features are added by the prophet's imagination. v. 11. *camp,* i.e., host; *who can abide it?* (cf. Jer. 10:10; Mal. 3:2). v. 13b. Almost verbatim from Ex. 34:6; *repenteth,* so also Jonah 4:2b. v. 14. *blessing:* by permitting the earth to yield materials for sacrificial offerings. v. 17. *that the heathen,* etc.: the probable rendering is: "that the heathen should mock them" (R.V. marg.). v. 18. *will be:* the past tense is better; read "was" (so R.V.). v. 20. *the northern army,* i.e., the locusts swarming from the north; *east sea,* i.e., the Dead Sea (cf. Ez. 47:18; Zech. 14:8); *utmost sea,* i.e., the western sea (so R.V.): the Mediterranean; *because:* rather, although. v. 21. *will do:* cf. R.V. "hath done." v. 23. *moderately:* the word means "according to righteousness," i.e., "as God's righteousness prompts him to give it" (Driver); v. 24. *fats,* i.e., wine vats. v. 32b. This should be rendered: "For in Mount Zion and Jerusalem there shall be those that escape, and the fugitives will be the remnant whom the Lord calleth."

Chapter 3. v. 2. *valley of Jehoshaphat:* the name means "God judgeth"; the location of this valley is uncertain, its symbolical name is the significant thing; *plead* = enter into judgment. v. 3. *cast lots:* conquerors divided captives by lot and then used them as they pleased. v. 4. The sense is: what are you to me? Are you paying me back for something I have done to you, or are you trying to do something to me? v. 5. *temples* = palaces. v. 8. *Sabeans,* i.e., the men of Sheba who lived in distant Southwest Arabia (cf. I Kings 10:2, 10; Jer. 6:20; Is. 60:6; Ez. 27:22; Ps. 72:15). v. 9. The thought of vv. 1–3 is resumed. v. 10. Note the strange contrast between this verse and Is. 2:4. v. 11. The nations having been bidden to assemble in all their strength, the prophet now prays the Lord to cause His angelic hosts to descend to meet them. v. 12. This is the Lord's answer: let the nations assemble; He is ready for them. v. 13. *fats* = vats, as in 2:24. v. 14. *decision,* i.e., determination or final settlement. v. 16. *strength* = stronghold. v. 18 (cf. Am. 9:13) ; *fountain* (cf. Ez. 47:1–12; Zech. 14:8) : Waters actually gushed out beneath the Temple area in a perennial spring (Is. 8:6; Ps. 46:4; John 9:7) ; these waters should be increased in volume so as to irrigate the barren wastes of Judah; *valley of Shittim:* probably the long desert valley stretching from Kidron at the base of the Mount of Olives southeast to the Dead Sea. v. 21. Either "I will declare innocent those who apparently were not innocent" (because they had died unavenged), or, "I will avenge their blood; I will not leave it unpunished."

JONAH

Chapter 1. v. 3. Tarshish: probably Tartessus, a Phoenician city in the south of Spain; Jonah was bidden to go northeast from his home and he fled in the opposite direction; *Joppa:* the well-known port on the Mediterranean, and the only one on this coast; the harbor is small, inconvenient, and even unsafe. v. 4. *sent out:* lit., hurled (so R.V. marg.) ; *was like to be broken:* lit., thought to be broken (cf. I Kings 22:48; Acts 27:41). v. 5. The sailors were probably polytheist Phoenicians, or they may have belonged to different nations; *the wares:* not the cargo, but dispensable furnishings, spare tackling, etc. (cf. Acts 27:19) ; *lighten:* either to lighten the ship (Am. Trans.) or to make things easier for the sailors (cf. R.V., "unto them"). v. 7. An interval of time has elapsed; prayer has not availed to still the storm; *cast lots* (cf. Josh. 7:14–21; I Sam. 14:36–46). v. 8. *for whose cause,* i.e., what in your conduct has caused it? Jonah is given the opportunity to clear himself in spite of the imminent danger. v. 11. *the sea wrought:* "grew more and more tempestuous" (R.V.). v. 16. *made vows,* i.e., they would offer other gifts to God aside from the poor sacrifice they were able to make on shipboard, when they had come safely to land.

Chapter 2. v. 1. Note the expression *his God* to whom he has now drawn near in penitence. So also v. 6. and cf. Pss. 22:1, 104:1. v. 2. *by reason of:* better, out of (so R.V. marg.) ; *belly of hell:* i.e., "the heart of Sheol" (the unseen world). v. 3. *floods,* lit., the river: used of the flowing or current of the sea. v. 4. *I will look again,* i.e., in prayer; Am. Trans., however, translates: "How shall I ever again look upon thy holy temple?" So also G. A. Smith. v. 5. *to the soul,* i.e., so as to endanger his life. v. 6. The mountains are conceived poetically to be rooted in the lowest depths of the sea: *with her bars:* the earth was barred against him forever; *from corruption:* rather, from the pit (so R.V.). v. 8. *lying vanities:* this expression refers not only to idolaters but to all who, like Jonah, have followed the devices and desires of their own hearts; *forsake their mercy,* i.e., their piety, that which binds them to God.

Chapter 3. v. 2. *preach:* lit., cry and so "proclaim." v. 3. *three days' journey.* i.e., it required three days to walk through the city: not the circumference but the diameter is meant; hence we must assume that the city and its suburbs are included in this statement. v. 4. *yet forty days,* etc.: Nineveh shall be destroyed unless it repents. v. 6. *for word came:* better, and the tidings reached (so R.V.). v. 9. *repent,* i.e., relent.

Chapter 4. v. 3. cf. Num. 11:15 and I Kings 19:4, where the same prayer was offered by Moses and Elijah. v. 4. *Doest thou well to be angry?* Rather, Art thou so very angry? (so R.V. marg.) ; a gentle reproof is implied. v. 6. *gourd:* a rapidly growing oriental plant, with broad, vinelike leaves, which give a dense shade; *grief,* i.e., the evil case, the discomfort he was in. v. 8. *vehement,* i.e., burning (see R.V., "sultry"). v. 11. *persons:* without doubt young children or infants are meant, who have no powers of moral discrimination and hence are not responsible agents.

Index

NAMES AND SUBJECTS